PRAISE FOR *HINTS OF HOPE*

"In an increasingly adrift world, Steven Garber has a gift for finding the precise words and analogies that our hearts and minds are longing for. When we encounter these truths in his work, it is as if they were always there, waiting to be named. 'Proximate' is one such word—a concept with such weighty consequences that once you grasp it, you'll wonder how you ever lived without it. The journey of the proximate is made possible by wrestling deeply with moral meaning, humility, and neighborly love. This is one of his most profound books, rekindling the moral and aesthetic imagination as he reflects on the nature of stories, of loves, of good societies, and on our knowledge and its responsibilities—*Hints of Hope* is at once beautiful, engaging, and practical."

—**Kwang Kim,** Chairman of the Board, Human Flourishing Foundation, and Director of the Asia Economics of Mutuality Center, Seoul

"Steven Garber offers us a poignant account of the nearness of grace in real time—the proximate. These are peace-making words, telling things as they are, while giving hope to the heart. Honest and effortless, Garber is at his most lucid and longing here, reenchanting us with reminders of the deep substance of real living."

—**Sandra McCracken,** singer-songwriter

"We all need hints of hope as we navigate a world marked as often by seasons of sorrow and grief as by those of joy and gladness. Steven Garber profoundly offers us those hints in the pages of this book, one that may well be his magnum opus. Garber draws on his own story, his engagement with interesting, full-of-life people near and far, and his decades of deep reflection on the arts, philosophy, and theology. It's a book that will accompany me again and again as I journey on in hope."

—**Jeff Crosby,** author of *The Language of the Soul* and *World of Wonders*

"How may we make sense of our very complex and challenging world as we attempt to unravel the mysteries of our existence? And how, then, are we called to live and act out of the human connection to Creation and Creator? The cry for answers has never been more desperate. Now, in Steven Garber's profound yet basic primer in human living and response we may hear God calling, talking to us!"

—**Luci Shaw,** author, poet

"Gentle. Wise. Sorrowful. Hopeful. Those words repeatedly echoed in my head, my heart, as I read the essays that make up *Hints of Hope*. As Steven Garber guides through his reflections on making peace with the proximate—which is what life in this world requires, after all, if we aren't to go mad, and if we are to be faithful to God's mission for us—he doesn't leave us with frustration and sorrow. Rather, he brings us over again to the God of hope, the God of resurrection, who ensures that our labor is not in vain, is not vapor or futile, in the Lord. As a result, life in this already-but-not-yet world is worth engaging, loving, fighting for. By the end of the book, I found my head and heart also crying out, 'Thanks be to God!'"

—**Sean Michael Lucas,** Chancellor's Professor of Church History, Reformed Theological Seminary; author of *God's Grand Design: The Theological Vision of Jonathan Edwards*; and Senior Pastor, Independent Presbyterian Church, Memphis, TN

"There are books. And then there are Books. *Hints of Hop*e is one of these rare readings which draws you into the heart of what life is about; about who we are, about what we see ourselves as, about who we are meant to become. Every chapter strikes very deep strings in Garber's unique way, containing questions and wisdom potent to make the reader *a little more like who God intended us to be*. It is a must-read for everyone eager to find and sustain hope and energy for continued work to improve the world, as our world again faces unprecedented challenges."

—**Hermund Adler Haaland,** Founder/Director Zebr Institute

"Steven Garber explores tough challenges but does not leave us clueless. When it is so easy to become dismayed and overawed by the scale of suffering in the world, hope must be turned into something tangible, life-giving and lifesaving—and *Hints of Hope* spells that out, for all of us."

—**David Alton,** Professor the Lord Alton of Liverpool, Independent Crossbench Member of the House of Lords, Chair JCHR—Joint Committee on Human Rights

"Beautifully conceived, magnificent in scope, this book is laced with theological wisdom. But above all it is Steven Garber's stories—and the Story of stories which enables us to make sense of our longings, and our hope. He writes from the heart, exploring the loves of our human hearts in the light of the loves of the heart of God, who has a glorious end in mind for the whole human story, a Story that makes sense of the story of our own lives. This is undoubtedly his masterpiece."

—**R. Paul Stevens,** Professor Emeritus, Marketplace Theology, Regent College, Vancouver, BC; Founding Chairman of the Institute for Marketplace Transformation; and author of *The Other Six Days* and *Working Blessedly Forever: The Shape of Marketplace Theology*

"Garber's magnum opus, *Hints of Hope*, is, in a word: Magnificent! If you're seeking to explore the big questions of being human—Who am I? Why am I here? How do I live with purpose and hope in a broken world?—Garber is your reliable guide. Join him, as so many others have, on the pilgrimage of the proximate and discover your own hints of hope along the way.

"If you only have time to read one book this year, read this one."

—**Uli H. Chi,** author, *The Wise Leader*; Founding Chair, Computer Human Interaction LLC; Board Chair, Virginia Mason Franciscan Health; Senior Fellow, The Max De Pree Center for Leadership

2026 First Printing

Hints of Hope: Essays on Making Peace with the Proximate

ISBN 979-8-89348-034-4

Library of Congress Control Number: 2025941219

10 9 8 7 6 5 4 3 2 1

Cover design: Paraclete Design
Cover art: Dmitry

Published by Paraclete Press
Brewster, Massachusetts
www.paracletepress.com

Printed in China

HINTS OF HOPE

Essays on Making Peace with the Proximate

Steven Garber

PARACLETE PRESS
BREWSTER, MASSACHUSETTS

"Choose a neighbor before you choose a house."

To my long friends who are neighbors of heart and mind,
Todd Deatherage and Mark Rodgers,
twined together we are in a common calling
with vocations born of visions of the way the world should be,
living for more justice, more mercy, and more humility,
longing for signposts of what should be, and of what someday will be.

CONTENTS

FOREWORD

Steven Garber is a treasure, and his writing reveals why, his resonant words echoing in the caverns of our cold and damp modern hearts, his precious, loving words reaching the depths of darkness that few words in the past, much like those of C. S. Lewis or Frederick Buechner, dared to have reached.

He has always spoken softly when reading his well-crafted and lovingly layered presentations. His gentle voice can be heard here in these pages; if we slow down enough and remove our armor of protection, we may begin to hear that tender voice. He is a guardian of stories, myths, facts, and history, and in this volume they are stewarded in his mind, heart, and soul, awakening us again and again to a greater Reality of myths, facts, and history that beckon us to reread some of the greats like Tolkien, Weil, Aristotle, or Havel.

Steven's writing also amplifies our own stories and histories. When he chronicles his father, a man of "integrity of heart," I think of my own father, and of how "proximate" means more than mere physical closeness, but is woven into generational roots of shared concerns and overlaps of experiences. His writing helps me to steward my own memories and stories:

> *For reasons of the heart that are as deep as we are, sometimes when we wake to the morning, the bright shining sun or the slow drip of rain, we are drawn to its complexity, wondering why and what and wherefore. Artists are folk like that—on canvases and pages, stages and screens, feeling things first before the rest of us do, seeing and hearing the world in its glory and its ruin, the vocation of their lives reflecting the longings of the heart. . . .*

And when he writes, "Artists are folk like that," Steven speaks into my own soul, wrestling as it does in prismatic complexity, never trying to reduce the beautiful mess into something neat and sanitized for the marketplace, but trying, as an artist, to be as honest as I can be. Indeed, we are "seeing and hearing the world in its glory and its ruin" as artists. That is a journey into the labyrinth of complexity, of multiple worlds colliding, and it is rare to find someone willing to let that tension live in words.

Few there are whose voice you "hear" intimately as you read their writing. Once you have heard Steven speak or lecture, his unmistakable cadence and his narration—which seems meandering but at the same time absolutely precise and certain—takes over your reading. Rarer still are the writers whose voice you have not heard reading aloud takes over our reading. Frederick Buechner was like that; even though I never had the opportunity to hear him speak, as I read his words I can "hear" his voice. Perhaps that kind of voice is becoming faint, drowned out by machines' droning, lulling us into utilitarian cadence. The experience of reading Steven's words, then, is like a rare opportunity to hear a writer deeply.

Steven reflects on people like Douglas Coupland, Bob Dylan, Josiah Wedgwood, or William Wilberforce in the same cadence, always honoring their voices, their marks in history and culture. But then he digs and, like an archaeologist finding a fragment of history in a piece jutting out from the earth, he carefully excavates the surrounding ground of these voices to find an entire story, magnifying the macro vision or his "metanarrative" of grace. He writes of his discovery of such a world:

> *Then as I now, I believe that ideas have*
> *consequences, that knowing something about*
> *the world is critical if we are to know our place*
> *in the world; and yet I am also sure that my*
> *questions and answers were born of the necessary*
> *innocence of my early twenty-something years.*
> *I know that I longed to know, and to know*

> *what possible connection there was between my learning and my life—and that longing finds its way onto these pages years later.*

This longing is a necessary and gentle corrective to a reduced view of false binaries, a Flatland ruled by Culture Wars, in which ideas are reduced without consequences into a pattern of power grabbing. Ideas do have consequences, and Steven writes to trace both into the roots of our thoughts, or the thoughts behind those thoughts, as well as journeys of becoming our true selves by dismantling our idols of power. That careful dismantling has been his journey throughout a life dedicated to deeper and purer knowing.

How are we to understand our faith in the context of where our weakened faith and our colder, more cynical hearts are today? Many have abandoned the miracle of the miraculous. The whole point of the Resurrection is that it violates everything we know to be normative. The Resurrected Christ is not the resurrection of our ideals or our normative lives, of the normative thinking of "good people" hoping for normal days. No, the New Creation journey is full of reminders of the extraordinary wounds, visible still, in the hands, feet, and side of the One we worship.

Steven looks at these wounds through the writers, artists, and sojourners he highlights in these pages. For him, the blind spots and modern quibbles are not an opportunity for rebuttal, but an opportunity to listen, to understand deeply, not just our human conditions but the deeper epistemological basis for such a misunderstanding of God. He seems to know that deep inside all of us lies a subterfuge of deception, whether religious or irreligious, that we harbor on the same dock in our storms of uncertain fears. He listens deeply, anchoring our vulnerable vessels first before commenting. We are all pilgrims voyaging into these sacred wounds, and he navigates us through the uncharted waters, dropping buoys of deeper wisdom along the way.

Yet, our own navigation will look different today, even with these markers, in an epochal shift of nature and culture. Steven invites us into prophetic living, giving us a nautical map for our shifting tides as if to say that if we look, observe, and listen into the depths of the ocean of mystery, we will find delight in doing so together.

Telos for Steven is a journey into discovery, into wonderment, and wonderings. If the Resurrection is true and real, then we are to practice it day in and day out, not just recite the truth of it in our creeds. We need to walk on our Emmaus roads and expect to meet the resurrected Christ with his wound markings. We are to inquire and, even in a stubborn, desperate heart like Thomas's, to demand proof. Many of us throw out faith without asking, "God, if you are who you say you are, please show us and show me." Then, when Jesus willingly shows us his wounds, we must be courageous, as Thomas was, to kneel and worship. Once we are shown the Savior's wounds, we do not need to touch them. We should demand to ask, not because God is provable, but because God is often right in front of us, inviting us to see his wounds.

Steven implores my own journey into my studio with encouragement, *to give courage*, to create anew based on the experiences of my encounters. He introduces me to various obscure writers and a king named Louis in these pages, reminds me of forgotten poets, and guides me to see tribal ways of living, not for knowledge for knowledge's sake, but for me to create as I walk into my studio.

If you have never heard of, for instance, Christopher Lasch, Jean Bethke Elshtain, or Oliver O'Donovan, then Steven will show you how to read their magisterial writings. Why is that important? Not so that we can be enlightened, but so we can learn to care deeply. He has already loved these lesser-known authors of the past and thought through them, weaving from micro to macro—what Steven calls the "interconnectedness of metanarrative to narrative." His reflections help us to embrace what it may mean to be human today, and why these writings are connected, and are proximate to the gospel. So he meanders precisely, like a homing beacon to our anxious hearts, guiding us toward a north star of significance.

Yes, Steven Garber is a treasure, and his writing reveals why. After reading his work, like many others before us, we may find ourselves wanting to talk with him: "Do you have time for a conversation?" And he will nod, saying "yes," with his soft refrain, a sojourner willing to share these pages with us, sojourners we all are.

—Makoto Fujimura, author and painter

SEASHELLS ON THE SEASHORE

An Introduction

Anyone who claims that I am a dreamer who expects to transform hell into heaven is wrong. I have few illusions, but I feel a responsibility to work towards the things I consider good and right. I don't know whether I'll be able to change certain things for the better, or not at all. Both outcomes are possible. There is only one thing I will not concede: that it might be meaningless to strive in a good cause.[1]

—Vaclav Havel, *Summer Meditations*

Broken hallelujahs.

Even walking along the beach in the first hour of the morning, I think about the image of a "broken hallelujah"—as my wife, Meg, said so plainly, so perceptively, "You think about that all the time." And I suppose I do. Step by step I see the shells of the seashore washed by the waves, each one wonderfully imagined, intricately formed, and yet and yet, not all that it could be and should be.

So very beautiful, but broken too. Like everything everywhere. Though in my heart of hearts I long for a different life, wanting with all that I am a different world, what I see is always marked by both joy and sorrow; never neat and clean, but instead somehow both at the same time. The work of my life is to find an honest way to live with both together; in another sense, more globally born, all of us work at that, because in some sense we all have to, the world being what it is—and over the years I have wondered and wondered again, reading and reading more, living in and through the days of life, feeling the tension of what is and what is not in my very bones. What is clear to me is that there are some ways of seeing that resolve the tension by denying that there is a tension,

[1]Vaclav Havel, *Summer Meditations* (Knopf Doubleday, 1993), 16–17.

but that is neither sufficient nor sustainable. The differences are real, and they make a difference. All day long we are confronted with both, and we have to somehow make sense of the world and our place in it, being honest about both what is glory and what is ruin.

But why "broken hallelujahs"? The words are from the poetic imagination of the singer/songwriter Leonard Cohen, and his words run through my very being. With an artful, haunting eloquence, the song wrestles with the tension of life, the beautiful and the broken together, open-hearted wonder and melancholic despair . . . a broken hallelujah.

Truth be told, I have been walking the beaches of the world for a long time, looking for a perfect shell, sauntering through the surf, hoping that sometime and someday there it will finally be. What I find instead are hundreds and thousands of shells that seem just about perfect . . . but are not.

So many, of course, are terribly broken, now only fragments of what they once were; in their very different ways they make me sigh. But the ones that trouble me are those that appear to be more than that, that seem to be perfect—until I stop and look more closely. The colors are always uniquely created, the shapes are always uniquely crafted, and from six feet away they are amazingly beautiful. But when I bend over, the cracks are obvious, the almost-perfect outline is not quite, the holes stand out, and I find that each one is uniquely marred.

I first thought of this walking along the Assateague National Seashore in Virginia many years ago, there to take part in the wedding of dear friends. They had asked me to give the homily, to muse over the meaning of marriage as they made their promises to honor and love "'til death do us part." So I did my best to celebrate the day, glorying with them in the happiness of the hour, standing as they were amidst family, friends, and flowers with hope in their hearts. But given where we were I also reflected on the shells I knew, each one so very special, but each one a reminder that nothing is perfect. Wonderful as they were, wounded they were too.

Like every marriage I know. Like every family I know. Like every life I know. From the most personal to the most public, nothing we know is perfect in every way, and only the naive imagine otherwise. Slowly, slowly we all realize that we have to make peace with the proximate, and simply said, that is the challenge of my life. Of proximate justice in the public square. Of proximate happiness in a marriage. Of proximate pleasure in the work of our days. Every day I cry out against that conclusion, yearning for something more, my inward being groaning with creation itself—and eventually sighing over the weight of the world, knowing that everything is less than it could be and should be. As Bob Dylan has so poetically and profoundly remembered, everything is broken.

"Broken dishes, broken parts, broken streets are filled with broken hearts. . . ."[2]

Yes, everything is broken. As true as that is for individual lives, it is true for the public square too—as it is true for the work and workplaces of our lives, as it is true for the friendships and marriages of our lives. All day long I live with disappointment and grief and pain, like everyone I know well enough to know. And while I live my life wanting more, expecting more, to remember another poet, Bono, I never find what I'm looking for.[3]

And why is that? Because I am a glorious ruin myself. In my heart and mind I am never more and never less than that, both truths threading their way through the fabric of my life—and with strange grace, what is true of me is true for the world.

Even the shells have a story to tell . . . if we have eyes to see.

And that, simply said, is why I have written this book, in hope that we all will see more clearly the meaning of the world and our responsibility in it, a responsibility born of love that it is. With windows into life and the world in the first chapter,

---

[2]Bob Dylan, "Everything Is Broken," *Oh Mercy* (Columbia Records, 1989).

[3]U2, "I Still Haven't Found What I'm Looking For," *Joshua Tree* (London: Island Records, 1987).

reflecting on what it is to work for something that matters, even when not all we long for is satisfied; on into the great question of my life, and of life, that of *telos* and *praxis*, connecting the point of life with the point of my life; into an examination of stories within stories, the reality that for everyone everywhere we live stretched between metanarrative and narrative, our beliefs about all of life and our lives, frail and finite as they are; then pondering the weight of love for all of us who care about the world, knowing that even as "it all turns on affection," that brings its own challenge and complexity; from there the stories of friends from throughout the world who in their places among their peoples live in and with the proximate. The next chapter is about the commitments that make marriages and friendships the gifts of long-loved loves that they are, proximately, tenderly incarnate as they will be. There is no one in the world, though, who lives very long without being wounded by the world, scarring us as we care for and about it, hoping for what has been broken to become beautiful again. And finally, our deepest yearnings for what the world should be shape the way we live, longing for something more than what is—we make peace with what can be, in hope for what someday will be.

This is the book, from beginning to end, learning to live with deepened faith, deepened hope, deepened love, keeping our hearts alive in and through the years of life, learning to keep on keeping on into a pilgrimage of the proximate.

1

GLIMPSES OF HOPE

Most of the time I'm halfway content
Most of the time
—Bob Dylan, "Most of the Time"[4]

But the Disease Was Not Cured

Slowly, slowly, the first light of dawn makes its way over the Sangre de Cristos, turning the sky from midnight blue to orangish red, and then over the next hour another blue-sky day spreads across the San Luis Valley, these grand mountains running from Colorado to New Mexico for 250 miles. With sagebrush everywhere, it is only with the melt of the winter snow from the 14,000-foot peaks that the valley becomes the remarkably fertile land that it is—for centuries known as a hunting ground for the Ute people, and in more recent generations for its ranching and farming, especially raising sheep and growing potatoes.

That history brought my family here, and in the beautifully named town of Monte Vista I was born to a mother from Colorado and to a father from Pennsylvania, whose college years together were torn apart by war. Letters of love kept their hopes alive during that terrible time, and when World War II was over, as soon as my father got off the boat he took a bus to Greeley, Colorado, and married my mother. As was the norm for many in America in the post-war years of the mid-twentieth century, my mother made our house a home, a vocation that she lived into with heart and mind for the years of her life, and

---

[4]Bob Dylan, "Most of the Time," *Oh Mercy* (Columbia Records, 1989).

my father went on to more schooling, his boyhood interests in the natural world eventually growing into a vocation that gave meaning to his work for the rest of his life.

Vocations and the occupations that grow from them are mysterious, never neat and clean, for any of us. Sometimes it is simply history, brute history, and the choices we make do not seem like choices at all—because in most every way that we understand, they are not. The work we do is just the work we do, and the lives we live are just the lives we live, and people the world over groan for something more. Politics and economics, wars and rumors of war are the push-and-shove realities for many people in many places, and life feels more like surviving than flourishing. For others, our experience of life is different, with unusual graces that run through our lives, common and ordinary as they may be. Our families and societies, our educations and the opportunities for more this and more that, make our lives full of decisions and more decisions, seemingly choosing the path before us, taking responsibility for who we are and why we are, and therefore what we do with our lives—even though, in the end, the hard truth is that we still find ourselves looking through a glass darkly, which is what we do at our best.

My father's life was like that. Born in an industrialized steel town in western Pennsylvania, my 18-year-old father was invited into the office of his high school principal, who, with strong encouragement said, "You need to go to college!"—a conversation with consequences that changed the course of his life. My father was the first in his family to go to college, beginning a pilgrimage through educational institutions that he never finished, as the work of his life became woven into the larger life of the university world. But initially his decision meant two years of undergraduate education, a plan in place until all the 20-year-olds in his town went off to war, my father spending three years in the Army Air Corps in Italy. With the motivations of early maturity formed through the war years, he finished college and began graduate school at the University of Michigan with the support of his undergraduate professors, who were sure he should know more. But our best plans sometimes fail, and the surprising death of his father so wounded my father that he left school, for a time disabling his deepest dreams, and my parents moved West to join my mother's family in Colorado.

As happens to many of us as we move through our twenty-something years, my father began to enter into the questions that became his life. Whether we are butchers, bakers, or candlestick-makers, or plumbers who want to know "how this works," or farmers who every year plant seeds in hope that "this will be the year," or a scientist who cannot sleep at night because he wants to understand "what makes this happen," all of us move from childhood to adulthood into questions that become us, shaping our labor for the rest of our lives. For my father it was his undergraduate interest in botany which drew him to a program of study that gave concrete expression to what had previously been a classroom fascination. Because Colorado State University was the state's agricultural university, at its best it existed for the sake of its citizens, stewarding the flora and fauna for the flourishing of the people and their place, colorful Colorado as it was and still is. Though my father had no experience on farms or in farming, he was an eager student, and his war experience had taught him that he could learn just about anything.

Learning rapidly like most men of his generation—the boys who became men very quickly, "the greatest generation" we have called them—he found that his first graduate studies gave him enough understanding of potatoes that he was sent to oversee the San Luis Valley Research Station of CSU, taking up the position as its director. But he was also given responsibility to develop a research program for the vast sheep ranching throughout the valley, a challenge that became very personal for my mother as she pondered her pregnancy with me in the late winter of 1952, knowing that the spring lambs were coming at the same time as her baby; in the end, all were born as hoped.

Encouraged by his professors at critical points along the way, first to take up the work in Monte Vista as a place to learn the ropes of agricultural research, a few years later, with his professors having made the necessary connections, he began PhD studies at the University of California in Davis, which was then as now one of the world's leading agricultural universities—all with the professors' hope that someday he would return and join them on the CSU faculty.

Now that my parents are both gone, I often wish that I could ask more questions. What about this? Why that? I want to know more, please. But now I can only imagine their drive into the Rocky Mountains, through its valleys and over its passes, finally seeing the grandeur of the Sangre de Cristos and the San Luis Valley before them—and then driving down the "Gun Barrel," as it is called, the highway between Saguache and Monte Vista. The road so long and so straight that the locals could only imagine their histories of hunting in the nearby mountains, which is still remembered in the "muzzleloader-only" season in the fall, when only a certain kind of rifle is allowed to hunt the deer, the antelope, and the elk that roam.

It was in those years at the research center that my father's questions began to become clearer, as he entered into the lives and labors of the farmers and ranchers of the valley. Their challenges became his challenge, their disappointments his disappointment, their hopes his hope. As must be, central to his oversight of the research program was the difficulty of disease, which in different ways afflicted both sheep and potatoes. But it was the diseases of plants that most intrigued him, and given that his professors were serious scientists studying potato disease, their interests became his, and he eventually took his young family across the Colorado mountains into the deserts of Utah and Nevada, and up and over the California mountains, making a home in Davis, where he began to study plant pathology.

If I grew up knowing about the Sangre de Cristos and the Sierra Nevadas, the San Luis Valley and the San Joaquin Valley, I also grew up with the words *verticillium wilt* as integral to who I was and why I was. That disease was my father's disease. After he finished his UC studies, much to the disappointment of his CSU professors my parents chose to stay in California, where my father spent the rest of his life as a research scientist for the University of California, his work focused on seedling disease in cotton, in particular the plague of verticillium wilt. In Colorado it was the agricultural economy of the San Luis Valley that drew my parents to Monte Vista; several years later it was the surprising reality that cotton had become the major cash crop in California—and so my father's study of cotton disease became his work as a plant pathologist at the University of California's Cotton Research Station. The San Joaquin Valley, with its hundreds of miles along the majestic Sierra Nevadas, makes it one of the most fertile places on earth—a geography similar to but different than the San Luis Valley in Colorado.

What he did at the research station interested me as a boy, though I did not know much about its details. I knew where he worked, and the name of his work, but I did not know the nature of his work until I got old enough to want to know. Regularly he traveled throughout the valley, far and wide, experimenting with different soils and seeds in research plots, and he also worked in a greenhouse next to his laboratory, pursuing his research under more controlled conditions; but what he did while he worked was a mystery—until I finally spent a day with him, seeing and hearing my father the scientist explaining what he had learned over the past year to those who were making decisions for the agricultural economy of the state with its one-variety rule for cotton production. Millions and millions of dollars were at stake in making the right choices about what to plant and how to plant it to diminish the deadly plague of cotton disease.

He gave the years of his life to that one question, over time developing insight that served not only California but also the world. I began to see that farmers throughout the valley came to him, wanting to know what he knew; but I also watched him travel throughout the world, giving time-tested counsel to farmers, universities, and governments who wanted to understand how to develop their own research programs.

All through those years—stumbling along, longing for grace as he always was—he offered me a window into the meaning of *ora et labora,* of someone whose life was more seamless than not, day by day praying and working, praying and working, all for the sake of the flourishing of his neighbors near and far. I remember him sitting down with me one night after supper, explaining that his vocation was a complex one, one that involved the whole of his life—being a husband, a father, a friend, a citizen—and that he would not be in his laboratory every night, "just to get ahead." Rather, some evenings he would be off to take part in the local school board meeting, another night to serve as an elder in his church, and every Thursday to lead a Bible study at the local prison. Even as a boy I was impressed with the way he understood his life with its many relationships and responsibilities. But before we finished talking, I remember him telling me that every morning as he walked into his laboratory he prayed for wisdom about his work, longing to understand more completely the questions that were his, the connections between last year's work and the work before him, hoping to make the most of his hours and days. He saw the work itself, the science of plant pathology focused on verticillium wilt, as very important, as worthy of both *ora et labora.*

All that affected me, forming instincts about the meaning of a life, the meaning of his life, the meaning of my life. But even with the *ora et labora* that was his, serious and sustained as it was, when he finished the work of his lifetime, heaven had not come to earth—even though the work of his life was done in the shadows of saints, San Luis and San Joaquin. What I do know is that he saw signals of transcendence in and through his vocation, and more and more so as the years went by; but when he left the laboratory for the last time not all good that could be done had been done. Plants still died, the disease of verticillium wilt still occurred in the cotton of California and the world. At the end of the day, and the end of his life, my father had to make peace with the proximate, choosing something that was good, even if it was not everything that could be good. He worked hard, and he even prayed about the work of his life, spending decades deepening his understanding of a question that threaded its way through the whole of his life, but the doctor of plant pathology that he was, plants still died.

What is "the proximate"? As a word it comes from the Latin *proximatus*, to draw near, and from *proximus,* nearest, next. Sometimes it is given as "neighboring," which is a gift to us; we are close, even next door, but not the same thing as. At best, we are "nearby." The word gives us room to long for and yearn after what ought to be, and what could be done; it is a strange grace but a good grace, knowing that in the frailty of this life we will never see everything we care about, everything we long for, made right.

The question of my father's life was not a cheap one, and even with gifted agricultural scientists at work on it, any good answer was not going to be cheap either. Good cotton was grown, and still is, of course, because over time more knowledge of the ways of cotton and its diseases was developed by my father and his colleagues throughout the world, who through long work together began to understand the nature of the disease, creating over time disease-resistant varieties that were not susceptible as centuries of cotton growing had been. If there is an epitaph to this story, it is this: He had done good work, and people the world over respected his insight, and yet, and yet, he did not conquer the disease.

My father's life has been a good window for me into the life we all live. Hopes and dreams, longings that we wake up to and go to sleep with, keep us keeping on for the years of our lives, and yet at the end, there is still more to be done. Not *everything* good happened in my father's life and labor, even with hope in his heart—but *something* good did happen. Perhaps along the way our best work becomes a signpost of what might be, of what could be, of what should be—though in the end, they are only a signpost, and yet they are a signpost.[5]

---

[5]In my undergraduate years, like thousands of others, I made my way to the community of L'Abri in Europe, first in England and then in Switzerland, spending months asking questions that mattered to me, meeting people and ideas that have shaped my life. In his book *True Spirituality* (Tyndale, 1971), Francis Schaeffer of L'Abri wrote about the

Konvergencie, and Yet

"It was a very dark time" was the way he described his growing-up years.

One evening I was on a train from Prague to Bratislava, sitting in an enclosed compartment with a man about my age. He was a theater director on his way home, traveling across Central Europe through the hours of the night, and neither of us knew the other's language—but we ended up talking for hours, about our lives, about the histories of our countries, about the work of our hearts.

As we talked, stumbling between English and Slovak, understanding and not some of what we hoped to say, I asked him what had happened when the Communists took over Czechoslovakia. "I was sixteen in 1968 when the Russians came. It was a very dark time. I remember seeing my father cry, tears streaming down his cheeks. In the weeks that followed, he was taken to the police station, and we didn't know what would happen. For a week we heard nothing. When he came home, all he would say was, 'It was very hard.' And he cried again. Those were dark days for us."

He had studied theater at the university, and for forty years directed a theater in Bratislava. A thoughtful man, a kind man, a practiced man, a man who has lived a life far from mine—and yet, we had much to talk about together in our halting efforts to find words we could understand. Both of us apologized for not being able to say more; but we talked, and kept talking, about my love for Czech films, my reading of Vaclav Havel and Milan Kundera and the ways their thinking has woven its way through my mind, influencing the very way I see the world. I think he was surprised that I would know anything at all about his world, that I would even care about his world.

But I do, and I have.

---

vision for "substantial healing," a healing of the hurts of this life and world—from the psychological to the ecological—a healing that is honest and true, but not everything. That insight was a gift then, and still is.

Sometimes questions find their way into our hearts—as was true of my father—and they do not leave, echoing into the days and years of our lives. “Would you please come and speak to us about the challenge of vocation for the common good, thirty years after the Velvet Revolution?” The question caught me, as over the previous 15 years I had become friends with some very good people in Central Europe, visionary people, courageous people, kind people, generous people, each one someone who has suffered more terribly than most of us can imagine. That they still care deeply about the world and their place in it should make all of us pay attention.

Depending on our times and places, we may or may not know of the great plague of communism over the 150 years of its dominance in Europe and beyond. Born of the deepening injustices of industrializing Europe in the nineteenth century, it is best known to us through the insightful storytelling of Charles Dickens in books like *Hard Times, Oliver Twist*, and *A Christmas Carol*. Most of us are unaware that Karl Marx was writing about the same issues in the same city at the same time.

But if we linger too lovingly on the transformation of Scrooge with his long, dark night of the soul, smiling with hope as Tiny Tim blesses us all, we forget that the “hard times” were in fact profoundly and terribly that, and that Marx saw something about the alienation built into the industrialization of the nineteenth century that was real and true and right. If it took another century before writers like Franz Fanon critiqued the conditions which brought about the global desolation of “the wretched of the earth,” in 1867 *Das Kapital* was a cannon shot across the bow of history. With surprising passion Marx understood that men and women felt profoundly alienated by the growing disparity between those who had and those who did not have.

A generation later, Marx’s ideas, together with long griefs embodied in the oppressive indifference of the ruling class of Russia, brought into brutal being a revolution—as all revolutions are—that was explained as a necessary response to historic political and economic wrongs. But revolutions always bring terror, and the Russian Revolution tragically justified its own political and economic violence before its utopia even got started, arguing that one must be willing to "break a few eggs to make an omelet"—a poetic metaphor for the great, great grief that brought about the deaths of millions of Russian citizens. And for most of the next one hundred years Leninist and Stalinist rule terrorized the twentieth century, bringing untold sorrow to the peoples in the broad geography that runs across Russia into Europe.

Everyone I have met of a certain age in my visits to the Czech Republic and Slovakia has born that grief. *Everyone*. The stories are all different, but the wounds and scars are cruelly similar, and they are remembered.

Perhaps ten years before that train conversation I was invited to speak for a week to a group of post-university students from throughout the former Soviet Union, all of whom had come to Bratislava to think about the meaning of vocation for life, for the years that would be theirs now that their schooling was done. *Who am I? Why am I in the world? What am I going to do with my life?* Over those days spent together I had many long talks, sometimes walking through the city—both on its cobblestone streets with its almost fairy-tale castle rising over the Danube, and on the miles of concrete pavement which butts up against the horribly imagined public architecture left behind when communism imploded in 1989—again and again listening to their stories of life and learning under the constraint of the communist governments of Ukraine, Romania, Georgia, and Russia. They told no happy tales.

A second invitation is the one that took me from Prague to Bratislava on the train. This time it was to speak to a conference convened around a question that was central to my life, and to theirs as Central Europeans, one born of a social experience almost a million miles from mine. And yet as I have lived with the weight of the world in my own life, I know that we feel the same burdens, that our challenges are surprisingly similar. Like all of us they long for their lives to matter, for the work they do to matter, not only personally but publicly. Simply said, they wanted to think more fully about what a recovery of vocation would mean for a renewal of their societies, wounded as they were after decades of Nazism and communism. *Why and how could a reconsidered vision of vocation bring about a healthier social ecology?* Their questions are very human questions—whether they are asked in North America or China or India or Africa or Latin America or Central Europe—because they are questions at the heart of good lives and good societies everywhere. And the man on the train asked them too, looking back on his life, even as he hoped for more time to live a life beyond the dark times he had known.

And now a third time, with another invitation to Central Europe—and a similar question. Given my deepening love for these people in their place, the question intrigued me: "Would you please come and speak to us this time about the challenge of vocation for the common good, thirty years after the Velvet Revolution?" From my earlier visit they knew that I have loved their culture, reading their novelists and political philosophers, seeing their films again and again, and in particular they knew that I had taken the work of Vaclav Havel with great seriousness, learning from him about what it means to be a human being in the world. And since it was his vision for a new Czechoslovakia that was integral to the Velvet Revolution—the political implosion of Soviet socialism in 1989—they hoped that I would be able to think between their society and its challenges, and my work on vocation and the common good.

Before the trip I read Havel again, wanting to make sure I understood him, even though I have been reading him for years—and I decided to see Prague again. I had visited this capital city of the Czech Republic on my second trip, principally to linger along the streets in which the protests of 1989 had taken place, to walk across the great bridge from one side of the city to the other, and to ponder the balconies on which important speeches were given, but I wanted more. This time I sat in Havel's favorite cafe, the Prada, where he spent days and years among his friends, thinking through what a new politic could mean for their people. I took it all in, always wanting more.

Through his essays and speeches, as wide-ranging as they are and addressed to peoples the world over, there were central themes that mattered most to him, given his own pilgrimage through the century. Because he was born into a family whose status made them suspect during the Nazi era, which too soon was followed by the Communist regime, the political czars did not allow Havel to go to university. Born into a family with deep commitments to the crucial relationship of good lives to good societies, through his reading of poetry and politics during his adolescent years he was not surprisingly drawn to the underground conversations in Prague, ones that were very serious but off the radar of official Czechoslovakia.

Havel was influenced by the absurdists of his time, a community of artists who saw their time as socially and culturally "absurd," because the most important questions that human beings always ask and answer were politically repressed—even the possibility of *being human* was severely skewed; they saw themselves living in an absurd moment in history. Full of hopes and dreams for the world that ought to be, Havel began to write plays, artfully poking fun at the "absurdity" of the Communist ideology as it forced its way onto the Czech culture.

Because his work was a political "poke in the eye," agitating the Soviet overseers, he was eventually banned from Prague and exiled into the Tatras, the mountains of Czechoslovakia, where he continued to write about the challenge of holding onto one's humanity under the constraints of the communist government, offering the world important pieces such as "It Always Makes Sense to the Tell the Truth." Those were hard years, a refiner's fire for him in heart and mind; he spent most of the 1980s in prison, joining thousands of others who were *personae non gratae* in that time and place of intense social suffering.

And when 1989 finally came, he was inexplicably taken from prison and made the president of the newly formed government of the post-communist Czech people, surprising his society and the world. Visionary and eloquent, his words gave life not only to his own people, but also to peoples in every society and on every continent. Though there are pages and more pages of his addresses, if one were to summarize his convictions about persons and polities, these words come very close: "The secret of man is the secret of his responsibility." Having come of age in the middle years of the twentieth century, feeling the burden of absurdism as a way of (not) making sense of his moment in history, he also understood the currents of contemporary thinking with remarkable insight and therefore knew that the social meaning of totalitarianism destroys human agency, the idea that human beings are responsible in history, able to respond to history—and he knew that totalitarianism is a death-knell for human flourishing.

In one collection of speeches, which are addresses Havel gave to parliaments and universities the world over—in *The Art of the Impossible: Politics as Morality in Practice*—there is one question that he asks, and asks again: "What are the conditions in which human beings can take responsibility for history?" Explored in hundreds of different settings, that problem both plagued and inspired him. He wanted to understand what makes us responsible, what it is in a society that allows human beings to see themselves able to respond to the weight of the world.

And born of his own suffering and the suffering of his people, seeing into life and the world with remarkable insight, he came to this conclusion: If we lose God in the world, we then lose access to the great words *meaning and purpose, accountability and responsibility*. He saw this as a philosophical and political line in the sand, though he made no public affirmation of theistic convictions, much less than of orthodox Christian faith.

It is this history, and more, that brought the question that drew me a third time to Central Europe. In November 1989 all things seemed possible. A political leader who believed that truth matters? that always telling the truth is critical for a healthy social and political ecology? that the art of politics is to see it as morality in practice? The Wicked Witch of the East was dead, the Soviet Union was no more, and the burden of totalitarian ideologies began to be lifted after 80 years of terror. Havel's years as president were exemplary in many ways; his vision for a new politic was a clarion call for all with ears to hear.

But even for his own people it was hard to imagine that something new was really possible. Within a year of Havel's becoming president of the new Czechoslovakia, with honest political choices that could now be made, the two peoples separated, going their own ways as the Czech Republic and Slovakia. Neither nation had ever existed before as a unique body politic—any study of Central European history shows the map has been drawn, and drawn again, repeatedly through the centuries—and there was a desire to return to some sense of rootedness in their own tribes and traditions.

Perhaps history itself sighs, as creation groans, but 30 years later, heaven had not come to earth. All things had not become well. Public justice still felt more like injustice. The corruptors only changed names and addresses. And the question "What does vocation now mean for the common good?" had emotional and historical meaning, felt by my friends with understandable urgency.

It was on my first visit to Bratislava that I met Jozef Luptak. Squeezed into a very small car, we talked for a few minutes, knowing something of each other from common friends, but we had no more time than that. But over the years since then we have become good friends, being in the same places often enough to see our lives twined together, dreaming dreams about the way the world should be.

The music of this wonderfully gifted cellist is known throughout Slovakia, and year by year his artful imagination has won him audiences throughout the world. There are few weeks of his year when someone somewhere does not call him into a concert, wanting to hear him play his cello—and when he does it is as if he is wrapping his soul around his prized instrument, bringing forth the most beautiful music most of us have ever heard. But beyond this daily vocational rhythm, for most of 20 years he has convened a society-wide musical festival called *Konvergencie,* which for the month of September brings musicians of all kinds to perform throughout the country, from small village bandstands to large urban concert halls. Of course there are string quartets, but there are also great orchestras and rock concerts. Day after day, night upon night, the music comes forth, reminding a people who too long have wondered if everything would always be sad, that there is still beauty in the world, and it is important to celebrate it.

Through these three trips I have met Jozef's family and friends, the community of saints who care deeply about the flourishing of their city and society. Over time they have started businesses and schools, they have created micro-economic development projects for both Slovakia and the wider world, they have begun a publishing house, and more—all for the love of the world, all for the life of the world. Not parochial, as if life could only ever be that, but in the very best way, individually and corporately seeing their vocations as common grace for the common good.

As much as I loved being with them, hearing again their stories, understanding more fully their history as a people and their histories as persons, in my own small way entering into their hopes for history, I felt the weight of their question even more as I left after the third visit. Having suffered as they have for as long as they have, they still awaken to the days of their lives "with gladness and singleness of heart"—as the Book of Common Prayer teaches us—ready to pray and work again, incarnating in their own Slovakian way lives of *ora et labora.*

And yet, when all is said and done—after everything has been imagined and accomplished—their best efforts are necessarily proximate. Heaven has not come to earth in Central Europe, nor will it any time soon. On the one hand I believe that Jozef's vision for "convergence," for bringing hopes and histories together through the best music he can curate on behalf of Slovakian culture, is as good a work as I know; but on the other I know that every year it is hard work, that every year he has to battle against principalities and powers that have no interest in beauty for anyone anywhere, that every year he must pour himself out for a vision of what might be, if his city and society are to flourish. When one more year of hard work is finished, Jozef must make peace with the proximate.

His community of trusted friends, diversely employed as they are throughout Central Europe, know that seeking the flourishing of their cities is difficult, that in many ways their history is against them, that generations of economic and political corruption have poisoned the possibilities for the good life and good society they long for. And yet they still do, coming together year after year to think again about the world that is theirs, and the vocation that is theirs—which is why I was among them for a third time, lighting a candle, perhaps, remembering reasons to keep caring about their culture, yearning as they are for what should be and could be, knowing that what is, is not enough.

Hobbits We All Are

"I think you're on the menu!"

Years ago I was in Santa Monica, California, taking part in a gathering of the Wedgwood Circle, the visionary community which believes that the stories we tell about the meaning of human life under the sun matter for the flourishing of America and the world. Whether the stories come to us through songs and songwriters, on screen, the printed page, stage, or canvas—or even through comic books and video games—stories shape us. All of this and more has been the work of Wedgwood; some of its work we all know well, and some not so much, more hidden as it is.

Our days in a hotel along the beach of Southern California were filled with conversations with folk who hope and dream for richer and truer stories, ones that creatively show the truth of the human condition in both our glories and our shames—and so the hours are for presentations of all kinds, both to see and hear what has been done, but also to ponder what might be done. One afternoon we heard from Sean Astin, the actor whose work is best known in the films *Rudy* and *Lord of the Rings*, in the one as Rudy the Notre Dame football player, and the other as Samwise Gamgee, the faithful friend and hobbit. A true son of the film industry, he wanted to make a movie born of an important book, and he spoke with integrity and vision about the project, showing an unusual understanding of the financial and technical implications of filmmaking. We were all impressed.

A few months later he came to Washington, DC, and we spent a morning walking through the Holocaust Memorial. He had reasons for wanting to know more about that era, and as it has been an important setting for me with my long interest in the moral meaning of totalitarianism, I showed him what he wanted to see—and, knowing the city, I had made a reservation at a restaurant in Alexandria wonderfully named *Bilbo Baggins,* smiling in my heart.

When we sat down, the waitress came to our table, looked between us, and said to Sean, "I think you're on the menu!" Well, whether Sam was literally there or not, at least there were hobbits and elves and wizards along with the delightful fare of the restaurant, and we eventually had our lunch, talking about the morning, movies, and much more.

While Sean may be known in ways that most of us are not, his primary roles have been about the most ordinary of folk. Remember the walk-on hopeful "Rudy" who was *not* recruited by Notre Dame, but who longed with every ounce of his being to play for the Fighting Irish. But clearly it was his role as Samwise that made him recognizable at *Bilbo Baggins*, in a film in which he entered into a character best known for his undying courage through ordinary and extraordinary adventures, and for his furry feet.

The vision which brought our conversation into being was inspired by the life of Josiah Wedgwood, the British businessman of the eighteenth century whose company made fine dinnerware. His friendship with William Wilberforce and the Clapham community implicated him in the questions of his time and place, connecting the work of his life with his life in the world, making him ask questions about what his company made and why they made it. For ten frustrating years bills were presented to the Parliament to abolish slavery, and each time Wilberforce was laughed out of Westminster's hallowed halls; slavery was the economic engine of the British Empire at a time when the sun never set upon it, and the politicians were never going to change the lucrative trajectory of their political economy. These men and women of Clapham decided to go another way, committing themselves to the longer work of changing the hearts and minds of the English people; in the words of the Wedgwood Circle, they believed that "the culture is upstream from politics," understanding that any political transformation must first of all come from the hearts of ordinary people in ordinary places who together believe in a justice that is more than "just us"—and so they took on educational, agricultural, and prison reform, the changing of child labor laws, animal welfare, and much more.

And for his part, the man of the marketplace that he was, Wedgwood commissioned a plate with a cameo of a slave in chains right in its very middle, with the words "Am I Not a Man and a Brother?" running across the top. Rather than offering these as charity, a wealthy man's philanthropy for a cause he believed in, he decided to sell them, believing that the artful integrity of the plates would make them marketable—and at the same time become a means of changing the cultural conversation about the meaning of slavery. Remembering this story, the Wedgwood Circle was created, believing that the best art, art that reflects the good, the true and the beautiful, can find its way into the marketplaces of the modern world, perhaps transforming our understanding of things that matter most.

But Sam Gamgee, and William Wilberforce too?

While millions have seen the cinematic version of Tolkien's tale, the books are the best way into Middle-earth, necessarily truer and therefore richer, with narrative complexity and nuance born of a literary and moral imagination that is unparalleled. With over 150 million copies sold, the trilogy has drawn in young and old the world over who read and read again these books about a world that seems so far from ours, and yet is not—principally because they are truthful about what it means to be a hobbit, and a human.

The novelist Walker Percy's wisdom still echoes into the world, arguing that "Bad books lie; they lie most of all about the human condition." With unusual insight he set forth a remarkably strong thesis that showed why and how that is played out in the stories we know best, literary visions from worlds and worldviews that are universes next door to all of us.

Why do people everywhere find themselves in Tolkien's world? And see themselves on the pages of his stories? While his own life was in the refined academic city of Oxford with its ancient university, Tolkien chose to write his stories about the most ordinary life of all, of a village in a shire where good gardening and good beer made for a good life. Even in the very urbanizing world of the twenty-first century, there is something about the imaginative universe of the hobbits that invites us in, awakening us to something more, to believe in more, to hope for more.

In hobbit lore, Samwise Gamgee is the steadfast companion of Frodo through the trilogy we know as *The Lord of the Rings*. When the call comes to Frodo, it comes to Sam too, and off they go on their long pilgrimage, there and back again.

We know the story of the quiet life of the Shire with good cups of tea, good pipes to smoke, and good friendships, at least until Gandalf enters in with a task to be taken up. After some months and with some reluctance, Frodo and his friends leave all that is dear to them for the sake of the strange call to be Bearers of the Ring. Along the way they find that there are taverns to be enjoyed, lingering as long as they can; that there are adversaries who relentlessly pursue them, intending to stop them before they have even left their homeland; that the respite of Rivendell is a great grace with its unbounded hospitality, a place to be as satisfied as anyone can be . . .; and then mile after mile over the course of months through the thick and thin of orcs and every other unimaginable evil, until finally Mount Doom is seen in the distance—where Tolkien tell us, "They clutched at their hearts," knowing and yet not knowing the terror that was before them.

The very reason for their pilgrimage now comes to bear on what will be. Can they make it to Mount Doom? And can they hold onto the Ring, all the way to its fiery end? Those questions carry us into hardships of every kind, with heartaches that make completing their journey seem impossible, and we take a deep breath, learning that, "In terror, they stumbled on."

But slowly they keep at it, in some way knowing that the quest has more meaning than they know. And then, after seeming to come to the very end of what they can do, Samwise is Samwise one more time, saying, "Come, Mr. Frodo! I've got one thing I wanted: a bit of light. Enough to help us, and yet I guess it's dangerous too." Which it is, all the way along, with more difficulties, and more dangers, almost too much to bear.

Hope is hard, especially with more knowledge of what is and is not in the lives that are ours. Often, the farther we go, the harder it is to hope. That is as true for hobbits as it is for the rest of us, as finally the way forward seems impossible for these two stalwart friends. How can they go any further? What is uncanny in Tolkien's vision is his ability to hold together both the worst and the best, the most wrenching of experiences with ones that awaken us to our bravest and truest selves.

> *But even as hope died in Sam, or seemed to die, it was turned to a new strength. Sam's plain hobbit-face grew stern, almost grim, as the will hardened in him, and he felt through all his limbs a thrill, as if he was turning into some creature of stone and steel that neither despair nor weariness nor endless barren miles could subdue.*[6]

And then, and then . . . "a glimmer of hope returned to him."

---

[6]J. R. R. Tolkien, *The Lord of the Rings*, "The Return of the King," (Houghton Mifflin, 1981), 211.

Enough so that they made their way to the very pinnacle of the dreaded mountain, and the last battle for the Ring takes place, with Frodo and Gollum at the very edge of the great volcano with its yawning chasm waiting for one of them. Back and forth, up and down, until finally Gollum bites Frodo's ring finger, and as he does he falls into the mouth of the mountain—with both the finger and the ring between his teeth.

When I first read this story, a long time ago now, it felt to me like the story should have been over. A grand climax, a final fight, the credits roll, and "The End" is the end. Some stories do come to that conclusion, and in my younger years I expected that, and wanted that; but I have come to see that the best books do not finish that way—because they are books that tell the truth about the human condition, about what it means to be human. The life we all know is not that one, a world where in one fell swoop all good happens, where everyone gets everything, and we smile forevermore. Rather, Tolkien takes us down from the mountain, with pages and pages of more pilgrimage before we see the hobbits come home to the Shire, and all of this is after Frodo accomplishes his great task.

What becomes clear is that the work is not yet done. In part because in the world that really is, there is now more work to be done, like the sorting out of political affairs in a particular time and place now that the Ring and its powers are no more; but also because in an adventure like the one they have had there are wounds that have wounded, and they must be healed. The long trek, the innumerable hardships, the deadly battles, the fierce conflicts, the fight to the finish, all this and more have broken our friends, heart and mind, soul and strength. And because Gandalf of course sees more than most, he offers this grace to Frodo and Sam: "If your hurts grieve you still and the memory of your burden is heavy, then you may pass into the West, until all your wounds and weariness are healed"—words that become life for them over the next days, on through to the end of days.

And they make their way home, staying for the crowning glory of a king and his queen, but in reality it is Rivendell that calls them, and beyond that, the Shire itself. After so many miles, full of so much travail, they long for the rest of home, the place they most love in their whole world. We all know that longing.

But it is not to be, for as they cross the Brandywine River, the beginning of the end of their journey, rather than home, sweet home, "the land looked rather sad and forlorn." Little did they know that in their year away, Hobbiton had been turned upside down, with greedy and malicious hobbits taking over its political economy, allowing Evil itself to make its dwelling in the person of Saruman, the fallen wizard whose powers were corrupted through a tragic disordering of his affections, whose malice has already affected everyone and everything in the story that is *The Lord of the Rings.*

Tolkien says it best, and we should all read him, taking his gifts to heart. Between two worlds, the world of all things being right, now that the Ring has been destroyed, and the world that is not yet right, because wrong still lives and moves and has its being even in the Shire, we realize that we are being guided on this pilgrimage by a wise man, someone who knows the hearts of hobbits and humans, marked by both glory and ruin as we are. Even home was not yet finally, fully "home"—but home they went.

> *The travelers trotted on, and as the sun began to sink towards the White Downs far away on the western horizon they came to Bywater by its wide pool; and there they had their first really painful shock. This was Frodo and Sam's own country, and they found out now that they cared about it more than any other place in the world.*[7]

But caring for it more than they cared for anything anywhere, they were still surprised by what they found when they rode into

---

[7]Tolkien, "The Return of the King," 283.

this place of long love, and the loyal Pippin exclaims, "Well, I am staggered! Of all the ends to our journey that is the very last I should have thought of: to have to fight half-orcs and ruffians in the Shire itself." But fight them they did, to the bitter end, Sam concluding, "I shan't call it the end, till we've cleared up the mess. And that'll take a lot of time and work."

Which it did, because it always does. Through the long adventure, up and over the terror and triumph of Mount Doom, and back home again, we might expect that "all's well that ends well." But because the best stories are stubbornly true to what it means to be human, living in this now-but-not world—where *everything* is never possible—there is still tension to be lived into, there is still sorrow to be lived with. With existential pain, a pain born of his very existence at the end of the journey, Frodo tells his friends that he is wounded, "and I may never really heal."

He goes on, wanting them to understand what he sees in his own self, and what it means for all of them. "But I have been too deeply hurt, Sam. I tried to save the Shire, and it has been saved, but not for me. It must often be so, Sam, when things are in danger: someone has to give them up, lose them, so that others may keep them."

But finally the Shire is "scoured," as one of the final chapters puts it, though even with that cleansing, all has not been made well, finally and fully well. It is in "the West" alone where that kind of healing will happen, and only when this story of the hobbits is placed within the Great Story of Middle-earth will their deepest longings and loves be satisfied. And so they make their way back to Rivendell, then to the sea where Gandalf awaits them, in his wizardly wisdom having the last word, "Well, here at last, dear friends, on the shores of Middle-earth. Go in peace! I will not say: do not weep; for not all tears are an evil."[8]

For not all tears are an evil.

[8] Tolkien, "The Return of the King," 310.

At the very end of his hundreds of pages, the final words of the final book, Tolkien reminds us that there are good reasons to cry. Even sailing off into the West, the place "where all wounds and weariness are healed," we still have tears. Not of bitterness any longer, but tears are still tears, born of our yearning for what should be, for what will be. There is written into the very heart of Middle-earth the realization of the proximate, of making peace with the proximate . . . of something that is real and true and right, knowing that we do not yet see everything, that not all sad things have yet become untrue.

That was as true for Bilbo and Frodo, even for Sam, as it is for any one of us. We are frail, even in our earnestness, and we never ever get everything right. There is a tension between what we believe and how we live, between what we know is real and true and right, and the on-the-ground lives we live—and so we have to make peace with the proximate, choosing for something that is honest. Not because we have given up our hopes, but because we begin to know the deeper reality of life in this wounded world, that not all hurts are healed now, and yet we still must keep our hearts alive, into the Shire and beyond.

Making Peace with the Proximate

Making peace with the proximate is the way we all have to live, if we are going to live, keeping our hearts alive to the meaning of our lives, and to the meaning of life. To believe that something true, that something honest, that something right, that something beautiful, that something good is a signpost for what matters most—and that that is enough in this frail world that is ours, a world stretched taut between what is and what someday will be.

But "proximate"? *Making peace with the proximate?* We can find our own word and words, but I am convinced that we all need a word like that, a word that is deep enough and true enough to keep our hearts alive in and through the years of life—because even with our best efforts, our most serious and sincere desires, all good things do not happen in this life. My father's integrity of heart, his rich understanding of vocation, and the professional insights that served the world—and yet even all of that did not eradicate verticillium wilt. For my friends in Central Europe, even naming their festival *Konvergencie*, as beautiful and rich an image as it is, has not meant that heaven has come to earth, that the deep wounds of totalitarianism over generations have now been wholly healed—and yet they still long for what ought to be. Frodo's and Sam's commitment and courage brought them to the top of their world, and to the end of their task—and yet there was still more work to be done when they got home: The Shire had to be "scoured," and even with that accomplished, there were still tears.

Like hobbits, we all live for and by "glimmers of hope," seeing something of what is real and true and right—signposts they are of our deepest desires—longing for more of what should be, of what will be, choosing to make peace with something, with the proximate.

2

THE QUESTION OF MY LIFE

I'm just a poor wayfaring stranger
Traveling through this world below
There is no sickness, no toil, nor danger
In that bright land to which I go

—"The Scarlet Tide"[9]

War is hell.

Always and everywhere—and only the romantics imagine otherwise.

Wherever we have fought, wherever we are fighting, wherever we will fight, there is terrible conflict and horrible death. For thousands of years we have gone to war, and thousands upon hundreds of thousands have lost their lives in those wars. Tribes against tribes, nations against nations—from the Trojan War to the Hundred Years' Conflict, from the English Civil Wars to the French and Indian War, from the American Revolutionary War to the Napoleonic Wars, from the Boxer Rebellion to the Spanish Civil War, from World War I to World War II, from the years of "the Troubles" in Ireland to the Six-Day War in Israel, from the Bosnian Conflict to the Desert Storm War, from Vietnam to the War in Afghanistan, from the assaults on Gaza and Ukraine—each and every time born of a sense of justice against injustice, of right against wrong, and at the end of the day there are more tears than we can ever imagine. Sometimes we can see some good that finally emerges, but often that is

[9]T Bone Burnett and Elvis Costello, "The Scarlet Tide," sung by Alison Krauss, written for *Cold Mountain* (Columbia Sony, 2003).

hard to reconcile with the sorrow that necessarily comes, the grief that is written into the very meaning of war.

When the novel *Cold Mountain* was published, winning the National Book Award for Fiction, I was intrigued because of the attention the novel received, but also because we live in Virginia amidst the scars and wounds of America's war against itself, the Civil War we call it—and even our neighborhood bears that history. So I began to read the story of a soldier who made his way to Virginia and its battles, taking up his duty to the people and place he saw as his, before eventually deciding that he had had enough of the war, and he began his long journey home to Cold Mountain in North Carolina. The story is one of tenderness and tragedy, and tenderness and tragedy again; perhaps the best stories are like that, drawing us into the human heart, full of great joy and great sorrow, into the longings and loves that make us human beings.

There are travails along the way, and we make our way, coming to know W. P. Inman, the main character, even to long with him as he faces the hardships and terrors of hunger and rivers, betrayers and bounty hunters, mile after mile, and as a good story will do, we are drawn into his heartaches and his hopes, as we should be.

But there is another soldier whose life is woven into the story, Stobrod Thewes. Not nearly the Odysseus-like character of Inman, this one has not endeared himself to anyone, and having seen all that he wanted to see of war, he wandered away from his own less-than-stellar soldiering. "The war just didn't engage him anymore. He became casual in his attendance—and he was little missed." He ends up in Richmond, not so far from his battles, playing his fiddle in the saloons of the city, not a very heroic figure; the reader comes to know him in all his shame, and a little bit of his glory.

A dirty, messy world it is, and the novel carries us into that world, from the bloody battlefields to "the dim regions of Richmond's taverns, rank places that smelled of unwashed bodies, spilled liquor, cheap perfume, and unemptied chamber pots." But it is here that Thewes flourishes, surprising himself as he learns about the ways of the fiddle, "play(ing) until dawn, and every time he did, he learned something new."

> *He first spent his attention on matters of tuning and fingering and phrasing. Then he began listening to the words of the songs they sang, admiring how they chanted out every desire and fear in their lives as clear and proud as could be. And he soon had a growing feeling that he was learning things about himself that had never sifted into his thinking before. One thing he discovered with a great deal of astonishment was that music held more for him than just pleasure. There was meat to it. The grouping of sounds, their forms in the air as they rang out and faded, said something comforting to him about the rule of creation. What the music said was that there is a right way for things to be ordered so that life might not always be just tangle and drift but have a shape, an aim. It was a powerful argument against the notion that things just happen. By now he knew nine hundred fiddle tunes, some hundred of them being his own compositions.*[10]

There is a right way for things to be ordered. The words jumped off the page, and I wondered what the story would be, if in fact it was rooted in an understanding of life under the sun that was more than "tangle and drift," that instead had "a shape and an aim." The answer is, sometimes "yes," and sometimes "no"—and the dissonance is at the very heart of the story.

There is more that could be said, but it is the end of the story that matters most here. The two have persisted in their pilgrimage home to Cold Mountain because what they want most is before them, even far off, and their deep desires have kept them going—getting home has kept both characters "alive"

[10] Charles Frazier, *Cold Mountain* (Atlantic Monthly Press, 1997), 153.

through their long journeys. For Inman, it is the longing for love for the girl he left behind; for Stobrod, it is more complex perhaps, but in part it is with hope that he will find his daughter again. Each one has traveled across fields and rivers, up and down mountains, been face-to-face with thc worst of humanity, and now at the end are only miles from the home they have yearned for. It is almost as if we are hearing the drumbeats, bringing them home, finally home.

And then, both are murdered.

In the final pages of the novel, almost near enough home to smell the bread baking in the farmhouse kitchen, both Inman and Stobrod are shot to death, cold-blooded, as they say. Meaningless murders that make no sense of the story, that make no sense of life. Yet to say it simply, the literary imagination of Charles Frazier comes to that terrible end, his novel earning acclaim as "the best book of the year" by the literati for its courage and vision—and I felt cheated.

I was not alone. The book editor for the *Washington Post*, Jonathan Yardley, at his work long enough to write 3000 reviews over 30 years, wrote this,

> *Even as Frazier is tugging away at our heartstrings, he's trying to show how tough and realistic he can be, but it feels strained and unpersuasive; my own hunch is that he thinks literary respectability can be earned only if sentimentality is served up with a hard-hearted twist, but it's the sentimentality that's believable, not the twist.*[11]

The great shock at the end of the book is as if Frodo and Sam had arrived in the Shire and were murdered—because in "the best stories," we are too often told, the stories that are truest to life in the world, evil wins in the end, because in a morally indifferent universe, *things just happen.*

---

[11]Jonathan Yardley, "Charles Frazier's Long-Awaited Second Novel Finally Arrives," 1 October 2006, Washington Post Book Review, 2.

In her hauntingly beautiful way with words, artfully bringing melodies into unusual being, the folksinger Allison Krauss poetically puts it this way in the score for the film version of the story, "Cold Mountain," with T Bone Burnett and Elvis Costello writing for war brides in every century.

We'll rise above the scarlet tide
That trickles down through the mountain
And separates the widow from the bride[12]

Rather than the satisfaction of a love longed for, we are given a love lost, terribly, tragically lost . . . with its scarlet tide "that trickles down through the mountain," this song one more in a long history of songs born of battles that are marked by too much blood, too many tears, severing hope from history right in the heart.

In what is perhaps whistling in the dark in his narrative of the story he has chosen to tell, the author offers a brief, shining moment after the murders, with a page given to a family-and-friends meal, smiles all around. But unpersuasive it is, profoundly so. Not because good stories avoid evil, or that they refuse to wrestle with great sorrow and terrible pain—the truest stories do in fact—but because the "hard-hearted twist" is sadly, tragically that. No one I know believes that everyone and everything is fine; there is too much sorrow in this world for that. And no one I trust wants every story to end "happily ever after." What is unsatisfying, psychologically and philosophically, is that after the long, long journey home, the ones we have been asked to love lose their loves and their lives, meaninglessly, in cold blood. *The end.*

A Shape and an Aim

But are other stories possible? Ones that are in reality more honest, more reflective of the truth of the human condition,

[12]Burnett and Costello, "The Scarlet Tide."

with storytelling skill that remembers both our ruin and our glory? Yes, but to understand why, we must take up even deeper questions about who we are and why we are, about the nature of human vocation—which are the questions that have mattered most to me for most of my life.

I have long loved the students who have come into the classroom of my heart, and because I have, it is their longer lives that I have cared more about. What will they learn to love? What commitments will form them beyond their student years, and into the rest of life? While I have assigned many books over many years, expecting my students to take them seriously because I do—knowing that good books become companions for life, writing their way into the way we see the world—I am convinced that there is a deeper kind of learning that transforms us, heart and mind, forming pre-theoretic commitments that shape our souls.

This pedagogy is always over the shoulder and through the heart, because there is something profoundly incarnational about the truest learning; words must become flesh. In fact, to press more deeply, we need to see that words can become flesh in order for us to believe them to be true. Nothing we learn that matters to us do we learn in any other way. From learning faith, hope, and love, to learning to ride a bike, we need more than what even the best books can offer. *Words must become flesh.* When we apprentice ourselves to wiser ones, learning to learn from those who have gone before us and beyond us, we begin to see more clearly what matters most to being human, understanding reasons for being that go beyond "eat, drink, and be merry, for tomorrow we die," instead entering through windows to transcendence and truth, to beliefs about God and the world that—in Havel's surprisingly insightful reading of the human condition—can begin to make sense of meaning and purpose, accountability and responsibility.

But many who learn, like many who live, stumble over this.

In every century and every culture, it is one thing to master what is read; it is something very different to master the meaning of what is read. With remarkable wisdom, the contemporary theologian J. I. Packer argued, seminally and simply, that we can know about God without knowing God; the twentieth-century scientist and philosopher Michael Polanyi made the same argument, that we can stand outside looking in at the world, but it is only when we indwell the world of what we study that we begin to know what we are studying. The best learning honors both, always. Probing where bone and marrow meet, the physician and novelist Walker Percy offered a warning shot across the bow of everyone's existence when he said that it is possible "to get all A's and still flunk life." Without a sufficient reason for being, we will falter, we will stumble, missing the point of learning and missing the point of life.

In one of the best-known of the stories of Jesus, this reality is painfully examined. "There was an expert in the law" is the way the Gospel begins, placing the parable within a social context that gives meaning to what we have called "the good Samaritan." The conversation begins in a time and a place; the question comes from a questioner. Assuming that he knows all that is required because he has mastered the letter of the law, the expert asks Jesus questions that only make sense within the worst of the academy. Why should anyone listen to you, rabbi? Who were your teachers? Where did you go to school? What kind of degree did you get?

The lawyer presses in, resisting the moral meaning of the conversation—but Jesus will not play the academic game, and given his own pedagogical practices, simply begins to tell a story about a man who was badly beaten.

> *What does it mean to love your neighbor as you love yourself?*

Two men much like the expert in the law see, but do not see; they know, but do not know. The eyes of their hearts failed to see a neighbor; for reasons of the heart they were unable *to know* that a human being was in desperate need, not seeing themselves implicated for love's sake in his situation. For historical, sociological, and theological reasons they passed on by, certain that no one who qualified to be "a neighbor" needed their help. The scandal and surprise of the story is that a Samaritan stopped, sure that there was "a neighbor" who had been hurt, and who needed help. The Samaritan bound up the man's wounds, got him to an inn, and promised to pay all that was needed for whatever help was required. And then Jesus asks the lawyer, "Who was the neighbor?" Because the lawyer always knows the right answer, the expert that he is, he responds, "The one who showed mercy." And Jesus's reply is simply, "Go and do likewise." Or we might say, "Your words have to become flesh for you to understand them. Apprentice yourself to the Samaritan. Look over his shoulder, then through his heart, and learn."

It is not a very long story. But it is one that insists on the difference between mastering the letter of the law and mastering the meaning of the law—because it has *always* been possible to get all A's and flunk life.

Finding our way to coherence is hard, for a thousand reasons. The unusually gifted, morally serious philosopher Simone Weil wrote these words on the last night of her life: "The most important task of teaching is to teach what it means to know." She believed in a deeper, truer knowing that gives us eyes to see what is honestly going on, to understand the meaning of what we see, calling this "learning to pay attention"—to see what is real and true and right in the concreteness of our study, making the surprising argument that when we begin to learn like this, our learning becomes "sacramental," because we see where heaven meets earth in our study. For her it was the movement from "knowing about" to "knowing," a kind of knowing that only comes with indwelling what we know, choosing to see ourselves implicated for love's sake in and by what we know.

True for everyone everywhere, this was true in the saloons of Richmond where Stobrod discovered that the fiddle tunes he had long played were not just "tangle and drift," but had "a shape, an aim." As he began to indwell what he was learning, spending the hours of the night listening to others play, he began *to know* what he was learning, that "things don't just happen," because instead there is "a right way for things to be ordered." These words are only possible within a world and a worldview where there is true right and true wrong, one in which human beings have access to the moral meaning of life in the world. If that is not true to the way things really are, then *things just happen,* and that is all that can be said—like the meaningless murders that brought *Cold Mountain* to its bitter, senseless conclusion. *Things just happen.*

But what if there is a true *telos* written into the human heart? into what it means to be human? into what it means to live in the world? In fact, what if there is a way to live in the world, a *praxis* that reflects a "shape and aim" to life for life, that is more than just "tangle and drift," one meaningless day after another?

Thousands of years ago poets simply sighed at the disorder they saw, the pointlessness of their lives and of life, leaving their epitaphs for the ages, "Why not then eat, drink and be merry, for tomorrow we die?" In both the Old and New Testament, this question is remembered, rippling through time, from the mouths of epicureans of every generation. For as long as we have a history that we record, these words have summed up what life looks like when we choose to believe that "things just happen," that it is all just tangle and drift. The words are born of a despair that should make us weep. But if they are ancient, they are contemporary too; the gifted poet/singer Dave Mathews offers them again for the twenty-first century, and thousands the world over sing his songs with him, lamenting lyrically as he does—even as there is a celebration of pointlessness.

The ancient words are weighty, echoing across the centuries as they do. But they reflect the reality that the idea of *telos* is more than just a word; rather, its meaning is written into the heart. In *A Christmas Carol,* the classic story by Charles Dickens, these poignant, tender words from Belle, the young love of Scrooge, tell this tale: "I have seen your noble aspirations fall off one by one, until the master passion, Gain, engrosses you. Have I not?" Tearful, terrible words, but true, and we understand them. We live that way, all of us, for blessing and for curse, following "master passions" in and through the years of our lives, to their end. Woven into the fabric of our lives is the longing for life to be about something, to be for something, whether that "something" is worthy of our hearts, or not. And when we eventually see that what seemed a passion worthy of our best energies and hopes is less than that—for whatever sad reasons we come to that conclusion, we join the chorus through the centuries, singing their sad song, *Why not then eat, drink and be merry, for tomorrow we die?*

Not a cheap question, and not a cheap answer. What is the point to life? Is there a point to learning about life? When we take the question seriously, doing our best to make sense of what we are seeing and hearing all around us, it takes time—but it is time from life, for life.

On Being Human

From my dropping-out-of-college days, hitchhiking wherever I wanted to be, making every ride a serious conversation about serious things, living in communes in the San Francisco Bay area for a year, and in the countrysides of England and Switzerland for another year, I longed for deeper reasons to be, reading and reading more, asking questions and asking them again. After miles and months of pilgrimage, what began to be clear to me was this: The way we understand what it means to be human affects everything else.

Sex and love, work and play, art and politics, business and economics, learning and life, the novels we write, the films we make, and the songs we sing: The meaning of everything about us, from the very small to the very large, grows out of what we believe it means to be human. In that interregnum, a time between times, from being in school to going back to school, I longed to understand my place in the world, to know who I was and to know why I was—and along the way I began to make more sense, finding words that captured the conversations of my heart, becoming pathways to know what had been written, and even what could be written.

Yes, words, words, and more words—and then sometimes we find a word that surprises us, opening windows into things we care most about, giving us eyes to see what we have longed to see. In my wonderings about everything, wanting to make sense of enough to live my life, the word "virtue" was like that. A word I knew, but only in a skewed sense, a reductionist reading of its meaning that had almost nothing to do with the world that I knew, the world that was mine to understand.

By definition it is a word about what it means to be human, pointing us towards our true end as human beings. Not all tangle, not all drift, but with a shape and an aim. Like most of the best words, "*vir*" comes from Latin, meaning "man," for what it means to be human. Always and everywhere virtues are habits of heart, the characteristic ways we think and say and do all day long in the push and shove of ordinary life for ordinary folk. And in the morally meaningful universe of the ethic of virtue—the way of life embodied in the virtues—*virtues* direct us to who and why and what we should be; in contrast, vices skew us, twisting our vision of the true meaning of our humanity, disordering our commitments and loves, insidiously offering reasons for being that are less than human because they distort the very meaning of being human.

If the first virtue is humility, which requires a truthful if painful recognition of human frailty, then its corresponding vice is arrogance and pride, making it "the great sin," warping everything about us, everything within us. In the ethic of virtue, to be true to our truest self is to be honestly humble, profoundly aware of our finiteness and our fallenness. Wise ones have known this for ages, while fools tragically cannot understand why it is that humility is integral to human flourishing, foolishly imagining that pride, to be full of oneself with myopic self-centeredness, makes for true happiness. In the end, a universe of self becomes a very small world.

If *vir* reminds us that there is a true north, that we are in reality made for a true end, then perhaps we have ears to hear the very first words of Jesus which are about the virtue of humility, "Blessed are the poor in spirit," knowing who we are and who we are not, knowing what we are and what we are not. The good life begins there, with a true knowledge of self; every other virtue is ordered by this first virtue, orienting us to our reason for being human.

As I found my way into the ethic of virtue, I discovered the great French philosopher Etienne Gilson, who argued for this vision with unusual anthropological and moral insight, setting forth the differences between virtues and vices:

> *Virtues are forms of habit disposing us more permanently to good actions. Habit is a disposition to the better or to the worse. Since habit measures the greater or lesser distance of the individual from his proper goal and causes him to conform more or less to his proper type, a careful distinction must be made between a habit disposing him to perform an act conforming to his nature, and one disposing him to an act in disagreement with his nature. The former are good habits, and such are also the virtues; the latter are bad habits, and these are vices.*[13]

Conforming to his nature . . . in disagreement with his nature. That definition draws us into a deeper reading of human nature, about whether there are truths that shape who we are and why we are, that matter for us and to us. In a postmodernizing world, a time and place beyond "the modern" with its assumptions about what is true and not true, can we even speak about truths that are like that, that form the contours of our existence as human beings? Or in the end must we conclude that there is no "right way for things to be ordered," because, as stark as it

---

[13]Etienne Gilson, *Moral Values and the Moral Life* (Shoestring Press, 1961), 260.

may be, we are just tangle and drift, with no shape or aim of consequence. Our answer becomes a line in the sand, and the way we understand its meaning has consequence for who we are and how we live. Given my commitment to the coherence of the cosmos, what is true for art—particularly for the work of fiddling—is true for biology, for chemistry, for economics, for engineering, for history, for mathematics, for politics, for philosophy, for psychology, for sexuality, and for literature, for the writing of stories, for a story like *Cold Mountain.*

The ethic of virtue is an ancient way to understand the integral relationship of belief to behavior, because it is formed by the vision of beliefs becoming behaviors; in sum, that is what virtues are. We cannot "know" if we do not do. Nor is it possible to know about justice, temperance, courage, wisdom, or faith, hope, and love without being someone whose very life embodies that knowledge, conviction becoming character, our beliefs becoming our behavior. Again, Gilson's insight guides us, setting forth that these are not only ideas, but ideas that must have legs—because they orient us to the way we must live if we are to live in a way that is true to our nature as human beings, to the truest of human nature.

As I kept at these questions, spending years reflecting on them, I slowly read *After Virtue* by Alasdair MacIntyre—a grand project, and perhaps the major work on moral philosophy of our time.[14] It took me days to make my way through, page after page, idea after idea, working hard to hold together the forest and the trees, the larger thesis and the smaller arguments that together made for the one book. From beginning to end my copy is underlined, full of side comments as well, revealing that I was sometimes certain of what I read, sometimes wondering about what I had read.

If there is one central argument that most intrigued me it was that of the purposeful, or teleological, nature of life, the idea of life as a *telos* that forms in us "a certain kind of life," one lived

[14]Alasdair MacIntyre, *After Virtue: A Study in Moral Theory* (University of Notre Dame Press, 1981).

with an end in mind and heart. To remember *Cold Mountain* at its best, it was Thewes's discovery that "there is a right way for things to be ordered," if we are to flourish, just as fiddle-playing is at its best when the player begins to understand that the art and craft of the instrument is dependent on "a shape, an aim" which is born of beliefs about the very meaning of music.

MacIntyre argues that rather than "tangle" and "drift," the point of human life is of virtue deepened and developed within a right ordering of *telos* to *praxis*, between what we identify as our reason for being and the way we live our lives, the practices that give shape and substance to daily life. By contrast, in a culture *after virtue,* where "emotivism" has won the day, that will never be because it cannot be. MacIntyre explains that emotivism argues that all evaluative judgments, and more specifically all moral judgments, are *nothing but* expressions of personal preference—with broad brushstroke, *the culture of whatever.*

Though there are a thousand ways to speak about what this commitment means and does not mean, the word *anomie* captures it well, *a nomos* meaning lawless, without law, against an ordering of life that makes any claim to transcendence and universality, describing "a condition of instability resulting from a breakdown of standards and values or from a lack of purpose or ideals." That does not work in families, on athletic teams, in businesses, or in society at large.

Because that is true, this is why the ideas of meaning and purpose, accountability and responsibility meant so much for Havel, why he saw them as critically important for the Czech people, and why he saw their metaphysical foundation as crucial—and it is why *absurdism* is a word that still has meaning, a morally meaningless meaning, echoing far and wide into worlds beyond Central Europe and its intellectual and cultural debates of the twentieth century. And why does it matter? So that life might not always be just tangle and drift but have a shape, an aim.

The Question of Telos, the Question of Praxis

In those long years of work, trying to understand the ways that belief and behavior are formed, that our ideas about the world become the way we live in the world—a question that has become the vocation of my life—I began to ask, "Do you have a *telos* that is sufficient to meaningfully orient your *praxis* over the course of life?" One can have a very good life without ever using the words *telos* and *praxis*; but whatever words we use, the question matters, and we will answer it well, or not.

I can remember a lunch one day, sitting under the grand columns of Union Station in Washington, DC, with an undergraduate whose questions about her study brought us together. A Latina-American from Los Angeles, she was intellectually eager about everything that mattered, an earnest smile that was willing to engage anyone and everything. As we talked she asked more about the reading, wanting to understand why we had assigned a particular book—not resisting, but more "I don't understand yet." I explained more of our vision for a pedagogy of praxis, a way of learning that took ideas very seriously, but which required the students to honestly enter into life on Capitol Hill, and the wider city and the world. Years later her words still run through my heart: "Then this isn't just about school, is it? This is about life, isn't it? This is what the rest of my life is about, of what I am going to believe, of what I am going to do, of how I am going to live!"

That conversation is only one of many, but the weight of the words between a student and her professor, both of them wanting the learning to matter, only deepened my desire to understand that the years we move from adolescence to adulthood are formative, shaping our souls into the future of who we will be and how we will live. From those years on I have wanted my students to think as carefully and critically as they can about what matters most to them, and therefore the life that will become theirs over time, their beliefs about the world becoming the way they live in the world. And because life is dynamic, and is never neat and clean, never 1-2-3, it is as true that the way we live in the world shapes our beliefs about the world, with equally deep consequence. Behaviors and beliefs work upon each other, mysteriously and profoundly, because in reality they define each other. As *telos* informs *praxis*, necessarily, so *praxis* informs *telos*, necessarily.

Wanting to learn from all who were willing to teach, in those years I spent months reading Aristotle, particularly his *Nicomachean Ethics,* eager to understand him and to take in his wisdom that continues to speak through the centuries. I did, listening carefully, pondering the complexity and nuance of his insight. But while I learned from the great teacher, impressed as true students have been for centuries, in the end I was certain that the Greek tradition was lacking. Its philosophical and theological anthropology, while rich, suffered from a poorly framed metanarrative, one that could not account for who we are meant to be, for who we are, for who we can be, for who we someday will be.

Without a grounding in grace, in a world that can see the centrality of grace, the Greek *telos* was insufficient to the task of meaningfully orienting one's *praxis* over the course of life. Even with its profound insight into what the good life requires—"both to delight in and to be pained by the things that we ought"—duty by itself is never a sustaining motivation—in part because we always fall short of what is expected, of what is required, even, and perhaps especially, when it is "a good man" that we aspire to be. And for the honest, sensitive soul, that is crushing.

Reading MacIntyre gave me perspective on this ancient way of making sense of life. The Greek tradition, yes, which is in a certain sense timeless, but it was not enough to make sense of the *telos–praxis* relationship. Something more was needed, a metanarrative that accounted for all of reality, all of life, all of history, every square inch, but that also made sense of the narrative of each person's life, every one of us—and I was drawn to the Christian tradition with its deeper roots in a world and worldview whose story begins at the beginning of time, offering an understanding of the moral life within a true knowledge of self and of God, the two being inextricably twined together. In fact, its best teachers argue that we cannot know ourselves truthfully without knowing God truthfully, and the reverse is also true, that we cannot know God truthfully without knowing ourselves truthfully—they depend upon each other, and cannot exist outside of each other. And within this vision of human life under the sun, the very heart of what it means to be human, to be "a man in full," is understood most comprehensively within this cosmos and its cosmology.

This way of seeing is formed by the Hebrew vision of what the world is like, and what we are like. There is no Christian vision apart from its grounding in the Hebrew world and worldview, whose beliefs begin with the God of heaven and earth requiring that human beings do justice, love mercy, and walk humbly with God. Beliefs about God and the good life are interwoven, with the meaning of justice formed by the character of God, the meaning of mercy embodied in God, the meaning of humility incarnate in God. Not the ideals of the Greek philosophical tradition, where justice, mercy, and humility exist beyond us because their reality is above us—*ideals* that they are, and *ideals* that they ever will be.

"What does Jerusalem have to do with Athens?" Taking up this age-old question, Louise Cowan of the University of Dallas, in her essay "Jerusalem's Claim Upon Us," with unusual insight analyzed the differences between these two perspectives on life in the world,

> *In stark contrast to the Greek, Hebrew literature assigns immense significance to humankind, made in the image of God, though it enjoins a necessary humility in the face of the creator's majesty and power. It affirms that mortals are not simply of nature or of Mother Earth but children of the God beyond gods—and obligated by the very fact of their existence.*[15]

[15]Louise Cowan, "Jerusalem's Claim Upon Us," *The Intercollegiate Review*, Fall/Spring 2001, 14-15.

She argued that the Hebrew God "fashions a cosmos out of love"—not the *eros* of the Greeks but the *hesed* of the Hebrews—making a covenant with the human race, calling forth "a creature like himself, in his own image, one that could know and understand and love." Seeing into the difference at the heart of what the good life means, she argued that "The object of the Greek way of life is to know rightly; the object of the Hebrew is to do rightly." And summing up the Hebrew vision, she concluded, "It passed down to us something radically new: not myth but history, a movement forward in time, and therefore a sense of an ending."

Though the words *telos* and *praxis* are Greek, the meaning of the words are universal, reflecting realities that are true for everyone everywhere, and are seen in Cowan's explication of the Hebrew way of life. *A necessary humility. Obligated by the very fact of their existence. Know and understand and love. A movement forward in time, a sense of an ending.* Is there a telos for human life under the sun? An end to which and for which we live and move and have our being? How do we live in a way that connects our deepest longings with our ordinary lives? Yes, in this way of seeing and hearing the world, there is a right way for life to be ordered, just as there is a right way for fiddling to be done.

Seeing and hearing are the primary ways we know about anything, and it is from our hearts that we make sense of what we see and hear. But as we have argued, it is possible to know about, and yet to not know. Only when we step in, only when we enter into, do we begin to know. Within the Hebrew understanding, we only know when we do; only when we see ourselves implicated for love's sake do we know. A profound and rich vision of knowledge, it stands apart from every other epistemological perspective because it is a kind of knowing that makes sense of "Adam knew Eve his wife," making the deepest intimacy a matter of knowing truthfully the inherent meaning of relationship to responsibility, just as it makes sense of "The righteous man cares about justice for the poor, but the wicked have no such concern," starkly contrasting a way of knowing that necessarily implicates one in the life of the world, with an indifference that is far less human than that. The same Hebrew word, *yada*, is used both times, as it is used hundreds of times in the Hebrew scriptures.

What does it mean *to know*, and why does it matter? Always brilliant, always committed, always passionate, always a woman who longed to make sense of the world, Simone Weil left us the gift of her last words—once again, "The most important task of teaching is to teach what it means to know." In these simple, yet profound words, written from her deathbed, this Jewish woman of the modern world who slowly and tenderly came to believe in "the God who has tears"—entering into the heart and hope of Christian faith—was a true daughter of her tradition, with its beliefs about the world and the way we are to live in it, intuitively knowing that "to know" rightly matters most in both learning and life, because it is central to who we are, to why we are, and to what we do with our lives, questions with answers that are the sum and substance of vocation.

And so for the years I have spent in the classroom, semester by semester opening my heart to one more group of students who have come wanting to learn, I have written into every curriculum a class on the nature of knowing, being as explicit as I can imagine being, giving examples and more examples, sources upon sources, pressing into the pedagogy of *yada*, hoping that our learning together will be marked by learning what it means to know, which always and everywhere is the first task of teaching.

The Christian vision of life in the world assumes these commitments and convictions, Jesus being fully Hebrew, as he is also fully God and fully human. His first teaching, what we call "the sermon on the mount," concludes with this hard truth: Only when we put into practice what we have heard will we understand what we have heard, because what we do with what we know is crucial for a good life. The conversation with Nicodemus only makes this a deeper truth, with *the* teacher of the law of Israel coming at night to ask questions of this unusual rabbi named Jesus, having stumbled over what he has heard in the public square, not sure what it could all mean. After a serious back-and-forth between serious people, Jesus ends the conversation with this sober statement: The reason you do not understand is that you do not *do* the truth. Always and everywhere, integral to knowing the truth is doing the truth.

Knowing and doing? Telos and praxis? Why do these ideas matter? In the secularizing, pluralizing, globalizing world of the twenty-first century, how can they be important to ordinary people in ordinary places? In different civilizations, in different cultures, in different centuries, we are still sons of Adam and daughters of Eve who live in the same world, where the sun still comes up, where daffodils still bloom, where we still long for justice because we believe for some reason that there is a right way for things to be ordered—for all these reasons and more, believing that everything cannot be only tangle and drift, but instead, when push comes to shove, there is a shape and an aim that is built into the fabric of the universe.

How are we to hold all this together? Never more, never less than proximately so. In this frail life we will never do more than that.

And yet, is it possible to find a way to make more sense of these ideas, complex as they are, in a way that is coherent and honest, that is meaningful and true? Yes, and to say it simply: Unless we do, we do not know, and unless we have a true praxis, we cannot have a true telos—even if proximately understood.

These words depend on each other; these ideas are bound up with each other. When we know but do not do, when we identify a reason for being that has little to do with the way we live, there is a dissonance built into the very heart of who we are, of why we are, of how we live our lives. And if virtues point us to our true end as human beings, to what it means to be a human being, then to disconnect what we know from what we do through the devices and desires of our hearts, distorted as they so easily are, disorienting to us as they will be, then it is impossible for there to be meaningful coherence between *telos* and *praxis* in our lives, between what we know and what in reality we do.

Telos and Praxis, Incarnate

Not so many years ago there was a conversation on K Street in Washington, DC, a street where there is not a starry-eyed person to be found; if there is one place where *realpolitik* meets *realeconomik,* it is here. Everyone knows the sausage-being-made character of the business done on this avenue, and everyone is professionally adept at the messiness seemingly required to get things done—at least the business that some people want done.

That day I was listening to an Israeli, a Palestinian, and a Jordanian, each one committed to the recovery of a healthier ecology for the Jordan River, which runs through the valley that is home for all three peoples. The water that is the source of their common life is a literal problem because sewage is dumped into the river from top to bottom, making it a surprisingly unhealthy ecosystem. But it is also a metaphor for their political life, which is what brought them to the Telos Group's meeting that day in the 1600 block of K Street in the Commonwealth Building.

And as I listened, I reflected on the word *commonwealth,* aware that it is an unusual word in the modern world. Still the name given to the 54 nations all over the globe who have historic roots in the British Empire, ranging from Europe to Africa to Asia to Latin America and North America, it is still used in the United States as the official name of Virginia, Pennsylvania, Kentucky, and Massachusetts instead of the word "state." An English word from the fifteenth century, "commonwealth" was created to communicate that human life is a common life, that individual good cannot be finally found outside of the common good, that individual wealth exists in, for, and by common wealth.

That is a hard truth for us, autonomous as we are disposed to be. *We will do what we want when we want it.* But in truth, no one flourishes with that belief, at least in a way that can be sustained:

Families, neighborhoods, and societies do not flourish, because they cannot flourish when they act against the very grain of the universe, a cosmos with justice, mercy, and humility woven into its being, a world that has an economics of mutuality with social and political meaning written into its very bones.

The Telos Group argues against that vision of the good life, insisting instead that it is only in an honest belief in a common good for all those who call "Israel" home that Israel will flourish. Almost no one believes this in either the church or the world, with fierce conviction insisting instead that "the Israelis are right because it is their land after all." Or the other side, "the Palestinians are right because it is their land after all." To believe in a commonwealth seems historically impossible, politically incredible.

But both peoples have histories, both peoples have hopes. And like the Jordan River, there is a social ecology that runs through the valley and its surrounding hills that is in crisis in thousands of long-suffering ways, sometimes manifesting itself in horrific moments that make all of us cry out.

The longer I listened to the Israeli, Palestinian, and Jordanian talk about the ruin of their river, the more I thought of the weighty words in the Epistle to the Romans that make strange sense of this wounded world, "The creation groans, waiting. . . ." Those words have been critically important for me: If the creation knows that things are not right, if the creation itself is groaning, then I can too—because I do.

Waiting for what? For the longed-for day when all hurts will be healed, when all wrongs will be righted, when groaning will all be done, because "Every valley shall be exalted, and every mountain and hill shall be made low; the crooked straight, and the rough places plain," as the prophet Isaiah promises. *Waiting for what?* In this now-but-not-yet moment in history, for us to awaken to being who we should be, where we are, to the vocation of being common grace for the common good.

The Jordan River Valley needs that, just as Jerusalem and Bethlehem need that, just as Hong Kong needs that, just as Paris needs that, just as Rio de Janeiro needs that, just as Lagos needs that, just as Chicago needs that—just as everyone everywhere needs that.

But knowing this to be true, the work of the Telos Group is terribly honest about what is, and what might be. Over the years of its life, its vision has been one born of a long hope. It is only those without much skin in the game who can afford the short-term fiction that it is possible to choose sides; it is only those who have not walked among both peoples in the deep conflict, hearing the stories of sorrow from both Israeli mothers and Palestinian fathers. They alone can pretend that the land can ever be holy without doing justice to both sides, without loving mercy for both peoples, without a humility that is rooted in a negotiation of their true commonwealth, the common good that must be if their land is to be.

This kind of deeper longing that marks the work of the Telos Group is distinctive to those whose "telos" is truer and necessarily more hard-won. By necessity it must take account of the very personal, very tender stories of families whose greatest hopes become their greatest heartaches; as it must also see into the complex character of twining together the ecologies of rivers and social identities, which is at one and the same time history and politics and economics—so from the most personal to the most public, which is what is required of true vocations wherever they are found.

And while the Telos Group has focused its work on the Middle East, particularly the land we call Israel, their creative vision has been drawn on to help make sense of other intractable conflicts with their own terrible histories. For example, the centuries-long wrong that is uniquely American, the poison pill of racial injustice born of slavery. Because Telos believes that the "come-and-see pedagogy" is uniquely transforming, that words have to become flesh for us to understand them, they have added a pilgrimage deep into the American South, taking people to Jackson instead of Jerusalem, to Birmingham instead of Bethlehem, to New Orleans instead of Nazareth. The days are long, the travel is intense, the conversations are difficult, but the consequences are remarkable. People who have read and read about the Civil Rights troubles in their own United States begin to know more completely and critically why things have been and still are, why the travesty of the slave trade continues to plague America's sense of "commonwealth" and "common good"—because they have moved from knowing about to knowing, from looking at history from the outside to indwelling the history itself.

These are questions that run through the stories that become ours, the rivers of our lives as they are, each one growing out of the primordial question: What will we do with what we know? The oldest question is remarkably contemporary. Are we becoming people who see ourselves responsible, for love's sake, for the way the world turns out?

And that, first and last, is about the meaning of *telos*, because it is rooted in the integral connection between what we believe about things that matter most, and the way that we live life in the ordinary days of our lives—longing for hope and history to rhyme in our time and our place. In this frail life, never ever will all that might be done, be done. While we groan against that, in this fragile world never ever will all that should be done, be done. But to give ourselves for what might be, for what someday will be, is a signpost of a good life, necessarily proximate as it must be, because that is the best we get, the most that we will find in this world, crying and waiting as it is.

A strange, but graceful juxtaposition—but that is the way of the Praxis Labs.

With a vision for the way the world ought to be, and perhaps even could be, year by year they bring together some of the greatest needs that we see and hear from every corner of the earth, with very good and gifted people who offer their hard-won expertise in addressing the complexities of the way the world is.

And while it is the whole world that is drawn into Praxis—from Asia and Africa, from Europe and the Middle East, from Latin America and North America—sometimes its work is in one neighborhood in one city.

Lawrence Sheffield is from the American South, and almost always is glad to be that—but he is someone who wrestles with the ancient tension of loving the world, and yet pushing back when needed, arguing for another way when needed.

It would be possible to imagine a profile for Praxis team members: eager, ambitious, motivated, and of course someone who has made his or her way through the Great Schools of this earth. Some are like that, but some are not. Instead some are people whose visions of what ought to be are ground out of lived experience in the most ordinary places among the most ordinary people, and yes, they are as eager, as ambitious, as motivated as anyone—and Lawrence is like that.

He loved baseball as a boy, and loved fishing and hunting too, a good boy who wanted to be a good man—and that took him to find his first work as a fireman in Birmingham, Alabama. Through the next years he began to learn about the story of his city in ways that were perplexing and troubling. In particular he was drawn to the problem of unemployment among African-American young men.

A good man in the very best way, Lawrence knew that he knew how to make things, and wondered if he could teach other guys to do the same, learning skills that could make a life worth living. The truest stories are the best stories, and his vision took time, trying this and that, trying again and again, but finally the Magic City Woodworks was created to address the need that he had seen.

Mostly hustle-and-sweat, born of surprising love, the shop is located in an old industrial neighborhood of the city, in the former steel capital of the South, a part of town that history has almost forgotten. But it is a busy place, with imagination meeting hard work, those who know coming alongside those who want to know, and over time "magic" is made. Yes, there are tables and chairs, benches and cutting boards—all beautifully crafted—and they are magic at their heart.

A few years ago I found my way to this shop, and listened, and watched, and learned. Most of the time the most ordinary work is the most important work. And the next day when I spoke to the city as a city about the recovery of the meaning of vocation for the renewal of the city, I talked about Lawrence, about his unusual vision born of an honest desire to see the flourishing of Birmingham come through apprenticing the next generation in the goodness of good work.

This is the vision and practice of Praxis. Creating cohorts of vocationally serious men and women who want to connect their hopes for history with the work of their hands, bringing ideas about life and the world to the way we live in the world—and *praxis* is the word.

The participants are mostly thirty-somethings, each one marked by an unusual maturity. They see the pains and problems of the world, and have chosen to be implicated, for love's sake, in the way things turn out. Each one is wrestling with the meaning of their lives and labors, wanting to understand the depth and range of what vocation means for them. Not a romantic among them—they have seen too much of what is not the way it's supposed to be—but every one a dreamer of what might be, a man or a woman choosing to step into history, willing to give themselves away for the sake of the others.

Often I was asked to offer an after-dinner reflection on being implicated in the way the world turns out. Not a new idea, but uniquely imagined for these people in this place. I talked about why it is that we see ourselves as responsible, for love's sake, for the heartaches and wounds of the world. Sometimes political, sometimes economic, sometimes educational, sometimes medical, sometimes social, and most of the time all merged together into an unholy mess that is ours to care about.

The good work of Praxis is to help grow these visions into being, forming a sustainable trajectory of well-conceived and well-planned growth over time that keeps hope alive—even when, as must be, the end in mind will be proximately achieved, resisting the temptation to even imagine that a perfect business plan or proposal will be found—deepening the work and developing their resources through the years. The heart of its work is drawing in those who have already given legs to their ideas, putting them together with mentors who offer years of wisdom and experience on behalf of the next generation, each one committed to being common grace for the common good.

In every different way each person, each project, is a signpost, a hint of hope showing that all is not lost, that sometimes some people are willing to give their hearts away for the sake of the world.

A Meaningful Life in a Meaningful World

Macabre is a hard word—the eyes of our hearts full of gruesome images so horrific that we recoil at what might be, its meaning so very terrible because death is both means and end. Like every important word, it began somewhere, and is likely a Latin variation on the Maccabean tragedy of the second century B.C., the Jewish revolt against tyranny that culminated with the tragic deaths of hundreds of men, women, and children, a horrific history that brought into being the festival of Hanukkah. What we know for sure is that the word is about death and dying—literally "the dance of death."

But macabre and a movie? There are horrible movies made about horror, but *Calvary* is not one. A surprising story set in a small fishing village on the western coast of Ireland, it was a film I was certain I would not want to see—with reasons that are complex and deep—but after reading a serious review I was intrigued, wondering what might be done on screen with a story written by a director who said he wanted to tell a tale about "a good priest," because there are plenty of stories about bad ones.

This tale of tenderness and tragedy begins in the village church with a priest hearing a confession through the screen, and the shocking words, "I'm going to kill you, Father." There is irony and mystery written into the words. The film is born of the terrible wrongs by priests in Ireland and throughout the world; but this priest is not that kind of priest. Instead, in the words of the confessor, "I'm going to kill you, Father, because you've done nothing wrong. I'm going to kill you because you're innocent." The unseen voice explains that he too was innocent once, but in his younger years he was abused by a priest, raped constantly for years, wounding him horribly—and a lifetime later the wounds still wound.

As the priest says, with sardonic wit, "It's a startling opening line." And as the weight of the words descends upon him, he knows that there is nothing funny about this at all.

The story takes place through the days of one week, a Sunday to a Sunday, which in and of itself makes *Calvary* very rich, a good word chosen for a morally meaningful movie. It is impossible to see it without thinking about the passion of Christ, the week between Palm Sunday and Easter; in fact, there are uncanny echoes of those days in the days of the film. But as Monday comes, and then Tuesday and more, the priest's life is taken up with the ordinary responsibilities of parish life in a small town, pastoring his people, seeing this person and that, meeting here and there—each man and woman determined to throw their distinctive sin in his face—and all the while we know that the clock is ticking, that the dance of death has already started.

Seven days later the sun is shining, a brisk breeze is blowing, and one more time the priest lingers, the shepherd of souls he is, hearing another "confession" of lament and longing from someone who has everything, but who sees it as nothing. In the messiness of life, and of ministry, the man yearns for something that will heal his heart, and the priest kindly responds, saying that he too stumbles in his faith. With pastoral attention, honest hope is offered, and he promises more—as he makes his way to the beach to meet the hurt man, Sunday morning that it is, a day that the Church has remembered for 2000 years as the day when death meets life, where despair is redeemed by resurrection.

The two talk, the wounded man full of deeply felt anger, and the priest full of compassion, knowing the worst of the human heart, yet still choosing to love. Simply said, that is his vocation, to care for the cares of the world, in Christ's name. These moments in the movie are weighty, with anger, and more anger; anyone who pays attention to the heartaches of history knows that there are righteous reasons for the rage. Watching as we are, we feel the justice of the man's wrath. But will he keep his promise, "I'm going to kill you, Father"? Or will he step back? The next moments are very tender, and very terrible, and the priest is murdered. In cold blood.

That the priest in the film is played by Brendan Gleeson, who seems to have been born for this role, is worthy of note, as he also played the character Stobrod Thewes in the film *Cold Mountain*. Murder is horrible however it happens, and in both films the deaths are awful; they have that in common—yet they are different stories in different times in different places, and their deaths are different, very different.

In the one, at the end of his long journey home, Thewes is meaninglessly murdered, and that is the end. The story is over, and there is no more story to be told. In the other, the priest is also murdered, but because the film takes place within the liturgical life of a community of stumbling saints—where ordinary life is made sacramental, if we have eyes to see—the meaning of the murder is something more than meaningless. As mysterious as the cross of Christ is for all who wonder, it is about the sacrifice of an innocent man who chooses, for love's sake, to take into his heart the wounds of the world.

The words in the confessional are chilling and stark: "I'm going to kill you because you're innocent." And while the filmmaker does his creative best to show us the priest as an ordinary man with a history like the rest of us—a very clay-footed man with a history of glory and ruin—he is also a good priest most hours and most days, loving his people through the years of their lives, doing his work for Christ's sake in the service of his parish.

And it is that man that enters into this week with a startlingly clear vocation before him. The hours pass, the days come and go, and in imitation of Christ he allows himself to be mortally wounded, knowing what he knows of the wounds of the wounded man. There is nothing happy here. In fact the visual shock of the murder is gruesome in every way, a scene most of us will not ever want to see again. But that is the story that we are given in *Calvary*, the director wanting to make a good film about a good priest. Is that possible? Can it be done? Was it done? Even with the grievous griefs? The terrible images and words?

What is astounding in the film is the director's decision to reflect on the vocation of a man whose calling in life is to see and hear and feel the sins of the world, and then to offer a true grace. While the film is not a theological treatise on the nature of salvation, or to be very technical, on the meaning of substitutionary atonement, it is an artfully profound treatment of the nature of vocation for people living in a world that has become skewed, where our loves and longings have become distorted. All of us are born with hopes for the truest intimacy, to know and to love, to be known and to be loved; little boys are, and priests are too.

All of us are. But in a wounded world, deep-seated desires are often terribly disordered, not only hurting others but hurting ourselves too—and the pain is pervasive, often overwhelming. That is why it matters that we know who we are and why we are, that we know what our true humanity is about, that we know what it means to be human. If we miss here, we miss everywhere else.

And that is why the ethic of virtue still matters. An ancient wisdom, but a profoundly perennial insight into the meaning of life as a whole, the virtues are by definition about the reason for life, our reason for being human in the world. *Vir* is that word, echoing across time, asking and asking again, "What does it mean to be human?"

Calvary is not a sermon, and therefore it has no "message" for its audience. But it is a story with moral meaning, as the best stories are, and if we have eyes, then we might see that it is about people just like us, from beginning to end. The priest, the murderer, the adulterer, the thief, the depressed daughter, the bully, the suicidal author, the scoundrel, the grieving widow, and more, each one a glorious ruin, in their distinct ways a son of Adam, a daughter of Eve. And threaded through is the story of the priest who feels called to his work, but who knows his frailty, feeling his own brokenness in the broken world all around him.

In a thousand different ways, that is what vocation is for everyone everywhere. To know that our truest self is found in giving up our selves, and instead taking into our selves the hopes and heartaches of others, in imitation of Christ, whose own vocation was to take into his heart the wounds of the world, for love's sake. Knowing the world in its great griefs, loving the world through his great grace—at one and the same time Christ is fully God and fully human, in his life showing what life is finally and fully about. That is the *vir* of every life.

But to see that in the story of *Calvary* is to understand that the story of which we are part is a story that is deeper than the here and now. In *Cold Mountain* the murder was meaningless, meaningless, meaningless, a hard-hearted twist in a flawed narrative that glories in what the Central Europeans of the twentieth century saw as "the absurd"—the starkness of a secularized world with no windows to transcendence. As Havel saw it, very plainly, very plaintively, "If we give up on God, then we give up on meaning and purpose, accountability and responsibility." In the reality of the world that is really there, none of us honestly believe that all we hope, all we need, is summed up in the creed "Eat, drink and be merry, for tomorrow we die." In our bones we know there is always more to life than life; but to live that way, for love's sake taking into our lives the longings of others, we must see the story as a deeper story that makes sense of our hope that this life, with its disappointments and deaths, its terrors and tragedies, is not yet everything that will be.

The final scenes of the film *Calvary* are signposts of that hope. As we see the whole village in a cinematic scrolling through of life after the murder, we see vignettes of the different people we have met during the week, and one is a woman whose husband was tragically killed in an auto accident on a country road near the village. On holiday in Ireland, they were only visitors to the area, and she was among those the priest pastored during the week, offering his care in her heartache. Flying home to Italy, her husband in a casket in the hold, she prays, crossing herself with belief that all is not lost, that some things are still true that give meaning to her life, that her love was real and true and right, a profoundly proximate love it was—that "Calvary" is still Calvary, and can sustain her in her great grief.

And then surprisingly, at the very end we see the priest's daughter—a complex story itself, which is the tenderest relationship in the film—who has chosen to visit the prison, and her father's murderer. In simple, sober quiet, she sits waiting for him to come to the glass partition, her looking at him, him looking at her, each pondering what to do, each picking up the phone for what becomes a conversation without words. The silence is weighty, but what is clear is that she cries, tears of grace falling down her face. And with that, the film is finished. *The end.*

The stories of *Cold Mountain* and of *Calvary* ask and answer in their own ways the question that has been the question of my life—and a question that runs through every life, and through every death: What's the point, anyway? Is there a point? Or in the end, when all is said and done, is it *point-less?* Can we find our way to a meaningful life in a meaningless world? Can we make sense of vocation in the void? Can we be called without a Caller? Human beings that we are, we long to know.

And from these questions, there are more, questions that long to be answered. Do I have a *telos* that is sufficient to meaningfully orient my *praxis* over the course of life? Does what I understand about the meaning of life, the reason for being in the world, give me an honest grounding for the longings that are mine, the loves that are mine? Can I form a vision of vocation that can make sense of who I am, of why I am, of what I want to do with my life? These questions, which are one question, asked or not asked, are the great questions of every life—and they must be answered, requiring that we press in more deeply, exploring the necessary relationship of metanarrative to narrative, of the Story we believe that makes sense of life, and the story of our own lives. The answers, necessarily, will be proximate, seeing through a glass darkly as we do; but weighty as they are, that we ask them, and then answer, matters; it matters very much.

3

STORIES WITHIN STORIES

Our curse as humans is that we are forced to interpret life as a sequence of events—a story—and then when we can't figure out what our particular story is we feel lost somehow.
—Douglas Coupland, Life After God[16]

I need God.

Vancouver, British Columbia, is one of the most beautiful cities in the world. Glory and majesty everywhere, from the great ocean to the great mountains, the waters of the Pacific Northwest winding their way in and through the landscape like fjords—all grand and all together.

But as full of wonder as it is, the shining city with its gleaming glass towers that so wondrously reflect the light of the sea and sky, there is also a metaphysical and moral weight, if one has eyes that see. A starkly secular city, and proud to be, having moved beyond any memory of transcendence and truth as defining realities, Vancouver is a city of the twenty-first century, the globalizing, pluralizing, secularizing twenty-first century. And while there is a sophisticated sense of communal self, one that requires attentiveness to all claims about the nature of reality—necessarily religious as they are, painstakingly acknowledged as they sometimes are—there is an aching undercurrent that is haunted by living in a city "after God."

But one would need to be very attentive, willing to ask searchingly good questions before that ache is acknowledged. Sons of Adam and daughters of Eve, we know, yet we do not

[16]Douglas Coupland, *Life After God* (Pocket Books, 1994), 223.

know—and to remember Simone Weil, it is learning "to know" that is central to human being.

Most of us find a thousand reasons to be disinterested in cosmic questions. There is a lot of life to be lived, our days are full of the stuff that makes life, life—and the people of Vancouver are people who love "life," especially the outdoor life found on the sea and in the mountains. Watching as I have, listening as I have, I have seen that "disinterest" in the great questions of life under the sun is often born of the distractions so easily accessible for those who love to ski and sail, to climb and hike. As a child of the West I understand those loves, but like all loves, they can be disordered, making them our first loves when they cannot be in the reality of the world that is really there, if we are to flourish as human beings.

But not everyone looks out rather than in. For reasons of the heart that are as deep as we are, sometimes when we wake to the morning, the bright shining sun or the slow drip of rain, we are drawn to its complexity, wondering why and what and wherefore. Artists are folk like that—on canvases and pages, stages and screens, feeling things first before the rest of us do, seeing and hearing the world in its glory and its ruin, the vocation of their lives reflecting the longings of the heart—and that is as true in Vancouver as anywhere else on the face of the earth.

Not surprisingly, to understand this city is to listen to its best-known contemporary artist, the novelist Douglas Coupland, who cannot write without one more time, one more book, wrestling with what life in the world means, if God is gone. His novel, simply if plaintively titled *Life After God*—which is autobiographically rooted, but not formally an autobiography—is the story of a long pilgrimage through the days of life, page after page until we come to the very end, and read, "I need God." We feel him sigh, and we do too.

> *Now—here is my secret.*
>
> *I tell it to you with an openness of heart that I doubt I shall ever achieve again, so I pray that you are in a quiet room as you hear these words. My secret is that I need God—that I am sick and can no longer make it alone. I need God to help me give, because I no longer seem capable of giving; to help me be kind, as I no longer seem capable of kindness; to help me love, as I seem beyond being able to love.*[17]

There is a starkness here. In his sober wisdom, Havel, the great Czech playwright who became his country's president, saw the line in the sand over being human grounded in this very idea, observing that when we lose God, we lose meaning and purpose, accountability and responsibility. A different man in a different place in a different time, Coupland longs to love, but feels unable to love, if God is gone.

I need God.

But do we? So modern that we are, so full of our lives *after* God with their complex relationships and responsibilities. So sure that our lives in the world are "quite well, thank you," certain that we have moved on because the world has moved on. What is Coupland seeing and hearing and feeling that his neighbors are not? And what can be believed about God, anyway? About what it means to be human? About the meaning of history? The questions matter, and they keep being asked and answered by and for all of us, wherever we are in the world.

On the Ordering and Disordering of Our Loves

As crucial as it is, the relationship of religion to life is perennially problematic—and even more deeply, the relationship of our deepest beliefs about God, and the gods to the whole of life, from

[17]Coupland, 359.

the most personal to the most political, from the bedrooms of our lives to the public squares of history. It is difficult to get this right, and mostly we miss.

At its heart, the history of the world is a history of loves, ordered and disordered, and frail as we are—intellectually, morally, and psychologically—more often than not we love the wrong things for the wrong reasons, and as must be, there are implications for persons as well as polities. There is public meaning to what we believe, and why, meaning for ourselves but also meaning for the way we live together in the commons of our lives.

What will we worship and why? Baals of every kind rise up, calling for our allegiance. Always and everywhere, we choose someone or something to matter most. Money. Sex. Power. And more. *Homo adorans*, we will give the cohering power in our lives to something. "This is why I get up in the morning, this is why I live." Try money, sex, and power again. This is true for all of us, whether we are conscious of it or not, whether we see ourselves as "religious" or not; the deepest root of "religion" is "to bind" in fact, and we do bind ourselves to someone or something, giving our loyalty and love. As Bob Dylan plainly put it in his song for the centuries, "You gotta serve somebody, it may be the Devil or it may be the Lord, but you gotta serve somebody." Yes, in billions of ways we do; yes, because that is at the heart of our humanity. Even if we flinch at his stark juxtaposition, resisting "the Devil" as the only other object of our service, we will make something matter most, and everything else in life finds its place after.

And as peoples, we come together with beliefs in common, ways of believing that become ways of behaving, ways of behaving that become ways of believing. Tribes and tongues and traditions, East and West, North and South, we are *cultured* people. Asian and even Indonesian *cultures*. African and even Kenyan *cultures*. European and even Irish *cultures*. Latin and even Brazilian *cultures*. We cannot not be. That the very idea of "culture" comes from "cult" is critically important, an etymological truth that is philosophically and psychologically profound as well. In premodern, modern, and postmodern times, someone or something is believed to matter most, giving explanatory power about the nature of being human in the world in a way that satisfies our souls—whether we believe in souls or not.

The sun and the moon, the sea and the sky, each one has captured the hearts of men and women over the face of the earth, seeing "god" everywhere in everything; and the pantheisms of the twenty-first century still make these claims, offering their own hopes for the now-and-the-not-yet of human life and history. Theisms also argue for a way to live in the world, setting forth liturgical rhythms that order the days of our lives, shaping our loves and our labors in the name of God. That is true for the materialisms of history as well, and they are in reality as "religious" as any other "ism," with confessions of faith in what is and what is not that are *cultic* in character, insisting that their way is "the" way. Whether we live in Jakarta or Jerusalem, in Mumbai or Manhattan, as human beings we are *homo adorans,* and in the unfolding of history, every variety of religious commitment makes its claims about reality, and necessarily about the reality of human life. Who are we? Why are we? What will we do with our lives?

At the dawn of the modern age, what we call the Age of Enlightenment, it was assumed that now that we "know" as we do; in order to see more completely what is true and what is not true about the reality of the world, we must leave behind "the dark ages," and all that was once believed, all that was once assumed about the way the world is and ought to be. *Who ever really believed that, anyway? How could they have?* Because, of course, moderns we are and enlightened we are, now we know!

In my undergraduate years I gave much of my final year to a thesis exploring these questions; it mattered to me to have answers that made sense of me and my world. Having left school because the questions mattered, after years away, thinking and traveling, reading and writing, working with my hands and my heart, I finally returned and began to study more seriously in the worlds of anthropology and psychology, history and literature, theology and philosophy. What my time away taught me was that learning was primarily my responsibility, that I was the learner before my professors were the teachers. While I came to love some of my professors, opening myself to them to learn all that I could, I began to see that I had to bring questions that mattered into the classrooms and courses, asking for guidance in my pilgrimage through my study. *What is more important here? What should I read? What do you think of what I have already read, of the conclusions I have come to? And if this is true, then what about this?*

Eventually I took up a question that still runs through my life most of life later. For my thesis I studied two Englishmen, both named Francis Bacon, relatives across the centuries. One was the encyclopedist of the sixteenth century, and the other the painter of the twentieth century; one first articulated the promise of the Enlightenment, and the other poured his outrage at its eventual meaning onto the canvasses of the modern world; one certain that our new knowledge would bring about a great new day, the other despairing over what we now know about ourselves and the world—and I named my study "From Instauration to Alienation: A Study of Two Francis Bacons." I read, and thought about what I read, working hard to make honest sense of my culture, of where it had come from and what it now meant for me and for my generation.

At the symposium in which we presented our work, I took my turn among the other students who, like me, had labored for a year to bring to conclusion their undergraduate learning. One was a question within history, another in literature, yet another in the sciences, and more, each a serious presentation, all aware of the weight of the afternoon, every student knowing that our studies looked both back and beyond.

To say it as simply as I can, I was just like everyone else. Having thought about a question for months, I was weary of the work I had done, but I also wondered what all that work might mean for my future—in fact for the future. No rockets went off, and no press releases were given. All in all it was a quiet day at the end of a long year, and I can remember an existential obligation to think about things that were woven into life in the world. Then as now, I believe that ideas have consequences, that knowing something about the world is critical if we are to know our place in the world; and yet I am also sure that my questions and answers were born of the necessary innocence of my early twenty-something years. I know that I longed to know, and to know what possible connection there was between my learning and my life—and that longing finds its way onto these pages years later.

When Ideology Becomes Idolatry

But again, what does this mean for the relationship of faith, of whatever kind, to the public life of a people? The relationship of cultic commitments of every kind, to culture, to the ways we think and live communally, culturally? Hard as it is, it matters that we work at getting this right.

The citizens of the world are weary of the words "And may God bless the United States of America," emptied of almost any moral meaning as they have become in the civil religion that makes America, America. Though founded on a commitment that there would be "no establishment of religion, for the sake of freedom of religion," in its 250-year history America has stumbled, and stumbled again. Whoever the "God" of these words is, it is not the God of biblically born faith, the God whose one requirement is that human beings "do justice, love mercy, and walk humbly." It is rather a feel-good god, a smile-on-a-sunny-day god, more often than not marked by a sympathy for transcendence without any belief in truth, and tragically, a god whose hopes are remarkably American hopes. People of honest faith wince when these words are the casual conclusion of political speech-making, knowing that what has been said has almost nothing in common with the blessing of God on anyone and anything.

This is not a new, particularly American problem, as the temptation for ideology to become idolatry is as old as we are as human beings. A perennial problem—at our best and truest, longing for our common life to be a common good—we are disposed to misusing beliefs in and about God to justify the most egregious behavior, seemingly unaware that the cynical state knows our frailty and uses those very same beliefs to bolster its own short-sighted ends, its ambitions knowing no end.

In his magisterial, six-volume *The History of the Decline and Fall of the Roman Empire*, the historian Edward Gibbon observed, "The various modes of worship which prevailed in the Roman world were all considered by the people as equally true; by the philosopher as equally false; and by the magistrate as equally useful." Yes, rightly ordering the relationship of God and the gods to life in the world is very difficult, and mostly we miss. Seeing and hearing the name of God taken in such terrible vain as it characteristically is in contemporary America has been cancerous for the body politic, wounding all of us, the United States and the watching world. Yes, we have a hard time getting this right. But perhaps it is because it matters so much that we miss so much. If this was of no consequence, why would it matter? But it does, and it does again.

It is an American problem, but it is a human problem more deeply, historically and politically incarnate all over the earth. In the notably and officially "godless" society of the USSR, which no longer is, as it began its movement away from its federated, totalitarian states through *glasnost* and *perestroika* in the 1980s, the first film to chronicle this surprise was one titled, for the English-speaking world, *Repentance*. Set in the Republic of Georgia, it is the story of a city in which the mayor has died, but is buried and unburied, again and again. Finally the police watch through the night, and arrest the woman who is responsible. Most of the film is her trial. She explains that she could not leave this man buried, as he did not deserve an honorable grave because he had tyrannized her family through his dictatorial political practices, telling the sad story of oppression and persecution that went on for years. Finally a recess is called, and everyone leaves the courtroom, except the deceased mayor's grandson, who sits in silence, pondering all that he has heard.

Eventually his father comes back, looking for him, and angrily asks, "What are you doing here?" The grandson and son responds, "Did you know all of this about Grandfather?" With more fury, the father asks, "All what? What's the problem?" To which the young man responds, "But wasn't Grandfather first of all a human being before he was a politician?"

And while the film could have ended there, the story only deepens, with the greatest questions of life asked, ones with the philosophical and political weight that people ask in every generation in every culture. The film ends with a poignant scene of an old woman, a babushka, walking up to a house, asking, "Is this the way to the church?" She hears a fierce "No!" and moves on. As she walks up the street, she says to no one—no one but to heaven above—"What's the use of a street that doesn't lead to a church?"

And the credits roll.

In my travels through Central Europe, this film has come into conversations time and again, its meaning still echoing through that world. Not in the pandering of politicians, whatever their allegiance, as that is almost always cheap, rarely connected to any coherent account of a vocation in service of the common good. And not because we can find quick answers for our present and future. But rather that in an ever more pluralizing and pluralist world, understanding what "faith" means for the public square is hard work for everyone—and that is not very appealing to most of us.

What do we do with God? Not a cheap question, not a cheap answer. As Coupland writes with unusual if painful honesty, "I need God." And in one of the greatest heartaches of history, one of the most tender dramas of the soul, this was true even and especially of Friedrich Nietzsche, who celebrated the death of God, but could not leave God dead. Amidst the growing chorus as the Enlightenment vision became increasingly secularized through the years of the modern and modernizing world, Nietzsche was the clearest, announcing with finality and formality the death of God, and with that death, "the revaluation of all values," setting forth the terms of life in the new world, a world where meaning and morality have necessarily had their own deaths. With surprising honesty Nietzsche argued that if God is gone, then moral meaning is gone too; and therefore the world needed to own that, to be honest about that, *to revaluate all values*. There was a price tag for *a*theism—the contrasting vision of life in the world to theism and pantheism—and Nietzsche knew its cost, insisting that we all be honest about the morally meaningless world that no longer exists.

And yet in one of the great ironies of history it is his thinking about the nature of reality, of what is and what is not, that has shaped "reality" for the modern world. We see through his eyes, we hear through his ears; the basic judgments about what was, what is, what will be, are born of what he believed and did not believe. That is indisputable, even though page after page of his writing is God-haunted. That God is in the grave is without question; that Nietzsche will not leave him there is troubling. And whether we have ever heard of "The Enlightenment" it still casts its shadow on everything. The modern world is Nietzsche's world, and as his heirs—whether we want to be or not—we live in a world without windows to transcendence, without windows to truth.

At least we do in public, in the public places of our lives. But in our quiet moments—as with Coupland—perhaps we are like him, and we know in the deepest places of our hearts that we too need God.

On the Meaning of Meaning

What do we do when we lose the story of the world? When we cannot find ourselves in a story that makes honest sense of ourselves, and of the world around us? Coupland's insight is worth hearing again: "Our curse as humans is that we are forced to interpret life as a sequence of events—a story—and then when we can't figure out what our particular story is we feel lost somehow." More politely put than the tortured canvases of the twentieth-century British artist Francis Bacon, crying out against the cultural inheritance of the Enlightenment with his angry and artful paintbrush, Coupland's post-modern prose is marked by a search for meaning in his life, and in all of life, *after Nietzsche.* With a surprising understanding of the integral relationship of a Great Story to the story of his life, his novels wrestle with the ideas of a *metanarrative* to the *narrative* of his life, feeling in his own bones the tension between the two.

These are the questions everyone asks and answers, and our lives depend on honest answers to these honest questions. MacIntyre's wisdom again: "I can only ask the question 'What am I to do?' if I have asked the prior question 'Of what story or stories do I find myself a part?'"[18] That is the conundrum Coupland faces, the life-in-the-world that perplexes him as he concludes his novel *Life After God.* "My secret is that I need God—that I am sick and can no longer make it alone. I need God to help me give, because I no longer seem capable of giving; to help me be kind, as I no longer seem capable of kindness; to help me love, as I seem beyond being able to love."

Because our reasons of the heart are deeper than reason can ever know, when we read Coupland we read him as a human being longing to make sense of who he is and why he is, and therefore of what he will do with his life. And for him, as for all of us, he lives stretched taut between what he believes is true for all of life and what he believes is true for *his* life. As full of meaning as the words *metanarrative* and *narrative* are, most of us never need to use them in the everyday lives we live—and yet they are ideas that we all live with because we all live in and by their meaning.

Everyone sees the world through a lens of the heart, the heart being the center of human being, forming beliefs about life, about God, about the human condition, about history, about justice and injustice, about all of reality. As the unusually gifted

[18]MacIntyre, *After Virtue*, 216.

professor and scholar David Naugle has written, we are "cardio-optic" in our humanness, making sense of life and the world in and through our deepest commitments about the things that matter most.[19] And because it is the ordering of our loves that forms us, our first loves form us most deeply, becoming our cultic commitments—whether we are pantheists, theists, or materialists, or imagining some other way of making sense of the universe. We will make something first in our hearts, binding ourselves to its claims upon us, and upon the way we see and hear the world.

Articulate or not, conscious or not, we live out of the stories we believe to be true, true to the way we see and hear the world, born from the loves of our hearts, *cardio-optic* as we are. Hindus and Buddhists, Jews and Christians and Muslims, evolutionary materialists and street-level hedonists are human beings first, and therefore people who hold together at the very heart of life the dynamic tension of metanarrative and narrative, which are other words for "all of life" and "my life." On some level, we expect our beliefs about all of life to form our lives, as our lives form our beliefs about anything and everything; and that back-and-forth is nothing if not a complex and mysterious reality.

There is no one who has written so widely and so well on this as Victor Frankl in *Man's Search for Meaning*. A survivor of the Holocaust, he kept notes during his prison years that became a book one year after he was freed, and millions and millions of copies later his name is synonymous with the meaning of meaning, of why and how we make sense of making sense.

Born of a Jewish family in Vienna, he was a gifted and serious student with a deep sense of purpose shaping his learning and his life. As hints of the coming horror began to be told about the Nazi vision, he chose to stay in Vienna to care for his aging parents, a sense of great obligation born of great love. But finally no Jews were allowed to remain in their homes, everyone was rounded up, put into cattle cars, and taken into the concentration camps from which most did not return.

---

[19]David Naugle, *Worldview: The History of a Concept* (Eerdmans, 2002).

Frankl began his pilgrimage of sorrow in Theresienstadt in Czechoslovakia, then on to Auschwitz in Poland, and then on to Kaufering III and Türkheim in Austria. His book chronicles those long days and years, drawing us into the dehumanizing character of the death camps. Human beings the world over have listened, reading his reflections on the nature of life and death, knowing that we must silence ourselves before his suffering, wrestling with the meaning of meaning as he did. Pushed to the wall of human existence, pushed beyond the wall of human imagination, millions did not make it through, either being forced into the gas ovens, or in despair giving up, sighing their last breaths on work details in the winter cold or in crowded, but lonely beds. What point could there be in all of this?

Frankl painfully wrote about his search for something that would make some sense of what "the point" was and why it was—a meaning to the meaning of it all. Because he lost so much in those years, his parents and wife, his health as a body and soul in community, when with his hard-won wisdom he insists that "meaning" means something, we pay attention, feeling the weight of his words, honoring him because his deepest commitments and loves emerged through the refiner's fire of terrible evil, still holding onto his humanity, to the hope of being human.

Given my reading over the years, giving the attention of time and heart to the meaning of Hitler and Nazism, I have wondered what Nietzsche would have done with the Holocaust. He lived in the world of ideas, and, as noted here, his ideas have had far-reaching effect, influencing the world as we know it. But tragically, he had a hard time with ordinary life, of living into the meaning of his ideas about the good society, his last years being full of pain and sorrow with diseases of heart and mind, soul and strength. The morally meaningless life he celebrated was not a good life.

There is a serious thread of intellectual and cultural history that connects the two, Nietzsche's arguing for an Übermensch and Hitler's vision of a master race, an Aryan people who were collectively "supermen"—and, terribly, the Nazi determination to exterminate all who fell short of that ideal. Again, history is complex, and honest people are humbled in its face. We know, and yet we do not know. We wonder, and at the end of the day, we see through a glass darkly, always.

But the question remains: What would Nietzsche have done with the Holocaust? Given all that he believed about life and the world, about the nature of power, about what it means to be human, what would it have meant for him to sit with Hitler and his chief collaborators, as they planned the deaths of peoples and populations? What would he have done watching millions walk from the cattle cars into the gas ovens? Would it have been possible to continue to argue that "enlightened" human beings are "beyond good and evil"?

To imagine a conversation between Nietzsche and Frankl is as fascinating as it is ponderous. What would they have said to each other? What could they have said to each other? There is a chasm between the two men, a world with worldviews that cannot be reconciled.

For Nietzsche, the denial of transcendence and truth meant moral meaninglessness; for Frankl, his struggle against personal pain and systemic evil brought him to the conclusion that the very heart of being human is our search for meaning, for some meaning in a seemingly meaningless world. While never in his writing does he draw on the words "metanarrative" and "narrative," it is clear that in the face of unimaginable loss, he longs to understand these questions: Is there meaning to my life? Is there meaning to life?

These are the most human questions, and in every time and place they are asked, and answered. Wherever we are, unique as each one is, we are first of all, most deeply of all, people who long for meaning, and we will do just about anything to satisfy our souls—sometimes painfully and poignantly concluding with the generations that we should all simply "eat, drink and be merry, for tomorrow we die." But others long for something more, something more worthy of us, a proximate meaning, if we are to be human. Frankl's search is that, simply that, even if profoundly that.

And the Longing of Longing

Having been apprenticed by a wise man who loved film and took me with him to the theater as I moved from adolescence to adulthood, teaching me to "see" cinema, I have long been enamored with gifted filmmakers. Years later, I still remember the lights dimming, and to my 20-year-old surprise my teacher taking out a pencil and paper as the movie began—I raised my eyes, wondering what he was doing. In the best of being British and wonderfully kind and proper, he said, "Of course I do not leave my brains at the box office!" He was serious, and I became serious too. For him, films were "confessions in celluloid," always one more cinematic argument for what it means to be human, "images of man" as he called them. I play, therefore I am. I work, therefore I am. I kill, therefore I am. I copulate, therefore I am—and I listened, and learned, beginning to see the stories of the screens of my life differently.

Cinema shapes both our souls and our societies, with each and every story a window into what it means to be human, each and every story a way of making sense of making sense. Conscious or not, intentional or not, every movie maker tells a tale that is a wager on meaning, on the meaning of meaning, and not only personal meaning but public meaning, skillfully making an argument about what it means to be human, human beings that long for meaning in the heart of our hearts. *What does this day mean? What does my life mean? And perhaps more searchingly, does anything have meaning?*

While most movie making passes us by, the stories told and sold and soon forgotten, sometimes there is a film that stands out as something more, as about something that matters more. In her directorial debut into the wider world of filmmaking, with *Past Lives* Celine Song has told a story like that, with surprising simplicity offering a film about the long friendship of a woman and a man who together wonder what their relationship means, about what they are supposed to "mean" to each and for each other.

Stretched between Seoul and New York City, and therefore between Korean and American cultures, the film begins on a school playground when the two are children, with affection and innocence forming a friendship that might have been forever—except that it is disrupted when the girl moves with her family to Toronto. Ten years later they are in graduate schools, and through the strange wonders of social media, they "find" each other again, as she studies writing in NYC, and he engineering, still in Seoul. They are overwhelmed with each other, young adults that they are now, and all through the hours of the day and night, the time zones of the world between them, they talk and talk and talk, each one aware of something deeper that binds them together, kindred souls that they are, almost sure that they always have been.

Early on the Korean word *inyun* is offered as a way to understand the almost cosmic sense they have for and about each other, a connection that they can hardly communicate and yet is at the center of the story. Fate? Providence? The way things are supposed to be? And all of that is interpreted through the lens of Asian Buddhism with its belief in "past lives," of the millions and millions of reincarnations that make us "us," the people who see and hear and feel in the ways that we uniquely do.

Twenty-four years after the girl left Korea for Canada, the two meet again in Manhattan, where she now lives with her husband, and they spend a few days together after most of life apart. Surprisingly, there are no love-triangles, at all, the inevitability of adultery of some sort creating dramatic tension; that is not this story. Instead, the film is a serious reflection on commitments and choices, and the consequences that they have for the lives we live.

If anything, the story is about the meaning of love, set within the tension of the meaning of life. Does "fate" make sense of being human? Do the connections that come in ordinary life "just happen," like the act of brushing by someone on the sidewalks of our lives, wondering who they are and why they are—and perhaps wondering whether we have known each other in a "past life" that somehow gives more meaning to this life? Is an idea like chance informing our "chance encounters" enough to make sense of what we experience?

A reminder of my teacher and his confessional cinema, seeing films as one more "image of man" played out on screen, *Past Lives* poignantly wrestles its way through the most understandable hopes of the human heart. To love and be loved. To know and be known. To make sense of making sense. To see my life as written into the meaning of life. Nothing cheap is offered. There is an unusual beauty to the story, full of longing as it is—and when the film ends, there is still longing, even with it being an unusual cinematic statement about a truer love than most movies ever imagine.

Though Song's story is a million miles from mid-twentieth century Europe and Frankl's "search for meaning," we cannot watch it without hearing again that human beings as human beings long for meaningful lives. All of *this* cannot just be about *that*? All that I am, all that I want to be, must be about more than what my senses sense, than what my experience can understand? There must be more.

If the materialist West gives us Coupland's lament born of the loss of a metanarrative that makes sense of narrative, then the pantheist East of *Past Lives* leaves us with longing for the same, caught in the same tension. Differently done, differently imagined, both ways of making sense are first and last impersonal, lives lived in a world that is in and for, by and of itself. Whatever meaning there is is self-imagined. Whatever moral order there is comes from within. The one is Nietzschean to the nth degree, an honest human being feeling what the world feels like when God is gone; the other is a world without grace, and the gifts of affection and hope that come with grace, all that is left being the chance-of-fate coursing through the cosmos.

And with the deepest ache, both cry out to heaven, feeling that they are forever "stuck in a moment that they cannot get out of," to remember U2's poetic lament.

All of us long. In fact, to be human is to long for more than we know, for more than we experience, for more than we imagine. *Past Lives* is a surprisingly tender story about life and love, with longing threading its way through, hoping against hope that an ordinary life has more than ordinary meaning. With "inyun" offered as a way to understand our past, our present, and our future, the question at the end is whether an impersonal universe can sufficiently explain all that is and will be, somehow in some way making sense of the days of our lives, our moments being mysteries that sometimes seem so mysteriously beyond what our senses and sensibilities can take in.

Films as films tell these tales, East and West, North and South, every one of us with longings for more, seeing the screen one more day, wondering if one more story will satisfy, somehow saying something that matters to who we are and to why we are. The twenty-first century has brought into being platforms and possibilities that the world has never imagined, with movies and more movies—even as the meaning of stories is still the same. And like it or not, cinema shapes us, explicitly and implicitly arguing for a way to "see" the world, for a way of living in the world.

The Father I Am and the Films I Love

No longer a boy, not even a young man anymore, but father that I am, for years I have awakened each day with my children in my throat. Wanting them to understand the stories of their day, to ask questions that mattered most about what they saw, to have a deepening sense of the power of stories to shape their souls, I began taking my children to the theaters of the city, the grand screens in the old neighborhoods as well as the art house cinemas, hoping that they would grow up learning to "see" what they were seeing, not leaving their brains at the box offices of their lives. At the end of the day, my best hopes were that, missing more often than not, but trying, and trying again.

Over the years they saw all kinds of movies with me. An after-school surprise for the box office opening of *Jurassic Park* on Washington, DC's grandest screen, with T-Rexes chasing us across the theater. An evening together with the playfully, theatrically rich *Much Ado About Nothing*, Shakespeare's classic made film, with Kenneth Branagh, Emma Thompson, Denzel Washington, and more, laughing when they laughed, crying when they cried. An intense afternoon with my sons, the weight of *Seven* with its macabre account of "the seven deadly sins," with hope that we could think about true evil in a culture of *whatever*. Pondering the wonderful beauty of marital intimacy in *Rob Roy*, amidst the grandeur of the Scottish Highlands and sword fighting extraordinaire. *The White Rose* too, with its story of university students who responded to the horror of the Holocaust with remarkable courage, bringing beliefs about the way the world should be to bear upon their moment in time. And more.

I can still remember taking some to see *Thin Red Line* by Terence Malick, having read a serious review that commended his skill and story, hoping it would be something worth talking about together. When the film finished, I was not sure, though again, we tried, all of us tried. But I did not give up on Malick, sometimes intrigued, sometimes perplexed by his vision, years later coming to see him as the preeminent filmmaker of his generation, writing into his cinematic storytelling the most important questions that can be asked. In film after film he raises the stakes on movie making, and while the local Cineplexes struggle to sell his stories—amusing ourselves to death as we are—more observant observers judge him differently. As one reviewer in *The New York Times* notes, "Very few contemporary filmmakers venture so boldly or grandly onto the primordial terrain of philosophical and religious inquiry, where the answers to basic and perennial questions seem to lie. Why are we here? How do we know? What does it mean?"

But in the body of his work, two films stand out, the one a metanarrative, and the other a narrative, the one a feature-length account of the whole of reality, the other an examination of one man's life—and if we have eyes that see, we will learn about the meaning of meaning from Malick.

In *The Tree of Life*, with neither footnotes nor hand holding, we are drawn into a vision of the way the world was meant to be, the way the world is, the way the world could be, and the way the world someday will be. Without a blush, this is the Story of Stories, from creation to consummation. Not parochial productions, movies made for an audience already sympathetic to his perspectives and presuppositions, Malick's movies are made for Everyman and Everywoman. When *The Tree of Life* was invited to Cannes in 2011, the most highly curated film festival in the world, it was judged the best of the best for that year. The world watches with wonder at his work.

The story begins on an ordinary day on an ordinary street with ordinary people in an ordinary town—and we are drawn into a family's life, marked by the intimacies and rhythms that people the world over know. But terribly and too soon there are tears as the mailman brings news of the death of a son, and it is that tender moment that threads its way through the film from beginning to end.

Why? Why me? How could this possibly be? They are the questions at the heart of every heart, living in the ruins that we do, searching for meaning as we are. Never cheap questions, and there are never any cheap answers. As the best storytellers do, he imaginatively asks questions which are everyone's questions; this family is in its own way every family.

In Malick's remarkable imagination, he chooses to begin at the beginning of beginnings, offering an incredible palette of grandeur and mystery, the complexity of creation itself. Nothing is said, no words are spoken, but we are drawn into wonder at what might have been. It is as if he knows that we know that sorrow must have meaning, a meaning that is cosmic if proximate, if it is to be meaningful, because the pain is too much to bear, if this is all there is.

From there we slowly make our way into the unfolding of the family's life, full of happiness and heartache as all families are. There is playfulness and tenderness, and over time the increasing responsibilities of a life together, even as we watch the fabric of the family begin to unravel. Angers and resentments, and through the years assumptions and expectations begin to form that are all too familiar, making us groan as we see our lives lived on screen.

But wounds wound, and left untended there is no future for a family that longs to be a family. As in all of Malick's movies, there are conversations and there are conversations, sometimes in the script for all to hear, and sometimes whispered for only God to hear. Along the way we begin to see that the choices made over time have not made anyone happy—in fact there is much that is very unhappy—and even those at the center of the story feel that pain, not wanting it to always be. What we are offered is grace, the grace of awareness and apology, and the grace of forgiveness.

Finally, with more mystery, Malick brings his story to an allusive end with a vision of the world that someday will be. All hurts healed, all hopes satisfied, every sad thing become untrue—the story of stories it is, a metanarrative, the one at the heart of the Christian tradition, taking up the sorrow of the son's death at the beginning of the film, thread by thread weaving a tapestry of the meaning of life and death. A great story, a necessarily complex story, it is a story with four chapters—the beginning of beginnings of the world that was meant to be, the aches and sorrows that slowly come into everyone's life in the world that is, the grace of grace in the world that could be, and our deepest longing for a world where there is no more death, no more grief in the world that someday will be.

If the first film is cosmic in its contours, *A Hidden Life* is a narrative born of the life of one man in the middle years of the twentieth century who saw himself implicated, for love's sake, in the way the world could be and should be. Living in a farming village in the Austrian Alps, far away from the troubles of the world—I have never seen a film that is as cinematically beautiful as this is—the townspeople and the farmers work together for their common life, practices that have kept them for generations. One reviewer simply wrote of it, "Cinema at its mightiest and holiest. A movie you enter, like a cathedral of the senses." And yet, and yet, the wounds of the world always at the door of our hearts, in the early 1940s the malignancy of Nazism finds its way in, bringing betrayal and division to what seems an almost pristine, if very hard life.

A farmer whose commitments and loves are so metaphysically and morally rooted that he cannot "Heil Hitler," Franz Jägerstätter is a husband and a father, a farmer and a friend, whose beliefs about God and the world, about work and worship, are so profoundly formed that he believes that a truer patriotism means he must not give his loyalty to the Führer and the Fatherland. Even when the Church of his day is grievously complicit in the ideology which becomes idolatry, Franz says "no," bearing the cost of his discipleship, painfully and terribly.

As in *The Tree of Life*, there are conversations in *A Hidden Life*. There is laughter and teasing, there are words born of faith and hope and love, there are words about the work to be done so the land will provide food for another year, and there are angry words between long friends who disagree about the nature of Nazism; but there is also a conversation with God that threads its way through the film. More quiet, necessarily subdued, sometimes with passion, if we have ears to hear, the dialogue graces us, hearing the hearts of human beings—quieter, necessarily subdued, sometimes with passion—who long to make sense of their moment in history, as difficult as it is, as dramatic as it is, as desperate as it is.

What Malick offers in this story is the gift of a greater story, an eschatological hope that Franz believes in with all his heart. As weighty as his days become, that he sees them as "now" but "not yet" allows him to live, facing the horror that is before him.

Differently done, his response is not far from that of Frankl, who in one of the great ironies of history quotes Nietzsche, the one who so searched for meaning, offering to the world the words of the one who gave up on meaning: "He who has a 'why' to live for can bear almost any 'how.'" When we read Malick we know he knew; when we read Frankl we mourn that he missed, so profoundly he missed. Not everyone will see these films, but it matters that we understand that the ideas of metanarrative and narrative are written into the stories of the screens of everyone's life, as plainly seen, as poignantly portrayed in *Past Lives* as in *The Tree of Life* and *A Hidden Life*.

Lest we imagine that this thesis is so far away from ordinary people in ordinary places, while most will not see Malick, auteur that he is, most have seen the films of Pixar, born of on-the-ground geniuses, telling tales that even the littlest among us love. So differently done, and yet in their own playful ways they are stories that reside within the same dynamic of metanarrative to narrative, of all of life to my life. Think about *Toy Story* and *Cars*, about *Inside Out* and *Soul*. We are invited in to ponder and smile as we take into our hearts the truest truths of the universe, each story one of surprising depth, asking questions about the human condition, about what it means to flourish as human beings—as the best films must.

From Song to Malick to Pixar and more, the best movies are always "more," because we see that ideas have "legs" in the world in which we all live—seeing and hearing out of our hearts as we do, our hearts being formed by pre-theoretic commitments that are so deep within us that we cannot live any other way. We live out of our loves, whether we intend to or not, whether we believe we do or not. The challenge is to be folk who choose well, finding our deepest and truest selves in beliefs that are true to the way the world really is, that make sense of our longing for a morally meaningful universe, and push come to shove, that give us the courage to live with an integrity of heart and mind that holds on to our humanity, making peace with something that is more beautiful, something that is more true—making peace with the proximate in and through the days of our lives.

When all is said and done, the vocation for every son of Adam and daughter of Eve is always the same, that of deepening the coherence between who God is and who we are, between what God's world means and what our lives mean—rather than dismantling that relationship of metanarrative to narrative, the revaluation of all values becoming a valueless life and world resulting in the abolition of human being, lonely people longing for something more than we are. . . . *I need God.*

The Fabric of the Universe

Born into a family that loves music, Wynton Marsalis has been composing and performing music that people the world over applaud and honor, becoming the best-known face of jazz in the twenty-first century. Growing up in New Orleans in what has been described as "the first family of jazz," he eventually made his way to New York City, becoming the featured musician at Lincoln Center, earning multiple Grammys for the excellence of his work, the only musician to win Grammys for both jazz and classical albums—even awarded a Pulitzer Prize for the artfulness of his craft and the importance of his music to the public square of America.

What is his music? Remarkably able to play across genres, he threads jazz of every kind through his work; but he has also offered his trumpet to the work of Bach and Beethoven, Mozart and Vivaldi; and at a profound level the blues too are written into his understanding of the art of his life. Of the latter he intriguingly writes, "The blues was not just a musical form; it was a rich legacy that is part of our national identity as Americans. It was only later that I began to recognize that the blues trains you for life's hurdles with a heavy dose of realism about life and love and pain and death and stupidity and grace."[20]

Of the over one hundred albums he has produced, *Blue Interlude* offers one of his most fascinating compositions, "Jubilee

[20] "Wynton Marsalis & Indra K. Nooyi - The Dialogues - Connecting Leaders," *Wynton's Blog*, April 14th, 2014.

Suite," a story set in song that feels as if it was woven out of the fabric of the universe. With a beginning, a middle, and an end, we hear the beautiful complexity of the world through Marsalis's trumpet, note by note entering into a remarkable depth of feeling, awakening us to nuance and wonder. But slowly and then more slowly those notes begin to be less consonant, with an uncomfortable dissonance unraveling in our ears, and we hope against hope that this is not all that is and will be. And it is not, as Marsalis begins slowly, then more slowly to weave the world together all over again, drawing in the beginning of the suite, but now with an unimagined richness, creating sounds that resound in the deepest places of our hearts.

The suite is a story of stories unfolding through time, one that begins with beauty, that brings brokenness into its very being, and that concludes with a renewal of what once was and of what could be, becoming even more beautiful, more than it was at the beginning, musically and mysteriously remembering the metanarrative.

Marsalis calls his final piece "Grace." Of all the words that might be chosen, this one captures the uniqueness of the Christian story unlike any other, its hope integrally rooted in the idea of jubilee. In the Torah "the jubilee" is a vision of the way life ought to be, of the way life should be, that is set forth in the Hebrew Scriptures, one that addresses the whole of reality. Formed by the holy rhythm of work and worship, of six days and then a seventh, this mandate from heaven is stretched across the weeks and months and years: social relationships and economic responsibilities, the way that people and place are bound together over time, the stewardship of land within a common life that remembered responsibility as the heart of our humanity. Seven days, seven years, seven times seven years, and finally the year of jubilee . . . when all things were set right. Debts forgiven, land returned, hope restored—all this because grace is written into who we are, why we are, and what we do with our lives.

Intriguingly, Bono and his band U2 offer their own artfully aching reflection on this story within stories in their allusively titled song "Grace," poetically setting forth what grace is and does, then starkly contrasting it with karma, with its dead end to our deepest longings. If the Nietzschean world is right, if "past lives" is the defining reality of human life under the sun, then all we have is karma of some kind, whether in the materialism of the West or the pantheism of the East. There is no beginning to the story, there is no end to the story, and we are stuck in the middle, with dissonance everywhere in everything; the reality running through both is the belief in a fated universe where everything is determined before time, and therefore where grace has no home. *It is what it is, and that's it because that is all that ever could be and should be.*

But it is in this very painful place that Coupland, who is first of all a human being and then an artist with an uncanny sense of our postmodernizing time in history, hopes for something more. Not able to figure out what the story is about—if *this* is all there is—he writes that he "feels lost somehow," his own humanness crying out in this "life after God." Longing for windows into the meaning of the universe, of what it means to be human in the world, he feels what we all feel, that without God we are alone, even lost in the cosmos. Nietzsche's brutal honesty is so stark that most shy away from his insistence that if God is gone, we must give up on meaning and morality, on the possibility of a morally meaningful universe.

But is *this* all there is? That is the great question of the ages, in every century and every culture. The deepest mysteries of all are born of this question, and in their different ways both Malick and Marsalis step into it with artistic seriousness. Seeing what they see, hearing what they hear, the answers they offer are bound up with God and grace, simply said.

And that is not small, because if *God* and *grace* are rooted in reality—and to say it as plainly as possible, *are* reality, the world that we do not get to choose or prefer because it is simply and profoundly there—then the heart of our human vocation is to see and hear what is there, remembering the story that was, the story that is, and the story that could be and will be, *proximately* understood as it must be.

The stories of your life and mine only make sense if there is a Story like this that makes it possible to connect what is real and true and right with our honest experience as human beings in the world, one where narratives are integrally written into the metanarrative that Malick and Marsalis so beautifully and wonderfully imagine.

4

THE WEIGHT OF LOVE

I have also decided to stick with love, for I know that love is ultimately the only answer to mankind's problems. And I'm going to talk about it everywhere I go. I know it isn't popular to talk about it in some circles today. And I'm not talking about emotional bosh when I talk about love; I'm talking about a strong, demanding love.[21]

—Martin Luther King Jr

"Do you have time for a conversation?"

Several years ago I was in Oxford for a seminar, sponsored by the University's Said School of Business and the Mars Corporation, on the doing of "responsible business," an idea that has captured my heart from its beginning, and still does. One morning a dear friend of a dear friend came to me, first explaining her own DPhil studies, then asking if I would be able to talk with a friend of hers. As she put it, "She has read your work. . . . Do you have time for a conversation?"

Intrigued by the words, and weighed down by them as well, I wondered who she was. What had she read? And would a conversation help?

And so we met at the little cafe next to the University Church of St. Mary's, the Vaults and Garden, a room in use since AD 1320. A South African doing years of graduate study at Oxford University, first two master's and then a DPhil, she was working hard to understand her place in the world, explaining the range of her studies over the last few years, developing an intellectual

[21]Martin Luther King Jr, "Where Do We Go From Here?" delivered at the 11th Annual SCLC Convention, Atlanta, Georgia, August 16, 1967.

passion for the aching needs of adolescent young people in the townships of post-apartheid South Africa. As she put it, "They want lives that matter, work that matters. They long for vocations too. But it is all so wrong, and deeply, systemically wrong. This is what I am studying, wrestling with what it all means."

If the desire for conversation is often the way in, surprisingly it is followed by something like this: "You have written about suffering, about heartache, about injustice, about vocations in the midst of a world that is not right, a world where we know much of the worst about life, and yet still want to hold onto what we believe to be true, working that out in the way we live. . . . But I am having a hard time doing that, knowing what I now know."

And while these have been the questions of my own life, reaching back into the first years of young adulthood when I began to see more, to know more, to feel more, each time the conversation begins with the wounds of the world I take a deep breath, knowing that this too will become a weight in my heart, knowing what I will now know. As must be, the older I get, the more I know—and as the poet Byron once noted, "The one who knows the most mourns the deepest." I understand that, now I understand that. These stories of sadness that begin with the most personal sorrows more often than not bleed into the most public wrongs, becoming only more complex.

For years I have been thinking about the responsibility of knowledge, particularly the ways that that reality implicates us, for love's sake, in the way the world turns out. *Knowing what I know, what will I do?* That has never been an abstract question for me, and so as we sat in the cafe, the history of centuries all around us, we stepped into the complexity of her study, the burden of her reading, thinking aloud and together about a way forward—for her, for South Africa, for the way the world turns out.

Though perhaps surprising, for searching souls it can be terribly difficult to care about the world, especially to keep caring once we begin to understand the weight of love. For her, someone who grew up under the long shadows of apartheid, yearning for a new body politic for her people and place, living into the hope of the Truth and Reconciliation Commission, she had entered into the seriousness of the challenges facing South Africa for the post-apartheid generation. And her years at Oxford had only deepened her commitment to a public justice for the public square, pressing her to broader and deeper analysis of what was and what ought to be.

If we are paying attention, we all know that tension.

How do we see clearly, and honestly, and still care? Byron's words are perennially poetic and prophetic. As I sat there that day, I could feel her feelings for those who suffered, for those being left behind as the nation forged a new future, one that promised to care for everyone, but tragically was leaving behind the neediest of the needy. And what would she do with her learning and her life? What would the responsibility of knowledge mean for her? What would it mean for her several serious and sophisticated degrees whose reason for being was *for* South Africa—and yet being unable to achieve the kind of "truth and reconciliation" that would honestly alter the hopes of those who only wanted to hope.

Her longings are hers, uniquely born of her time and place, and yet they are not new, not hers alone.

Cry, the Beloved Country were the words of the eloquent and passionate story of South Africa by Alan Paton, a novel in 1948 whose powerful prose drew in readers from all over the world who began to watch this nation with more than passing interest, sensing instead that its history and heartaches were global, affecting and implicating all of us. So very beautiful, and yet so full of tragedy, the novel tells the story of a nation torn apart by apartheid, by the systemic wounds of racism that alienated generations of people, Africans and Afrikaaners, the black and white peoples of South Africa.

Over the next decades the question of apartheid—the social, economic, and political separation of the races—became a *cause célèbre,* with the world sitting in judgement over what was happening in South Africa. Great evils and great wrongs seemed to go unchecked, with protests bringing imprisonment for many, best-known among them Nelson Mandela, who eventually spent 30 years in jail for his outspoken argument in favor of the dismantling of apartheid. When he was finally released, to the surprise of his own people and the world, he was elected President, bringing long-suppressed exaltation in the streets of Cape Town and Johannesburg, and throughout the land. What had once seemed impossible under the constraints of institutional racism had happened—and the people came together to vote for a new future.

A national anthem was created that honored all the tribes and tongues of the new South Africa, each with their distinct identities: the Zulu, the Xhosa, the Sesotha, the English, the Afrikaans—a new song for a new day.

Lord bless Africa
May her glory be lifted high
Hear our petitions
Lord bless us, your children
Lord we ask You to protect our nation
Intervene and end all conflicts
Protect us, protect our nation
Protect South Africa, South Africa
Out of the blue of our heavens
Out of the depths of our seas
Over our everlasting mountains
Where the echoing crags resound
Sounds the call to come together,
And united we shall stand,
Let us live and strive for freedom
In South Africa our land.

Words to live by and with, a vision that inspired a nation to imagine a new way forward—and it is not too much to say that the whole world hoped.

Twenty years later, almost a generation after this song had been written, I met the young woman in Oxford, so full of longing and love for her nation—and not all the hurts had been healed, and not all the wrongs had been righted. So thoughtful as she was, willing to do the hardest work she could imagine so that she could understand her place and its people, she was perplexed. "But it is all so wrong, deeply, systemically wrong."

What am I going to do with what I am learning? Now that I know what I know, what am I going to do?

Not the first one to feel the weight of love for her land, a truth which neither relativizes nor glamorizes her sense of responsibility for her moment in history, but her longings offer us another lens on the reality of the perennial tension between metanarrative and narrative, between what we believe about all of life and what we believe about our lives, between what we imagine should be and what in fact is—yes, about the nature of the proximate.

It All Turns On Affection

Several years into the twenty-first century Wendell Berry received the Jefferson Prize from the National Endowment for the Humanities, an honor given annually to one person for exemplary contributions to American culture and life. The occasion takes place at the Kennedy Center for the Performing Arts, as grand a setting as there is in Washington, DC, and that night it felt as if the whole city was there, the largest of the theaters filled to capacity with people whose hearts and hopes had been fired by the good work of one known as "the most prophetic writer in America."

A husband, father, and grandfather, he is also a farmer and friend, living most of his life on a family farm near the Kentucky River. But he is also an essayist, a poet, and a novelist, through his many books reflecting on the character of our life together, the nature of the "membership" that keeps us as a people in these United States. In one of his short stories he puts it this way, "The way we are, we are members of each other. All of us. Everything. The difference ain't in who is a member and who is not, but in who knows it and who don't."

Berry titled his address "It All Turns on Affection,"[22] beginning with a story of his grandfather's life and labor in Kentucky. Tobacco was the crop that kept his grandparents alive. In the spring they planted, in the summer they cultivated, in the fall they cut and cured, then sold the tobacco at the Louisville auction. On the night before his grandfather took the train from their farming community into the city to bring to a conclusion the hope and hard work of the growing season, his grandparents talked through what they needed to make if they were to keep farming another year. With their costs in mind, he went off the next morning—and came home that night with terrible news. "We made nothing." All the work, all the need, all the longing . . . nothing.

But someone did make money that year, and his name was James B. Duke, the president of the American Tobacco Company. Like robber barons before him, he manipulated the markets, making sure that he made millions, leaving those who brought the goods into being with *nothing* for their long labors.

In Berry's address, he drew on E. M. Forster's novel *Howard's End,* with characteristic insight rooting his analysis of the industrializing world of the early twentieth century in the life of a businessman who saw the business of business as solely about the maximizing of his own profit, "a capitalism without conscience" for anyone and anything beyond his own economic ambitions. It was the failure of this man who owned both the work and the worker to "only connect" that makes the story one we are still reading.

"Only connect" to what, though?

Quoting Forster, Berry's long argument is that "it all turns on affection," because as human beings living together in the world, we are bound up with each other, whether we want to be or not. That "truth, nature, imagination, affection, love, hope, beauty, joy" are the habits of heart that make for human flourishing, for healthy persons and for healthy polities, always and everywhere.

---

[22]Wendell Berry, *It All Turns on Affection: The Jefferson Lecture and Other Essays* (Counterpoint, 2012).

"Affection" is not a small word for Berry, one that only accounts for personal and private dispositions. Do we "like" chocolate? Do we "like" flowers? Do we "like" the mountains or the ocean? Instead Berry sees the word as a deeper word, one crucial for our well-being, arguing that the love of self embodied in the business practice of Duke was cancerous for the body politic, even as it made him a rich man able to build a well-endowed university. Instead of an all-consuming self-love, Berry set forth a vision of life together born of relationship and responsibility, a sense that we are implicated for love's sake in the lives of others, that our well-being is integrally woven together with the well-being of others.

Thousands came to listen to Berry that night, taking in his criticisms, his observations, his pleas, and for the most part going home to the fragmented, isolated lives of those who live in the metropolis that is Washington, DC—in their many different ways keenly aware that the contours of their days and weeks are formed by institutional shapes and structures that are indifferent to "affection" of any kind. The ways we worship and work, and the streets and neighborhoods of our lives, have almost nothing to do with the sense of a life together in which "my" flourishing has anything to do with "our" flourishing.

These issues are never finally "theoretical," only possible in the ivory towers of the world. Rather it matters that we work them out, dreaming of what could be, living for what should be.

The Economics of Mutuality

But what *could* be, what *should* be?

These have been the serious conversations of my life, for my life; but in the last 20 years they have been focused on a project we have called the Economics of Mutuality, a surprisingly serious effort to rethink the business of business. Brought into being by the Mars Corporation, still a family-owned and therefore privately held company 100 years after its beginning in the 1920s, its footprint is global, selling M&Ms and much more to the wide world.

Because it must be, the great question for a business like this is, How do we sustain profitability? With no pressure to maximize shareholder profit, and formed by an unusual conscience within the family, the perennial issue is making money in a way that acknowledges stakeholders far and wide: not only the owners and senior executives, but managers of all kinds and at all levels, as well as the scores of thousands of employees who make Snickers Bars and Dove Ice Cream Bars, as well those who grow cocoa in western Africa. Could we honestly bring into being a business that believes in an "economics of mutuality"?

One evening we hosted in our home a table full of folk from throughout the city of Washington, DC. Some graduate students, a bank president, economists from the World Bank, business people, and two Mars executives, gathered to think through Berry's essay "Two Economies," which begins here: Wherever we look in the world there are two economies, one that is the lesser economy, and one that is the greater economy. The lesser economies are a company like Mars, then a state like Virginia, then a capital region like the District / Maryland / Virginia, and then the United States, each one responsible to take a sharp pencil and work out "the numbers" for the coming year, drawing in the best advice, through the year, quarter by quarter, evaluating the relationship between expectation and reality, and finally seeing what in fact happened over the previous months. What are our numbers? What went right? What went wrong?

With his unflinching insight into what makes for human flourishing earning him respect among the youngest idealists and seasoned practitioners alike, in his essay Berry sets forth a way of discerning the difference and the difference it makes to disconnect work from the worker, as the modern capitalist economy does, arguing instead that when "the lesser economy" becomes dissonant with "the greater economy," when a particular business pretends that it can exist in and for itself, apart from a grounding in the reality of human being in the world, eventually the lesser economy fails, unable to sustain its promise.

To keep making money requires acknowledging a more complex bottom line, at least if we want to do business in the world that is really there. In the greater economy of Berry, justice can never be "just us," or even "just me." Whether we want to be or not, we are implicated in the life of the world around us, responsible, for love's sake, for the way the world is and ought to be. Very simply, Berry calls this greater economy *reality*, naming it as "the kingdom of God," and while noting that we can call it what we want to call it, what we cannot do is live for long as if it is not true, because it is beyond our choosing or preferring, *reality* as it is.

The project has grown through the years, becoming increasingly grounded in the truest *realeconomik* possible—an economics forged in the fire of reality of the global marketplace—and over time has moved from Washington, DC, to Geneva, Switzerland, with the mandate to spend its next years developing business partnerships with companies throughout the world who are willing to enter into the moral seriousness of honestly examining the business of business—what we might call the "telos" of business, which is necessarily about the purpose of business.

At our best, there has never been the belief that all good will happen in and for the world if an "economics of mutuality" can be developed, even if its argument is seriously made and heard the world over. That is not our view of history, or of hope. Heaven will not finally and fully come to earth. What we do believe is that it matters to work for signposts of what could be, of what might be, of what should be, even in our heart of hearts, of what someday will be. And so a signpost of something that is right, something that is true, something that is real—for *some* reimagining of the meaning of the marketplaces of the world, for *some* rethinking of the purpose of a life and of our life together—yes, for *some* justice to be done on the face of the earth. It is neither more nor less than a choice to make peace with the proximate.

And for that to be, for even some of that to be, in truth *it all turns on affection.* We do not live in any other world than one in which mutuality matters, as we are inextricably connected with each other, whether we want to be or not. As Martin Luther King Jr argued, "We are caught in an inescapable network of mutuality, tied in a single garment of destiny. Whatever affects one directly, affects all indirectly." And his insight is not far from Berry's, that it is "truth, nature, imagination, affection, love, hope, beauty, joy" that are the habits of heart that make for human flourishing, for healthy persons and for healthy polities, in every time and every place. Wise ones will listen, hearing in these prophetic voices visions for the habits of heart that make our life together more healthy and honest, a social ecology that is sustainable for one and all.

What Do You Love?

"The Devil laughs because God's world seems senseless to him; the angels laugh with joy because everything in God's world has meaning."[23]

Milan Kundera watched the world of Central Europe fall under the weight of totalitarianism, over most of a century being crushed, first by the Nazis and then the Communists. With remarkably artful eyes he saw the despair of his own people and place, in his books and essays writing again and again of the philosophical and political burden of those years. *The Unbearable Lightness of Being* is his astute reading of the modern world through the eyes of the Prague Spring in the 1960s. This story of love and loves explores the meaning of life and labor: If God is gone, then there are no windows to transcendence and truth. There are bare bottoms and more in the filmed version of the story, but always with questions about the meaning of sex without love, and slowly by slowly the realization that to make

[23]Milan Kundera, *The Book of Laughter and Forgetting* (Penguin, 1981), 232.

love without choosing to love is unbearable, bringing about a lightness to our being that is unsustainable.

As the story unfolds, with the tensions of life and love and longing, we hear the aching words from a woman who innocently, if naively, has opened herself to a man's affections and desires, in her heart wanting more than he is willing to give, finally asking, "Then what do you care about?"[24] Not abstract, her question is born of an intimacy without commitment, a willingness to offer oneself to another in hope—but beginning to see that being in bed together is not the same as a life together. The question Kundera asks is crucial, at least if we are to know ourselves and our world with any degree of honesty. What we care about is central to who we are, to our sense of self and of our place in society, the choices we make about anything and everything born of our answer to that question.

As contemporary as Kundera is, a modern-becoming-postmodern writer, we read him because he wrestles with the reality of the human heart, the truth of the human condition, and the best books, the truest books, always do that—which is fundamentally why we are still reading *Confessions* by Augustine of Hippo. In his time and place a man whose life without love came to its own sad end, a man living in the world that honestly is, in the very deepest way Augustine knew he wanted more than he had known, more than that which the headlong pursuit of love lost in lust had given him.

To love and to be loved are the greatest of gifts. But we can skew that, getting it wrong, loving the wrong people in the wrong places, forming loves that are profoundly and tragically full of the wrong things in the wrong ways. Certain that our commitments and cares fundamentally form us, Augustine offers one of his great gifts: his understanding of the ordering of our loves. With insight that runs through the centuries, he knew the human heart well enough to know that we must get our "affections" right, we must love the right things in the right way, if we are to flourish as human beings.

---

[24]Kundera, *The Unbearable Lightness of Being* (Harper Perennial, 1984), 121.

In his magisterial *The City of God*,[25] with its hundreds of pages centered on one great question—what is the nature of our life in the world?—Augustine reflects on the words charity (*caritas*), love (*amor*), and fondness (*diligis*), arguing that in the end, nuanced as they are, they are about the same reality. Different faces, but each one a dimension of our deepest and greatest affections, of what we care most about and for. For this brilliant professor of rhetoric who became the theologian for his century and the centuries, everything does in fact "turn on" what we love and why we love what we love.

The depth and range of *The City of God* are astounding, with page after page full of probing, thoughtful analysis of what it means to be human in the world—from beginning to end a contrast of two cities, of two ways of living in the world, the City of God and the City of Man. They are marked by a line-in-the-sand difference: One is fixed on the love of God and the other on a love of self—and there are implications for both persons and for polities, for "me" and for "we," realities that taken together as they must be are integrally woven together throughout the book, and our life in the world, whether we are of the fifth century or the twenty-first.

In the most simple way, *Confessions*[26] is Augustine's account of his life, a book-length reflection on his life from conception on, not knowing and then painfully knowing the ins and outs of his days and years. With unusual self-awareness he allows us to listen in as he remembers his childhood, his adolescence, his adulthood—the story it is of one man's pilgrimage through time. On the other hand, *The City of God* is a broader analysis of the larger world, one begun in the heart but one that necessarily has meaning for the public square too. In a word, it is the metanarrative that makes sense of Augustine's narrative; or, to reverse it, the narrative of *Confessions* takes place within the metanarrative of *The City of God,* Augustine finding the meaning of his story within the deeper story of Everyman and Everywoman.

---

[25]Augustine, *The City of God* (Penguin Random House, 2004), XIV, 7.
[26]Augustine, *Confessions* (Penguin Classics, 1961).

To press the point: In the modernizing post-modernizing world, there is much written about "narrative theology," with books by gifted people articulating a vision of theological meaning that comes from the biblical narrative. I am intrigued, but I have never seen this as "new." The truest truths cannot be that, and never are. In the fifth century Augustine was the first to set forth the biblical story of creation / fall / redemption / consummation as the Story of Scripture, of all of reality and of every human heart—a metanarrative if ever there was one. Threaded through his work we hear of human beings made *posse peccare, posse non peccare*, able to sin and able not to sin; of *non posse peccare, non posse non peccare*, not able to sin, not able not to sin; of *posse non peccare,* able not to sin, and finally, *non posse peccare*, not able to sin.

In its uniquely Augustinian way, with his own remarkable ability to write about himself as a self—the first autobiography we know—this framework makes sense of all of us, the story it is of all of us, a searching examination of one's choices over time, of one heart wrestling with the nature of true love as the deepest of motivations; as opposed to false love, which disorders us and the world around us. It is the story of the world that was meant to be, the world that is, the world that could be, and the world that someday will be, with meaning for human beings wherever we may be found.

Much more could be said, and while we might imagine that because of their substance *Confessions* or *The City of God* are the best of Augustine's work, over time *The Enchiridion*[27] has been more widely read, published time and again, becoming a catechism for the Church through the ages. "The Handbook" was born of a correspondence between a Roman businessman, Laurentius, and Augustine, the bishop of Hippo. Watching the world as he was, having no historical categories of "decline and fall" to even imagine, Laurentius was trying to make sense of his time and place, of what seemed to him the disintegration of the

[27] Augustine, *The Enchiridion on Faith, Hope and Love* (Gateway, 1996). (*Enchiridion* means "handbook" or "manual.")

Roman Empire. What is happening? What does it mean? What do we believe that can make sense of this?

Augustine responded, setting forth the Lord's Prayer, the Apostles' Creed, and the theological virtues of faith, hope, and love as the core commitments that give grounding for a life that can make it through the crumbling of Rome, the city and empire that promised to be "eternal." Centuries later it is still a great city, a very beautiful city, and yet at its heart it is a city of memories, of what was but no longer is, a glorious ruin with loves disordered through time having consequence for the people and the place that is Rome.

The bishop wrote that it is only as we take into ourselves the convictions that come from these creedal confessions that we are able to keep on keeping on. Idea by idea, he sets forth their meaning, weaving a tapestry of belief and behavior that has stood the test of time. People all over the world are still listening, still learning.

As he moves into the final section of his letter, explicating the virtues—the commitments about life in the world that direct us to our true end as human beings—he first takes up faith, then hope, and finally love. With insight into "us" that is not surprising given his almost timeless reputation, Augustine distinguishes one from another, first this, then that, and then this. When he comes to the meaning of "love," he retraces his steps with the other virtues, explaining their part in the whole of one's understanding of self and the world. But then he presses in, arguing that the *telos* of faith and hope is *love*. After every other question has been asked, the most important question is this: What do you love?

For Augustine, that question probed most deeply, going to the center of who we are and why we are.

Given that I have spent the years of my life with people who are learning to live in the world, coming into the classroom of my heart in many different kinds of ways, after listening to their lives and longings as well as I can, I have offered Augustine's question as the most critical question. At the end of an undergraduate degree, of graduate study, in fact over the years of life beyond schooling, the question for all is, "What do you love? What have you learned to love?" After we have read all the books, passed the final tests—even sometimes affirmed every creed—the question that awaits us is Augustine's: "What do you love?" What is it that matters most to you? What is it that is most important to you? What is it that is at the center of who you are, of why you are, and of what you are going to do with your life? Yes, a *telos*.

Augustine believed that our loves shape us, for good and for not, for our flourishing and for not—because our *telos* forms our *praxis*. In *Confessions* he argues that "our weight is our love," understanding that what we care most about, what is at the heart of our hearts, forms and shapes us. At the end of the day, in whatever century and culture we find ourselves, it all turns on affection.

Not surprisingly, Berry's argument in his address for the Jefferson Prize threads all of this together. Everything. All of life. All of learning. All of labor. From the most personal relationships to the most public responsibilities, our affections shape our selves and our societies. This is a hard truth, a weighty reality—but Augustine knew it, and in a very different time and place, Kundera did too.

The question of what we care about is the weightiest of questions, one we ask and answer all day long, in and through the days of our lives. Learning to care about the right things in the right way is what a good life is all about—and when we miss, we miss the meaning of our lives, and of life.

Four Modern Augustinians—Arendt, Niebuhr, Newbigin, Elshtain

In the last century there were four folk, two women and two men, whose thinking has shaped the world of our lives, each one wrestling with the most complex ideas and issues imaginable, and not surprisingly, each one was an Augustinian, rooting their thinking about life in the twentieth-becoming-twenty-first century in the insights of someone from the fifth century. Who is my neighbor? And what does "neighbor" mean to me, and for me? Very human questions for everyone everywhere, these questions were at the heart of Hannah Arendt's life.

Seeing herself as a twentieth-century Augustinian, Arendt focused her dissertation at the University of Heidelberg on Augustine's understanding of love, of love for the world. Increasingly burdened by the horrific horrors of the twentieth century, she chose to ground her thinking in the ancient wisdom of the great saint, whose own deepest reflections on the same questions drew him to see that "it all turns on affection," on what we believe about love, which could never be a simple word, a romantic ideal uprooted from its necessary place in the push and shove of history.

It was after all the civilizational decline and fall of the Roman Empire that was the fulcrum for Augustine's thinking about the nature and direction of the "two cities," the one a city with a common life that could be sustained, the other a city with a common life that would disintegrate; for Arendt it was the weight of the world between wars, with the very idea of Europe being called into question. What was it? Could it still be? What should it be? While she finished her dissertation in 1929, it was 20 years later that she wrote *The Origins of Totalitarianism*, now knowing the nearly unbearable horror of the Holocaust. Was love a rich enough idea? A deep enough word? Could it carry the weight of the world?

And she took up Augustine's vision of "neighborly love" as a means of analyzing human responsibility in history, a question that she spent her life answering,[28] she found a means of understanding human responsibility in history—a transcendent love, a world-oriented love, and an existential love, these loves threading their way through his thinking about the meaning of the city and the world. For him they were love as craving or desire (*amor qua appetitus*), love in the relationship between the

[28]Hannah Arendt, *Love and Saint Augustine* (University of Chicago Press, 1929).

human (*creatura*) and the Creator (*Creatura*), and neighborly love *(dilectio proximi*). Nuanced, complex, she wrestled with the greatest questions of the human heart throughout her life, and yet was always attentive to the reality of her moment in history, deeply formed by her apprenticeship to Augustine, for whom the personal and the public were held together in one life, *Confessions* and *The City of God*, the narrative and the metanarrative. A woman of the twentieth century, Arendt lived within that same tension, knowing that both mattered if we are to flourish as citizens and cities.

But these ideas are never abstractions. To the surprise of many in the West, so enamored were they by the promises of the Enlightenment for "a better, brighter future" for the world—now that we *knew*, of course, enlightened about all that made for human happiness—after two world wars had brought ruin to Europe and Asia, Arendt's sensitive yet piercing study of the twentieth century's great plague of totalitarianism is still seen 75 years later as the seminal analysis of why and how human beings are drawn into ways of life and living that are by definition against our happiness, against what our flourishing means, yes, against what neighbors mean and must mean.

A decade after her book appeared, and the watching world was still struggling to make sense of what had happened in the Holocaust, she decided to see its horrible incarnation in the Nazi Adolph Eichmann's trial. Thus she began writing weekly reports for *The New Yorker,* an effort that from the beginning was controversial because of the way she interpreted what it meant, and did not mean. Eventually titling her collected reports *Eichmann in Jerusalem: A Report on the Banality of Evil,* she argued that there was an ordinariness to the horrific evil of the Holocaust, a "banality" that surprised her. It was never that Eichmann was anything other than guilty for his crimes against humanity, but that she began to see him as so very ordinary, someone like every one of us.[29]

[29]Arendt, *Eichmann in Jerusalem: A Report on the Banality of Evil* (Penguin, 1963).

Week by week she listened, sitting in the courtroom so that she could observe what was said and done, wanting to accurately account for the moral meaning of the corporate evil of Nazism, which as she famously said, "Does not begin in the gas ovens, but more often than not is processed in triplicate." The starkness of her judgment is that many eyes of many people have seen, and not seen, have heard and not heard, have known and not known, choosing the indifference born of a hard heart, refusing to see themselves as complicit in evil. Eichmann himself protested that he was only obeying the laws of his land: "My job was simple: to save the country I loved from being destroyed—the battle of destiny for the German people" (*der Schicksalskampf des deutschen Volkes*).

She wrestled with this, given what she believed about human responsibility born of love, seeing in Eichmann an ordinary German citizen who failed miserably to understand the meaning of "neighbor." In her profoundly perceptive account of Eichmann's trial, she concluded her book,

> *And just as you [Eichmann] supported and carried out a policy of not wanting to share the earth with the Jewish people and the people of a number of other nations—as though you and your superiors had any right to determine who should and who should not inhabit the world—we find that no one, that is, no member of the human race, can be expected to want to share the earth with you. This is the reason, and the only reason, you must hang.*[30]

Terrible words of judgment, but ones that are necessarily grounded in both "the city of God" and "the city of man," stretched taut between an honest knowing of "neighbor," and therefore a true love for neighbor, and the historical unfolding of a love of self, its severe consequences destroying persons

---

[30]Arendt, *Eichmann in Jerusalem*, 279.

and polities. For a thousand complex and perplexing reasons, Eichmann could only see the outcome of the war in terms of his own self, of who he had been in the war, and what the war now meant for him. There was nothing to be sorry for, no one to be sorry to—because neighbor and love for neighbor were never the issue.

But they were for Arendt, as she saw their meaning threading through all that matters to us and for us in our relationships with others, near and far. *Dilectio proximi* gives us "neighborly love," which is always a most difficult love, one that is much easier to talk about, or write about, than to actually love. What do we do with real neighbors, when the words literally move into the neighborhood, having to account for those who live closest to us whose lives are intertwined with ours as family and friends? "Am I my brother's keeper?" is a question that echoes across the centuries, into every city and every civilization. What do we do with neighbors whose dogs bark into the wee hours of the night? Whose bamboo creeps ever so slowly but eagerly across and under the fence? Ideas about the world are more often than not very hard to work out in the world.

And then if we move beyond our own neighbors and their houses and begin to ponder "neighborliness" in the wider world, we find another level of complexity—and the question becomes very global. Why and how do we care for those in the majority world, whose lives with their distinctive aches and hopes are so far from ours? Or to localize the question within particular geographies: Are the English true neighbors to the Scots? the Croatians to the Serbians? the Indians to the Pakistanis? the Hutus to the Tutsis? the Japanese to the Koreans? the Portuguese Brazilians to the African Brazilians? the North Koreans to the South Koreans? And on and on. *Who is my neighbor?*

But when we begin to take seriously the questions of human responsibility in history, seeing them written into the vocations that make us "us," we soon realize that we cannot do everything. That not every hope, not every need, not every question, not every longing, is one to which we can respond—and those with the tenderest hearts feel this most keenly. Remembering to remember *dilectio proximi* is a grace, reminding us that love must be proximate, never everything for everyone, but something for someone.

On a Sunday morning in 1932, on his way into a church to be the guest preacher, Reinhold Niebuhr scribbled out a prayer on a piece of paper, aware that he would be the one to lead the congregation in its worship that day. Knowing his own commitments and loves, knowing enough of the challenges that others faced, understanding that we all long for something, even if everything we want is beyond our grasp, he wrote these words, "God, grant me the serenity to accept the things I cannot change, the courage to change the things I can, and the wisdom to know the difference."

There are few prayers that have been prayed so fervently and frequently as this one, written from the heart of someone whose theological vision became profoundly public, being drawn into a vocation marked by serious conversations about the way the world is, and the way the world ought to be. A public theologian who was also a pastor, he knew that questions about our common life can never be honestly addressed if they are not attentive to individual lives, that what we see and hear most intimately is felt most personally. Born of one people in one place, over time this heartfelt prayer began to be prayed by many people in many places, and is often best-known within the community known as Alcoholics Anonymous, which named this "the Serenity Prayer." That Niebuhr's pastoral vision, ranging across the nation and the world in the middle years of the twentieth century, could so simply find welcome in one congregation and one circle is a window for all of us into the moral and spiritual intelligence of a man who became the theological conscience for his generation.

In the years of his life, not only did he find avenues into theological education, teaching graduate students for most of his life, but also his understanding of the world, the push-come-to-shove world, was prized by leaders in business and politics in ways that we cannot imagine a century later. A man of the Word, Reinhold Niebuhr was a man of the world too, with an unusual grace living between the two for the years of his life.

But *dilectio proximi*? What did that mean for Niebuhr? His thinking ran far and wide, his writing taking up the most important questions of life in the world. When we read titles like *Moral Man and Immoral Society*, *Beyond Tragedy*, *The Nature and Destiny of Man*, *Christianity and Power Politics*, *The Children of Light and the Children of Darkness*, *Christian Realism and Political Problem*, and more, we realize that he was drawn to the complexity of our callings as human beings, and as people of faith, wrestling with the great challenge of living in but not of the world.

Central to Niebuhr's thinking was his understanding of the *proximate* character of life, a life of faith and hope and love set within the contours of honest responsibility for one's neighbor. In the journal *Foreign Policy*, he is described this way,

> *Niebuhr cherished the democratic enterprise. It was his belief that man's capacity for justice was what made democracy possible—and man's inclination to injustice was what made democracy necessary. But as a Christian theologian, Niebuhr also understood human weakness and frailty, which in the end produced "proximate solutions for insoluble problems." Niebuhr sought the middle ground—the space between the utopianism of the moral idealists and the despair of the cynical realists.*[31]

Proximate is a rich word—from *proximatus*, from *proximi*, both meaning "a neighbor" or neighborly, to be near, to be close at hand. If the second of the great commandments is to "love your

---

[31] Aaron David Miller, "In Search of Reinhold Niebuhr: America could use a little philosophical humility right now," *Foreign Policy*, May 1, 2013.

neighbor as you love yourself," the insistence on theological convictions about the life in the world becoming coherent with the way we live in the world, formed from first commitments and first loves, is deeply biblical, born of the very heart of God. Those who are nearest must see and hear and feel our love, as hard as that is to offer, as difficult as that is to do.

For a thousand reasons the wounds of the world bear down on us, making the loving of what and who is near a great challenge for us, frail ones that we are. The ancients have called this the problem of the world, the flesh, and the devil, and it is all that and more. From the most personal demons like alcoholism, to the most public burdens like national hubris, Niebuhr as an Augustinian wrestled with the range of responsibilities that we have. And because it cannot not be, because it always must be, is no surprise that he saw Augustine's understanding of being human, his theological anthropology that is the core of the analysis and argument in *The City of God*, as fundamental in forging an honest political vision, one that is true to who we are, to why we are, to what is ours to do in the world. Plainly stating his apprenticeship to Augustine, Niebuhr writes, "We must acknowledge his immense superiority both over those who preceded him and those who came after him . . . due to his reliance upon biblical rather than idealistic or naturalistic conceptions of selfhood . . . and [he] proves himself a more reliable guide than any known thinker."[32]

A professor whose scholarship was made profoundly practical, Niebuhr today is as relevant as he was for those who first heard him; he was a man for all seasons and centuries, drawing as he did on another whose insights have shaped critical conversations for centuries. Knowing what we know of the perennial temptation of *realpolitik*—the Machiavellian cynicism of the political arena in every century—it is astounding that Niebuhr's wisdom continues to influence those whose vocations are set within the public policy debates, even generations later.

---

[32]Reinhold Niebuhr, "Augustine's Political Realism," *Christian Realism and Political Problems* (Scribner, 1953), 123.

His hard-won realism about the human heart in the public squares of history makes his thinking significant for generation after generation, working hard as he did to answer questions that serious, thoughtful folk ask about the nature and meaning of the work of their lives, about the nature and meaning of our common life.

Still another Augustinian, Lesslie Newbigin was a pastor and then a bishop, not unlike Augustine himself. A man whose profound understanding of the gospel in and for the world was substantially shaped during his 40 years of life in India, early on he committed himself to a global conversation about the nature of Christian faith in the twentieth century, a promise he kept for the whole of his life.

With a deep sense of call to the Tamil people, he entered into their world, seeing that their Hindu convictions permeated everything—cultic commitments forming cultural mores as they do—the meaning of life and love, of worship and work, the whole of reality. They were serious about what they believed. *What was he serious about? What did he have to offer?* From the West, socialized by a very different account of reality, did he bring anything more than something foreign, a way of making sense of making sense that was inimical to his new neighbors?

Aware that his questions about moral meaning were not just his questions, sons of Adam and daughters of Eve that we are, he made the choice to enter into the religious life of the Hindu people. Never drawn to syncretism of any kind, he decided to become friends of heart and mind with Hindu scholars, reading their sacred texts with them, asking and answering questions as human being to human being. Having earned their trust through days and years of conversation, his Hindu friends seeing that he was willing to listen, he was invited to bring them his sacred text, choosing the Gospel of John to study with them, right in the middle of their Hindu temples.

One of the most instructive windows into Newbigin's long life in India comes from a conversation with a Hindu scholar, a man with whom he had been friends for 30 years, who said to him one day,

> *As I read the Bible I find in it a quite unique interpretation of universal history and therefore, a unique understanding of the human person as a responsible actor in history. You Christian missionaries have talked of the Bible as it were simply another book of religion. We have plenty of these already in India, and we do not need another to add to our supply.*[33]

Having read the best of religious books from every conceivable perspective—Hinduism, after all, being the great "all roads lead to the top of the mountain" religion—he saw the Hebrew/Christian Scriptures as completely unique, as different as different could possibly be on two great lines in the sand, its view of history and its view of the human being in history. These are the differences that make a difference, and are what deeply distinguish Marxism from Islam, existentialism from Judaism, hedonism from Christianity, i.e., what we believe about history and the human condition.

But to say it again, Newbigin was never a syncretist, smiling at all who wanted a smile, assuring them in his benevolent way that all beliefs are basically the same, that Hinduism as a religious vision of life in the world was as "true" as any other way of seeing life in the world. And yet, and yet, for love's sake he entered in, walking into their temples, leaving his sandals at the gate, passing by their golden calves, spending hours and years in honest conversation about the most important things of life and death, of God and history—agreeing when possible, and disagreeing when necessary.

---

[33]Lesslie Newbigin, *The Gospel in a Pluralist Society* (Eerdmans, 1989), 89.

In his profound *Foolishness to the Greeks*, a remarkable analysis of "the gospel and Western culture"—a question which he asked and asked again through his life because it was the very heart of his own vocation—Newbigin writes, "In order to view this task with some historical perspective, I would like to go back to Augustine. . . ."[34] And then he proceeds to ground his understanding within *The City of God*, arguing that there is nowhere else to go if we want to make sense of history in light of faith, perennial people that we are, in different times and places living in the same world.

Always attentive to the way that what we believe about being human affects everything else, he notes that "Augustine was very realistic about the evils that tear human communities apart—the family, the city, the nation," arguing that the Great Teacher had "no sentimental illusions about natural brotherhood among human beings." And yet, "He insists that love is the basis of society; even in their wars men are in fact speaking peace." Newbigin deepens this thesis, drawing on insights from Augustine about the ordering of a common life, of public justice, to the globalizing twentieth century, then driving home the point that everything depends on love. Words we have heard before, because yes, it all turns on affection, and it does because it must.

Lesslie Newbigin was a uniquely gifted man, living between the West and the East, deeply committed to the biblical vision of life in the world with its implications—beliefs about God, about human beings, about history—having learned from Augustine to hold together the Great Story of all of history with the stories of men and women he came to love through the years of his life as pastor and bishop.

Never a romantic, like Augustine he was realistic about the human heart, whether that was in his long labor of love in India, or after he came back to England, seeing the meaning of his own culture with new eyes. Honest as he was, he knew that in

---

[34]Newbigin, *Foolishness to the Greeks: The Gospel and Western Culture* (Eerdmans, 1986), 102.

this frail world we must have eyes to see what he called "signs and foretastes" of what is real and true and right, understanding that eschatological hopes inform us, affecting what we see and hear and feel—which is as true for Hindus and Marxists as it is for Christians. His friend the Hindu scholar had asked the great questions that everyone asks, in some way on some level: What is life all about, and what is my life about? What is the metanarrative, and what is our narrative? Does history make sense, and do our lives make sense? And in the Hebrew and Christian Scriptures he found a surprising answer.

At the end of the day, we live for windows into what is, to what could be, and to what someday will be, signs as they are, foretastes as they will only be. Seeing them for what they are, and are not, is another way of making peace with the proximate.

Born into a German Lutheran farming family in northern Colorado, Jean Bethke Elshtain lived her life in the most ivory of towers the university offers, but her soul was formed by the most ordinary questions of the most ordinary people. Who are we? Why are we? What difference does this all make in the way we live our lives?

A political philosopher at the University of Chicago known for her intellectual integrity, for being impossible to caricature, to "box-up" as liberal or conservative, as feminist or traditionalist, Elshtain was drawn in both by Democratic and Republican presidents because of the substance of her moral vision for responsibility in public life. She could not not think about the most serious questions without seeing them in light of her own deepest commitments about what is real and true and right. Against the spirit of compartmentalization, she did the hard work of redefining her discipline, always a political philosopher but always a theologian too. Certain that Machiavellian cynicism was a dead end for cities and societies, with a certain uncanny brilliance she wrote essay upon essay about *Real Politics*, insisting that there is more to the good work of the public square than we are willing to imagine, and that a healthy body politic requires a strong dose of truth about human beings and their societies, about *real politics*, not Machiavellian *realpolitik*.

In her study *Augustine and the Limits of Politics*, she sets forth for the modern world the ancient wisdom of the man who lived through one of the greatest political crises in Western history, the fall of the Roman Empire, who asked his own generation and every generation that has followed, "What is our business in this common mortal life?" In the simplest way, *The City of God*—monumental that that book is—is an answer to one question: *What does it mean to be responsible in history, knowing who we are, and what is ours to care about?* That Augustine acknowledges our mortality is telling and profoundly instructive.

We see, in part. We act, in part. Not all that we hope for will be seen. Not all our longings will be found. Mortality remembers our frailty, that we too shall die, *memento mori*. For the realist Augustine was, as committed to the real as Elshtain was, fundamental to the Augustinian and Elshtainian insight is the proximate nature of politics. Something is possible, but not everything, not ever everything—because there are *limits* written into politics.

In her essay "Politics Without Cliche," she reflects with characteristic wisdom on the political vision of Vaclav Havel of Czechoslovakia, calling it "a brief civic sermon."[35] The great visionary of his people, imprisoned for the courage of his convictions in the 1980s, Havel embodies a different way to imagine politics, one that is almost impossible to achieve in this wounded world, so much more accustomed to more Machiavellian twists and turns that we are. If he could say with moral meaning, "It Always Makes Sense to Tell the Truth"—having been born and bred under totalitarianism, knowing the cancerous character of public lies—most of us groan, wincing because we do not know a politics like that, nor politicians

[35]Jean Bethke Elshtain, "Politics Without Cliche," *Real Politics: At the Center of Everyday Life* (The Johns Hopkins University Press, 1997).

like that. Tragically, the majority of those who find their way into public office will say and do anything, the words of their work sold to the highest bidder; it is not for nothing that we become cynical.

More often than not, partisanship is poisonous because ideologies become idolatries. Rather, we are called to a deeper loyalty, to commitments for the common good that transcend party politics. That Elshtain could not be captured by one side of the social and political wars says much about who she was and why she saw the Czech poet and politician as a kindred spirit, writing that "What Havel insists upon is that whether something is right or left is the last thing that should interest any alert and concerned citizen. Rather, what we should be about is eschewing political labels that fail to capture the complexity of social life, fail to come close to the content of our actual beliefs and actions."

The rest of her essay focuses on Havel's understanding of responsibility, which is one of the most important contributions he made for those whose vision is for what matters most. In speech after speech, all over the world, he raised the question of responsibility in history, time and again, knowing that for his own long-oppressed people, the recovery of responsibility was crucial to their future.

Reading Elshtain and Havel together is as if we were sitting at the feet of the very wisest ones, the most astute ones, a political philosopher and a politician, both committed to a vision of the way politics could be, knowing its limits—and when we draw in Augustine too, hearing them think aloud and together about the vocation of politics, of what it can and cannot be, with each weighing in on the reality of political life, we have nothing less than a conversation with consequences about *real politics.*

It is those lovers of the pristine Havel challenges,
for they are the ideologists who disdain the
messiness of the human condition and want
to clean things up, the sooner the better. In

> *doing so, however, they must falsify what they see, color it out, blur it over, somehow do it in: everyday life in all its ambiguity is not grand enough for them. The humanly possible work is tawdry and unworthy by contrast to creating some earthly paradise—if only we can get the clutter cleaned up.*[36]

Central to Elshtain's vocation as a woman of the world was that ideas be honestly worked out, knowing "the messiness of the human condition," resisting utopian fantasies of whatever origin, whether of the left or the right. Instead she insisted that she was implicated, for love's sake, in the "tawdry" of history, in and through her academic work becoming a voice for the silenced, ignored, abused, and invisible members of society, writing with eloquence and power on their behalf, seeing that the love of neighbor has necessary social and political meaning—even as she would fly off that same week to take part in weighty discussions about what it means to be America and American. These ideas were her life, a seamless life fixed on the truth that it all turns on affection, of what we understand about the nature of love as it becomes flesh in and through the days of our lives.

It All Turns on Affection, One More Time

The weight of love—and the labor of our lives.

Why do we work? What does our work mean? Though these questions are at the heart of every heart, for most of us they do not wind their way into the conversations of our lives. For a thousand reasons we deeply sigh, and with the ages we resign ourselves to one more day, one more night, singing the words that echo through the centuries and cultures, "Eat, drink and be merry, for tomorrow we die."

But the next generation of South Africans has not done that, yet, though their national anthem yearns for a life and a

---

[36]Elshtain, 6.

world that is something more. They too long for good work, for vocations that matter to them and to the world—and their question is this: Can we possibly connect the loves of our lives with the labors of our lives?

We live in a world full of tensions of every sort, where we all feel the strain of things that matter to us and for us—from the plagues that keep plaguing us, changing the whats and wherefores of life in every way, bringing death wherever they go . . . to the deepening dislocation of all things political, with ideological allegiances distorting the common good in every nation and state . . . to the growing economic divide, fragmenting haves and have-nots into castes and classes that cannot be a commonwealth in any honest sense . . . to the ongoing sorrows of racial injustice among tribes the world over, a wound that is always wounding. And more.

And some days, with the youth of South Africa, our longings overwhelm us, so full of yearning for our lives to matter, so full of hope for work that matters. There is not much that is deeper for us than that, written into the very meaning of being human as it is—even more so when we are willing to think about who we are and why we are, and therefore what we do with our lives, which are the threads woven into the tapestry of vocation, always and everywhere.

And then sometimes, if we listen carefully, we find a story that tells this tale.

From the artful imagination of one of Europe's most distinguished filmmakers, Agnieszka Holland, the Polish film *In Darkness* is a story set in the 1940s of terrified men, women, and children who spend fourteen months underground, overwhelmed by rats and smells that are beyond what is imaginable. Though at the beginning he does not know what he is seeing, having no heart to see—therefore not having eyes that see—a sewer worker in Lvov is forced to see things he had never imagined, the opening salvo into the horrors of the Holocaust as its destruction comes to his streets and his city.

A very ordinary man in a very ordinary place, a glorious ruin in his own body, more local burglar than great hero, he is antisemitic, dismissive of the Jews, knowing very little of them, and indifferent to them. But when the Nazis begin to terrorize his town, one day, to his great surprise, he sees that Jews have made a hole into the sewer system, hoping to find safety underground. His first motivation is mercenary, charging them an outrageous amount of money to keep away the Nazis, who on the streets above, fired by their dreams of a truly evil empire with a callousness that knows no end, murder the innocents wherever they may be found.

As in all of the best stories there are strains: The demands of those being hidden, desperate for life, secreted away amidst never-ending tunnels filled with waste, come into tension with the sewer manager's heart, and there is a moment when he simply walks away, freeing himself of their needs. But the more he watches the sordid work of the Nazis above ground, the more he feels himself responsible for those living underground, and he returns. Called as he is to care for the pipes of the sewage system, he sees that he is called to care for human beings too, holding them together in one vocation, feeling the weight of love in and through his labor. That they find safety in the sewer is possible because this man comes to see his work as *dilectio proximi*, loving his neighbor in and through his work, and that is the story of the story.

Why and how can human beings choose to act with such inhumanity, living out of a world and worldview that is murderously myopic, a perverse self-love that despoils everything it touches? And yet, at the same time in the same story we are drawn in by portraits of the truest humanness, of people being the people they were meant to be. That both are true is the *raison d'être* of *The City of God,* in hundreds of pages exploring what it is that makes cities flourish, setting forth for the centuries the profound truth that the ordering of our loves matters supremely—to learn to love the right things in the right way is the only way to have a good life and a good society. When our loves begin with us, with me and mine, it will be alienation and anger, grief and sorrow instead, not only in the stories of our lives, but in the story of all of life.

What is remarkable in this film is the transformation of the man's loves, and therefore of his life. In one very poignant scene, born of a moment of great crisis, a little girl gives him her hand, offering her trust; with true affection he takes it, leading her to safety—and we all cry, watching him move from a hard-hearted "so what?" as he hears the aching cries of the Jewish people of Poland, to an open-hearted affection that is willing to do whatever is needed to keep them safe, at the very end exclaiming, "These are my Jews! My Jews! These are my work!"

In Darkness is the story of that pilgrimage, a pilgrimage of the proximate because it is a journey of grace from here to there, from disordered loves to ordered loves—and always and everywhere, it all turns on affection.

5

LOVE IN THE RUINS

***Indeed, there is something new in this valley, some spirit and some life, and much to talk about in the huts. Although nothing has come yet, something is here already.*[37]**

—Alan Paton, *Cry, the Beloved Country*

From Birmingham to Beijing, and back again.

A few years ago I had lunch with artists and artful people in a beautifully imagined home, full of paintings and furniture that were glories, each one. They represented a community of folk who care deeply about the city of Birmingham, Alabama, longing for their work as painters, sculptors, and musicians to bring renewal to their hometown.

Not far from the boyhood home of Walker Percy in the city's Mountain Brook neighborhood, I decided to reflect on his vision of the best and truest art as a way into our time together—and so it seemed right to draw on his collection of essays, *Signposts in a Strange Land*.[38] One more day in my life I mused over his thesis that "Bad books lie. They lie most of all about the human condition." But this time I connected Birmingham to Beijing, remembering a lecture I had given at the Beijing Film Academy to the cinematic storytellers of China's twenty-first century, arguing that it is also true that "Bad films lie. They lie most of all about the human condition." A truth as true for filmmakers in Beijing as it is for artists in Birmingham.

---

[37]Alan Paton, *Cry, the Beloved Country* (Scribner, 1948), 300.

[38]Walker Percy, *Signposts in a Strange Land* (Picador MacMillan, 2000).

That evening I was with a houseful of good people from all over the city: men and women whose vocations are in business, education, medicine, the arts, and the church. To a person they love Birmingham and long for it to be more what it might be, more what it could be and should be. I was asked to draw on Percy again, but this time in another part of the city. In the scope of his literary vision there is one question that runs through his work from beginning to end, from *The Moviegoer* to *Love in the Ruins* and *The Thanatos Syndrome*, and his insight is worth remembering. In the complexity of the modern-becoming-postmodern world, full as it is of personal and familial wounds as well as systemic and societal wrongs: What is our responsibility? What in fact does it mean to be responsible? Can we do anything? Should we?

Everyone there was passionate about these questions. Several hours later we walked out, both more burdened and more hopeful, realizing that there are others who care too, there are others who understand that those with resources of many kinds are responsible to enter into the lives of others who simply, sadly, do not. It was a tender time, historically born as it was, as in that city it is impossible not to remember the tensions of the Civil Rights conflict of the 1960s, captured so eloquently by Martin Luther King in his "Letter from Birmingham Jail" and the horrific bombing of the 16th Street Baptist church. What does it mean to care about this kind of complexity? Now, a generation later, what is our responsibility?

And then the next day began with a lingering breakfast at the Broken Egg with a tableful of people who wanted to move their great hopes to feet-on-the-street granularity, asking hard questions about what this will mean for their lives in their city. I offered more Percy, this time the image of "signposts in a strange land," seeing that language allows us to live amidst the ruins that are ours, with hope. Could we live towards being signposts, towards creating signposts? To work for something, even if it is not everything?

For two more hours a few of us pressed even more deeply in at the local Starbucks, and then we moved downtown to a wonderfully remade warehouse that has become a very popular co-working space for companies of various sizes and purposes. Over lunch we talked even more specifically about what it will mean to "seek the flourishing of the city" of Birmingham, with assignments and promises about who will do what when. My last word brought Percy in again, this time from his rejoinder to the New York literary critics who were sure that in him they had discovered "an American Camus," someone who looked the heartache of the human condition squarely in the eye, and did not blink. Percy politely protested, saying, "No, that's not me. In all I write, I want there to be some hint of hope."

A hint of hope. We can all live with that. In fact we cannot live without that—if more is required of us than being "hints of hope," then it is too much. How is anything else possible, given the sorrows and pains of life that are not only so personal, but so public? Not only individually experienced but institutionally driven? It is enough to have to live with ourselves and our disappointments and hurts; but to have to live with the rest of the world too? We groan, and we should.

Being a hint of hope sounds almost possible though. And so I gave Walker Percy back to Birmingham, honoring as I could his own wrestling with what might be done in this very wounded world, trying as he did to find a way to "love in the ruins" of his time and place. At our best, that is our vocation.

"I'm Still Angry, and I'm Going to Be"

A few years ago I spent several days in Memphis, Tennessee, speaking on vocation as "common grace for the common good." Believing in the ancient wisdom of "even your own poets have said," I want to listen to where I am, to speak to where I am, and so I thought a lot about the meaning of Memphis in American culture and history.

That meant drawing in the music of Elvis Presley and Johnny Cash, even the classic tune "Memphis Blues," but also the novelists Shelby Foote and John Grisham were remembered for their story-formed insights into the Delta region, the South, and what it means to be human. But also I showed a clip of the film *Mudbound*, which tells the tale of generational grief in the Delta—the geography in which Memphis is the center—the story of those who have and those who do not have, of class-born injustice, and yes, of the terrible wrong of racism in the post-World War II years.

Over the days I gave my heart away, coming to see and hear about a people and a place that was new to me. And while in each address I quoted Martin Luther King Jr, and the importance of his words in and for the city, I did not pretend to know very much about their life, so I chose to reflect on my own, growing up in the very middle of "the grapes of wrath" of California's San Joaquin Valley, with its own history of lament and longing, of class conflict and racial tension. We are perennial people the world over, and mostly we do not have eyes to see the ways that wrongs have to be righted—if there is to be an honest sense of life together that makes for a healthy social ecology, for a commonwealth with meaning for all.

One morning I began with a breakfast with one of my dearest friends, Tim Russell, at his favorite place, "Brother Juniper's," and then we spent hours driving through the story of the city, especially the story of racial conflict that has afflicted Memphis for most of its history. We drove here and there, getting out of the car to see this, walking to see that, all the while Tim giving me a window into what it means to be from Memphis, a unique city with its own glories and shames.

After we lingered at the Lorraine Motel where Martin Luther King Jr was assassinated, we walked back to our car, and I insisted that we stop at Makeda's, a little shop on the corner that promised "the best butter cookies in the world!" I asked the woman at the counter about her work, about the business of baking cookies for the city, only blocks from where King was murdered. Before we left with our box of her best, she told me that every cookie was baked with "lots of love!"

I have not forgotten the words, weighty as they were. A central thesis of my time in the city was that vocation is at its heart about seeing ourselves implicated, for love's sake, in the way things are and the way things should be. That she saw her work that way impressed me, specially so in light of where she worked, only a short walk from a place better known for hatred and heartache. As we drove back across town, I asked Tim to tell me more—and he did.

An unusually good man, a remarkably able man, a very thoughtful man, a specially sensitive man, a deeply passionate man, he said, "I'm still angry, and I'm going to be." You see, my dear friend Tim was an African-American man. Socially aware, historically conscious, politically astute, theologically trained, if there was anything true of Tim it was that he knew who he was and why he was, and therefore what his life was all about. To say it very simply, he saw into the heart, and into the heart of life.

Perhaps it was that we had driven through the city of Memphis, stopping at the iconic places that tell the tale of tragedy; perhaps it was remembering the long history of racism that has plagued Memphis, and in too many ways still does. But for whatever reason, Tim spoke plainly and passionately, wanting to make sure that I knew that the wounds of the city had wounded him. A friend for most of my life, he and I had talked about a thousand things over the years, about love and learning, about work and worship, about the whole of life. And given that my reason for being in Memphis was to keep that long conversation alive, arguing that a recovery of the idea of vocation is integral to the renewal of the city—a thesis that is as true for Jakarta as it is for Bratislava, as true for Singapore as it is for Nairobi, as true for Rio de Janeiro as it is for Sydney, as it is true for Memphis—it is only if we see vocations as common grace for the common good will our cities and societies flourish.

Martin Luther King Jr, so visionary, so eloquent, in his own unique way understood that, believing that street sweepers, like painters and composers and playwrights, are called to work in a way that brings heaven to earth, because work itself has sacramental meaning, connecting the truest truths of the universe with the ordinary lives of ordinary people.

> *If a man is called to be a street sweeper, he should sweep streets even as Michaelangelo painted, or Beethoven composed music or Shakespeare wrote poetry. He should sweep streets so well that all the hosts of heaven and earth will pause to say, "Here lived a great street sweeper who did his job well."*[39]

After speaking on behalf of the sanitation worker's strike in Memphis on April 3, 1968—poignantly speaking into history with the famous words, "I've seen the Promised Land. I may not get there with you. But I want you to know tonight, that we, as a people, will get to the Promised Land! And so I'm happy, tonight. I'm not worried about anything. I'm not fearing any man. Mine eyes have seen the glory of the coming of the Lord!"—by the power of his presence standing with those who swept the streets of the city, the next day he was killed for these very convictions about God and history, about work and the world, about what matters most and what does not.

A generation later, my friend Tim lived his life for the same vision. A different man in a different time, too soon he lost his life to the plague of COVID-19 in its early days. His wife mourned his death, his friends mourned his death, the city mourned his death, even the angels of heaven mourned his death. For the years of his life Tim was known by all as someone who gave himself away, for love's sake, understanding the way things are, longing for the way things should be—which is why he was angry at the wrongs of his city and society. But being Tim, his anger was born of love, and in that he taught us all,

[39]Martin Luther King Jr, "Speech." Barratt Junior High School, 26 Oct. 1967, Philadelphia, https://www.goodreads.com/quotes/21045-if-a-man-is-called-to-be-a-street-sweeper, accessed May 23, 2025.

his great heart holding both sorrow and joy together with remarkable integrity.

And those butter cookies? The ones made with "lots of love"? Of course Tim loved them, and I did too—sure we were that heaven and earth had paused that day, saying for all with ears to hear, "Here was a baker who did her work well." Good work is like that, a signpost of what someday will be, peering into the Promised Land as we still are.

A signpost of what someday will be? In those few words we have one more window into the meaning of the proximate, of something that is there, but not yet. Not expecting that all will be made well, that all wounds will be healed, that all wrongs will be righted, a *signpost* is set within the tension of our finite, frail lives, narratively understood as they are; and our beliefs about all of history, the very meaning of life, metanarratively constructed as they are. At our best, this is who we are, all of us, living between the story of our days and the Great Story that makes sense of every day—frail, finite, as it so often feels. As the agrarian theologian Norman Wirzba argues, "The way we name and narrate the world determines how we are going to live within it."

True for the whole of life, it was true for Tim. Contracting the coronavirus when he did was because of his love for a woman whom he had long honored, a distinguished art historian and librarian living in New York City, a woman more "mother" of faith and hope and love to him, a woman he wanted to see, for love's sake, in the last days of her life. In his own body both anger and love were twined together, the meaning of the one written into the other, seamlessly. But without a word like *signpost*, his anger can only be seen as finally futile—but because it was so profoundly born of love, it was not that, never that.

A Foretaste of What Someday Will Be

Over the years of my life I began to find that an honest way in with people I meet is the question "What do you care about?"

Maybe not the first thing said, but before too long I will ask, if the conversation seems one that can carry that seriousness.

There is no one anywhere who lives a life without cares, who lives very long in the world without seeing and hearing, and then caring about what has been seen and heard. We are not blank slates, ever, and so our cares will be for our flourishing, or not, for the flourishing of our communities, or not. And as he must be, the great teacher Augustine is our teacher: Knowing the human heart so well, he knew it was in and through our loves, our commitments and cares, that we are most completely, most truthfully known. But then his question was: How will we order our loves? That mattered in the fifth century A.D. as it does in the twenty-first century A.D., as true in Mediterranean society as it is in every society. The people we meet in the days of our lives are people just like that, on the sidewalks and streets of everyone's life.

Allison Beadle, for example, a woman whom I met over several days when a group met at the Laity Lodge in Texas to explore "seeing seamlessly," learning to understand the whole of life as a whole life, seeing everything in life, from the most personal to the most public, as a vocation from God for the sake of the world: As we talked, I began to hear about her cares, about who she was, about why she was, and about the way she lived her life.

Growing up with grocery stores whose aisles were full of bread and bananas, and much more, she spent her years of undergraduate study at Texas A&M University studying food—particularly why we eat the food we eat, with good questions about where it comes from and how it gets to us. Slowly a vocation was born, and she entered in more deeply with another degree in Boston, coming home to Texas to begin working for the HEB grocery universe, a company that has been serving the Lone Star State for 120 years.

Because of her deepening insight into marketing, she was employed by the Central Market division of HEB, the "Whole Foods" side of the larger corporate brand. Always one to ask good questions, even the most important questions, she was drawn into helping the stores make the health of their products more understandable to those who walked along with their grocery carts, seeing this and that, wondering about the difference between need and want, choosing what to eat for the next week.

The more Allison worked to understand, the more she understood her work, and she eventually made the decision to create her own firm to help farmers and ranchers market the fruit of their labor to Texas and beyond, calling her company "Wild Hive." Her business is the business of business, working with those who grow cattle and pecans in Texas, who grow raspberries in Washington, who grow avocados in Mexico—and those who grow mangoes, potatoes, and raisins all over, too—telling the truth about what they do, and why it matters, so that ordinary people in ordinary places are able to make informed consumer choices.

To say it very simply, and deliciously, Allison helps set the table at your house and mine, doing her best to make sure that what we eat is both healthy and tasty—not a trade-off, but both together.

She loves to eat, and she knows that we do too. But in the corporatization of eating, of buying and selling fruits and vegetables, of meats and grains in a globalizing marketplace, we have very little knowledge of the whats and whys and wherefores of what goes into our mouths. Where did these bananas come from anyway!? It was because those questions mattered to Allison that she began her study, and now years later she is engaged with good people all over North America and the world to do her best for the sake of all, immersed in the global nature of the marketplace of food and agriculture, "full as it is of true friendships and the messiness of politics," is the way she describes it.

It is an uphill battle. Too often both producers and consumers care very little about these questions, calculating that "the bottom line" will always be the bottom line, i.e., how much money will this cost? Rather than seeing that our common good requires more of us and from us, we resist infringements on anything, from the most intimate to the most institutional. In the tender underbelly of America there is a long history of "Don't tread on me!" A predisposition to autonomy runs very deep, and is mostly unacknowledged, simply assuming that what is, is what ought to be. *Who are you to call into question what I want to be, what I want to do, what I want to buy?* These are challenges, with difficult questions written into any honest answers that make sense to us and for us, because they go to the heart of our identity, personally and politically, with far-reaching economic implications.

A longing to understand more brought Allison to the weekend retreat in the hill country of Texas, pondering together the possibility of seeing more seamlessly the integral relationships that make our lives "ours"—and one afternoon we met, thinking through the world of work in general, and with her husband, Brian, their work. That day became more days, and the more I knew the more intrigued I was with the depth of her sense of calling to care about who we are and how we live.

Those commitments and loves have only deepened through the years, creating a holy complexity to the work that is hers, giving an unusual texture to her labor that has come from the questions that first took her into the study that has become her life: What do we eat, and why do we eat it?

Because she represents those who work the land, Allison knows more than most that those who raise sheep in America, Australia, and New Zealand need to make a true profit, if they are going to stay in business—and Wild Hive promises in fact to increase their profitability through more creatively imagined and critically analyzed communications. But she understands that sustained profitability, to keep making money, requires an honest commitment to a more complex bottom line, one that is more than merely the last numbers on a spreadsheet. That is a difficult proposition for most of us, short-sighted as we are, wanting everything now, if not yesterday.

But that she knows that "now" is not everything allows Allison to keep at it, not only in the daily work of Wild Hive, which as a business has its own complex bottom lines—year by year persuading the raspberry growers of Washington to sign on again for help in bringing their fruit to market—but in the longer sensibilities that are written into the vision of the vocation that is hers. Like every daughter of Eve, she lives her life stretched between the realities of metanarrative and narrative, between what she believes about all of life and the world, and the way she lives in the world, especially the way she works. While watching the world carefully is her work, facilitating trust between the growers and the consumers, she knows that in the twenty-first century many consumers expect their brands to honestly account for their reason for being in the marketplace, and they hold companies to an unprecedented high level of integrity. That that is true is not only right, as it must be for us to flourish together as a commonwealth, but is a foretaste of what should be, of a day when trust will be the language of life.

So, yes, a foretaste, a good word that it is for Allison, and necessarily proximate too, a prism into the tension that is hers, with all those "complex bottom lines"! But she knows that the work of Wild Hive, born of an honest confidence, is a window into what could be for those who eat to live and who love to eat—especially for those who eat well to live well.

Still Longing for Peace on Earth

"When the Zionists came here in the 1930s, my grandfather and his brothers welcomed them: 'Please make this your home too. There is room for all of us.'"

We were standing near the table in the Copty family home in the hills between Jerusalem and Bethlehem, a few miles from each of these ancient cities. Mr. Copty was a respected, trusted builder, owning a construction company that built in that geographic region. To build his own house he had quarried the stone from his property, probably not very far from the hillside on which the shepherds once heard the angels sing, "Glory to God in the highest! Peace on earth!"—arguably the most weighty words ever, a promise for life as it should be, and someday will be, but very much not the way it is, then and now.

Beautifully imagined, the garden had flowers and fruit trees everywhere, not a blade of grass anywhere. Plainly a place for his family to flourish, their table was known throughout Israel and Palestine for its Middle Eastern hospitality, Mrs. Copty herself being the author of highly regarded cookbooks featuring the cuisine of her heart and history.

I listened carefully to Mr. Copty, telling me of his family's choice to welcome the Zionists who came longing for their own land. He then looked at me, with his hands open, and plaintively said, "But now they say that there is no room for us. What am I to do? What will my family do?" It is an evening I will never forget, the conversation so poignant that it is written into the deepest places of my heart.

I was there at the invitation of their daughter Gina, who had been my student. While I was in Jerusalem, she was a guide for a time, taking me here and there, showing me something of the place that had been her family's home for hundreds and hundreds of years. Both Palestinian and Christian, their history of faith and hope and love is one that is as old as we have recorded history—and yet 30 years later there are not many of her family left, because the economic and political policies of the Israeli government make little room for the Palestinians of Palestine.

Being a crossroads, bounded by the seas we know as the Mediterranean, the Galilee, and the Dead, bordered by the Jordan River, with time-worn highways connecting the Roman world with the Egyptian world and Arabic history with European history, for thousands of years empires have been won and lost in and through the strangely named place we call "the holy land." Through the centuries its residents have been "blood brothers," in the profoundly insightful reading of Elias Chacour,[40] with ethnic and religious differences that are distinct,

[40]Elias Chacour, *Blood Brothers: The Dramatic Story of a Palestinian Christian Working for Peace in Israel* (Baker Books, 2022).

unique, with far-reaching implications—and that reality creates a question that echoes throughout history: "Whose land is it, anyway?"

In the nineteenth century, Jews who had long been scattered like the wind began to hope for a return to their historic homeland, the "Zionists returning to Zion," as it came to be over the next century. Through the first decades of the twentieth century, a trickle became a wave, and by the 1930s thousands had come, among them those who were welcomed by Gina's great-grandfather's family. In the aftermath of the horror of the Holocaust, the Western world, reeling from what had happened in the death camps, wanting to do something that was just and merciful for those who had suffered so terribly, insisted that the Arabic people of Palestine make room for the European Jews. History is always messy, and more often than not, more messy than we can even imagine. In justifying their decision to divide this historic homeland—drawing lines through villages and hills that had been home to human beings for thousands of years—the language of the United Nations Partition Plan in 1947 argued to the world that this was "a land without a people for a people without a land," words which were never true, a view of history that was far from what was and still is.

Because most of life is autobiographical, after her undergraduate study Gina stayed in Washington, DC, to work for Human Rights Watch, putting the shoulders of her heart into the injustices that human beings experience the world over; but she wanted more, to know more, to have more to offer, and eventually she entered an MBA program in Cape Town, South Africa, where she met her husband, who was from Belfast, in Northern Ireland.

Should they stay where they were? Or should they go somewhere else? Those were their questions, and they chose to return to his home, entering into the family's business, beginning to be and have a family. Because *vocation* is always a deep word, covering the range of our relationships and responsibilities, as the years passed Gina's sense of self deepened, with her commitments and loves becoming richer, more textured—even as she was always tethered to the moral meaning of being a Palestinian growing up in Israel, but never being an Israeli.

But the choice for Belfast had its own weight, as decisions must, Belfast being its own troubled place, known throughout the world, very literally, for "the troubles" between the peoples that make the place we call "Ireland." If in Israel the divisions are between tribes of Christians, Jews, and Muslims—though more than not born of envies and jealousies that are more social and political than religious—in Ireland the same dynamic exists, the Church riven with alienation between Catholics and Protestants, with complex identities that are more deeply social and political than ecclesial.

That that is true in Ireland has had meaning for Gina, time and again choosing to step in, believing that "peace on earth" must be seen first of all within the church, if it is to leaven the culture. For many years now a member of the Church of Ireland, she began to go to this meeting, and then that meeting, agreeing to this, and then that, always believing that hope and history should meet between people whose deepest affections are born of a love for God and neighbor. Years later she has now given herself for this vision, in Belfast and beyond, throughout Ireland and the world, in mind and heart committed to "the congregation as the hermeneutic of the gospel,"[41] as Lesslie Newbigin argued. What is the mission of the Church, and what does it mean for the world? Because being a Copty means that she grew up between centuries of Catholic and Orthodox family faith, so these longings for mere Christianity are in her blood.

Being a mother of four children, she has spent years loving them as they too learn to live in the world; Irish they are, embedded in a neighborhood, a city and a society, and yet Palestinians too. Wanting them to know something of those roots, along the way the family chose to live for a year in Jerusalem, simply if profoundly so that their children would

---

[41]Lesslie Newbigin, *The Gospel in a Pluralist Society* (Eerdmans, 1989).

know more of what "family" means, and must mean—to see more, to hear more, to feel more.

As the little ones have grown, so has Gina, and with her husband they chose to keep on keeping on with the Copty family's long history of hospitality, seeing life itself as an invitation for others to "come in"—to our land, to our home, to our table, "what is ours, is yours." With unusual creativity and generosity, they have given these last years to philanthropic efforts in Belfast, and also to ones that connect the Middle East to Northern Ireland, seeing themselves implicated for love's sake in the history that is theirs. Whether it is in support of women as entrepreneurs in her homeland, or of scholarships to schools and universities in the United Kingdom, they are living into the habits of heart that are written into Gina's own history. To give, to give and to give again, in hope.

Always a daughter of Eve, even as she is always a Copty, born in the hills of what we call "the holy land," Gina still chooses to live within this grounded vision of life in the world, in the now-but-not-yet of history. She is not a romantic about anything, having seen too much that is wrong, having lived through sorrows that are not only personal but also political, bearing in her own body the bruises of history. Now living her life far from her homeland that no longer is, she lives in another divided land with its own deep wounds, yearning for what could be and should be, still believing in the song the angels sang, still longing for peace on earth.

Responsible for Those That Have Been Forgotten

And the doors clanged shut, which is very sobering.

The few times I have walked in, I have walked out. A long time ago now, I was asked to spend a week of my 19-year-old summer with a group of youthful offenders in the Sierra Nevada mountains of California. I did, and I still remember some of those days and nights. Hope and longing, anger and hurt, hikes up and down the trails—and a visit to the state prison nearby, which was meant to be an inoculation, taking these 15-year-olds into a place that no one would ever want to be in, hoping that seeing and hearing would make them do everything they could to stay out.

The door clangs shut in places like that.

Years have passed, and not so long ago I walked into another prison, spending an afternoon in the Kansas State Penitentiary in Hutchinson, a maximum-security prison housing men who will be there for a long time, if not for life. I was with a friend, Pete Ochs of Wichita, someone I have known since we were ten-year-olds spending summer weeks in the Rocky Mountains of Colorado at a camp near Estes Park. He was from Kansas, and I was from California, so there was not much of an opportunity to get to know each other well, the summers being the only time we were together.

We lost touch after high school. I imagined him staying in Kansas, forming a life in the farming economy that was his as a boy, but did not really know. And then, surprise of surprises, most of life later, I was walking down a hallway in a hotel in Florida one day, and heard a deeper, older voice, but one I recognized, "Hi. I'm Pete Ochs," as he introduced himself to someone. I turned around, and it was.

We had a meal or two together the next couple of days, and hoped for more. When I knew I was going to be in Wichita, I wrote Pete, and he welcomed me, wondering if I would have "four hours or so" to go visit a prison with him. As I was speaking on the theme of vocation and the common good at Friends University, while honestly nodding to the Quaker history of the school, wanting them to know that I had thought about them and their history with its unique-in-the-world *raison d'être,* I also brought into the address my friend Pete, who I now knew more about after the years of silence.

He had chosen to study business as an undergraduate, and began a career in banking, all the while dreaming of more. Wanting to learn the ropes of money and the marketplace, by the time he was 30 he had set out into the creative, imaginative, and sometimes risky world of becoming an entrepreneur. First one idea, then another, then more and more, and by the time he was into his 40s he had brought into being several healthy businesses—and was still wanting more. Not more money, so much, but more meaning.

And he found that in a company of other guys like him, scattered about the country, all about the same age, each one a serial entrepreneur like him, each one someone of honest faith who longed for more accountability, for more friendship, for more relationship between what they believed about the world and how they lived in the world. Together they set out on a pilgrimage, meeting several times together each year, listening to each other, prodding each other, encouraging each other, even opening their bank accounts to each other. They wanted to know, and to be known.

That experience of iron sharpening the truest iron forged in Pete a surprisingly deep sense of responsibility. While he was born into that ethos of heart and mind as the son of parents who loved God and their land, his father and mother making unusual choice after choice so that their children would learn to love what was worth loving, the years after college are critical years for all of us: Who do we want to be? What do we want our lives to be about? How will we live?

The moral philosopher Iris Murdoch has written for the ages that "At crucial moments of choice, most of the business of choosing is already over." Not a soft determinism, at all; instead, a profound understanding of character, and the ways we see and hear the world characteristically.

True for everyone everywhere, it was true for Pete. With unusual discipline and focus, over the next 20 years he learned all he could about the work of his life, developing habits of heart that became "him," affecting his hopes, influencing his dreams. But with all of that true, he would say that the chapter of his life in which he is now living, the 25 and more years of praying, thinking, and working together with these other men, has been critical for him in becoming the man I met in the hotel lobby in Florida. Able and responsible, committed and generous, always eager to know more about the world and what he might do to form and shape it in ways so that more people and places would flourish—whether in his native Kansas, his home in Wichita, or far and wide in cities and countries beyond those worlds.

After I finished speaking, he picked me up and we drove to Hutchinson. We had years to talk about, and we only got started. But before too long, the high walls of the prison were visible, and we drove into the parking lot. He told me that he had imagined himself doing something "good" for the men, that he could use his business experience to bring change to their lives. But in his own very plainspoken way, he said, very simply, "They have changed me."

We walked into the prison, through gate after gate, door after door, locks and more locks, guards and more guards. Finally we were through, walking along the razor-wire-tunneled fence past the high stone wall, to a long, low, blue building that houses Pete's company, a business at work within the prison.

About 15 years ago he began thinking of another way to do business, one that would be within the walls, an honest business where prisoners could learn honest labor, earn honest money, and become honest men. He is no romantic, and the Kansas State Penitentiary has no romantics on its staff. But for the sake of trying something that might matter a lot, Pete persuaded the warden to allow "the best prisoners," the ones who over time had earned trust, to become his employees. It was a proximate proposition, from Pete to the warden, an idea born of hope of what could be. Still a prison, still prisoners, but a willingness to enter into a place desperately in need of something more, creating a signpost of more justice, more mercy, more humility.

As we walked around, Pete knew their names and asked about their lives, sometimes about their kids. Everyone was hard at work, which is the order of the day, and the prisoners seem to understand that good work well done is its own reward—and of course that they are paid an honest wage matters too. Some of the men are there for life, some are there for years to come, but each one we talked to seemed glad to be known and respected. Like every one of us, they long for dignity, and in a fragile place on the plains, a frightening place in the middle of Kansas, they have found something that they had not known.

As I thought about it all, watching Pete walk through the prison, I wondered why. What is it that makes someone see himself implicated, for love's sake, in the way the world is in all of its hurt, responsible for the way the world could be? Simply said, he sees with his heart, and knows that what he knows can be a gift to those who have lost their way. His business interests are far and wide, and they do not demand that he work with prisoners; in fact, for most of his life he did not. But over the years he began to see himself as a steward of good gifts, in fact seeing his whole life as a stewardship before God in service to the world—and then he began to see himself responsible for folks that had been forgotten.

I kept thinking back to the mountains of Colorado, ten year-olds that we were, sitting beside each other, learning about the most important things in life in one of the most beautiful places on earth—right below the majesty and glory of Long's Peak—having no idea that we would someday walk into an uglier place, for love's sake, a place where most of us never want to be.

But it is also a place where Pete belongs, because of his own calling to care about things that matter to God and the world. His vocation has become a common grace for the common good, serving Kansas and beyond in and through his entrepreneurial imagination. In a strange calculus, while his hope was to bring change, the most surprising change is in his own heart, giving him eyes to see that good work matters for everyone everywhere—even in a place where the doors clang shut.

These Neighbors in This Neighborhood

"Hello," she said, "I am Kikuyu, and I work for Médecins Sans Frontières."

The day before I had flown to Kenya, spending most of my hours reading *The Africans* by David Lamb.[42] Like everyone I had impressions of Africa, but only impressions, and so I had asked a Kenyan friend at the World Bank what I should read to know more. A long flight, a long read, and yet years later I still remember the gift of the book, painting with a necessarily broad brush and yet making honest sense of the many people and the many places that are "Africa." People by people, place by place, he looked through two lenses: 1) to understand Africa is to understand that it is a continent of tribes, not a continent of nation states, and 2) that throughout African consciousness, the hearts and the hopes that thread their way through its almost incomprehensible diversity, the idea of fate is somehow, somewhere present—and over the next days I began to see and hear the reality of his analysis, from city to village, wherever I went.

When I boarded my flight from Nairobi to Kisumu, and the woman in the next seat introduced herself to me with the words, "I am Kikuyu . . ." explaining that she worked for Médecins Sans Frontières (Doctors Without Borders), that she too was traveling to the west of Kenya—as the plane took off, I realized with an unusual poignancy that I was in Africa, seeing the words I had read become flesh in the seat right next to me.

Most Kenyans are Kikuyu, but there are other tribes too, the Akamba, Luhya, Kisii, Meru, Mijikenda, and the Maasai, Turkana, Samburu, and Kalenjin as well. When I stepped off the plane in Kisumu, I stepped into the Luo culture, somehow African and Kenyan, even if deeply distinct, with no intention of becoming lost in the larger world—the Luo are Luo, after all.

Why was I there? What had taken me to Africa? Several years earlier I had given a lecture for the Veritas Forum, and after the students had asked all of their questions, a group of guys maybe ten years beyond their student days were still standing there, with their own questions—and so we talked late into the night.

That evening I had addressed the challenge of the responsibility of knowledge, which is at the heart of every vocation within

[42]David Lamb, *The Africans* (Knopf Doubleday, 1987).

the academy, whether student or faculty, administration or staff. *What will we do with what we know?* Beginning with a conversation I had had with a good friend whose own work with USAID had taken her to Africa the previous months, tasked with evaluating its complex medical needs in light of growing disease and famine—concluding that the situation was "outrageous!"—on into a reflection about the film *Magnolia* with its surprisingly profound treatment of the most cosmic questions, the ones that rumble through every century and every culture because they are asked by every son of Adam and every daughter of Eve, *viz.*, Do our choices matter? Do we have true responsibility? Or in the end is it a fated universe? A world where the dice has already been rolled, the pretensions of "choices" and "responsibility" only that, ideas pretending to be something that is not and cannot be? And then finally into the rich vision of learning rooted in the Hebrew and Christian understanding of knowledge, where if we know we must care.

The guys were a band called the Jars of Clay, and over the next months we talked and talked again, focused on what they could do in light of the global health crisis in the early 2000s brought about by HIV/AIDS in Africa. "What could they do? What should they do?" In the years since then much good work has been done in and through the Blood:Water Mission, the organization that was birthed out of those months, and at least one good book written, *A Thousand Wells* by Jena Lee Nardella, a beautiful, thoughtful reflection about her own pilgrimage into the hopes and heartaches of Africa.

My trip to Kenya was with members of the band, and Jena. That first day we met with a public health nurse, Elizabeth Obiero, who already had experience with the very questions we had entered into; she was willing to help us know what the needs were, and how they could be met with the help of our newly birthed Blood:Water Mission. Amazingly, and yet not, 20 years later she is still helping, now working throughout the western region of Kenya, with the village of Lwala as the center point, with its confluence of the community of houses, a school, and a medical clinic. Over the next days we listened, learning more about these people in their place, beginning to understand more of the necessary complexity of their history, of who they were, of why they were, of the way they lived their lives.

And yes, we began to feel the weight of fate—agriculturally, educationally, socially—that "We are acted upon, more than that we are actors." While one word can never capture the complexity of a continent, one seemed to be in the air we breathed—i.e., that whatever we did would have to be against the spirit of "what happens, happens." In the Yoruba language of Nigeria, the word is *ayanmo*; in the Swahili language of Kenya, it is *hatima*. But more than these relatively isolated words and their usages, windows that they might be for us, what is true for Africa is true the world over, overwhelmingly so, in the Northern Hemisphere as well as in the Southern Hemisphere. In the pantheist East it is called karma, while in the materialist West it is called evolutionary determinism. "A life has been chosen for me" is the meaning of *ayanmo*, while it is "I am my DNA" in the Enlightenment-formed cultures of the twentieth and twenty-first centuries in the Western world. Time, chance, matter—there it is, and that is it. There are nuanced differences, but at the end of the day it is "I have been acted upon."

There are exceptions, though, by grace there are always exceptions. In a thousand different ways they are signposts of something more, signposts for something more. From the first conversation on the first day, Elizabeth stood out to me, formed within a worldview that saw human agency, honest responsibility born of love, as integral to being human. Very accomplished and serious in the best ways, she knew the Luo people, and she knew the most important questions to ask about health and well-being, offering not only her medical training but also her additional study in economic and social development. With well-formed eyes to see the deeper, truer needs of the women, the men, and the children of Lwala, for 20 years now she has overseen the W.A.S.H. program in the village—Water Access, Sanitation, and Hygiene—knowing the important relationship between clean water and clean blood in the fight against HIV/AIDS.

One cannot know Elizabeth without being taught by her commitment and resolve, given with open-hearted gladness and profoundly grounded maturity. Her labor of love as a life among *the vulnerables* of Kenya through the Lwala clinic serves over 30,000 people, offering good care for heart and mind, soul and strength. And while many others have come and gone over the years, each someone with eagerness and passion, willing to work hard with hope, she has stayed, choosing to keep on keeping on, pouring out her life for her neighbors near and far, in Lwala and beyond.

But "beyond" is a weighty word. She has a great heart, and very good gifts. Her work would be judged excellent all over the world; she knows what she is doing, and she does it very well. But she has chosen her own "neighborhood," one that stretches across miles and miles, including thousands upon thousands of people, while choosing to center her care in one village, knowing that she can do something, even if she cannot do everything. In a deeply Augustinian way, she embodies his understanding of *dilectio proximi*: While the whole world is there to be loved, any one of us can only love a small part of it, that which is proximate to us. A good life is one that makes peace with that reality, feeling the responsibility for more, while living within the responsibility for this and not that, of these neighbors in this neighborhood, for this time and this place.

To have sustained her vocation as she has, Elizabeth has lived within the ancient and holy rhythm of *ora et labora,* and is profoundly conscious of its ordering of her days and years. Praying and working, working and praying, hour by hour, week after week, giving her good gifts to all who come, to all who have need, especially to those on the frontiers of medicine, the faraway places that even most Kenyans have never visited—called to care for those who feel their own vulnerability. With a holy heart, born of a life given to God and to his world, she has loved her people in her place, a Luo who has loved the Luo.

Over the Shoulder, Through the Heart

The truest learning is always like that, *over the shoulder, through the heart.* While my life is full of books with shelves in every room of our house, books upon more books—my study itself wall-to-wall with hundreds of books—eventually words have to become flesh, if we are to understand them, if we are to know what they mean. Incarnation matters; in fact, it is crucial. We have to see what it looks like, to see if the words mean something in life, to see if the ideas really have legs.

In the first chapter of the Gospel of John, these few words, "the Word became flesh" are first of all the very center of Christian theology as they summarize the meaning of the Incarnation—but they are also a statement of pedagogical genius. And because the Story is a story, with threads of meaning woven from beginning to end, the words of Genesis 1 about the origins of the cosmos are crucially embodied in the life, death, and resurrection of Jesus, echoed as they are in the prologue of the book of John; chapter by chapter the Gospel gives us windows into what "incarnation" means; every conversation and question is one more story that shows what it means for the "Word to become flesh."

The first question in the first chapter is in fact answered with, "Come and see." None of us would have blinked if Jesus had responded with, "Read this scroll," or even, "Come hear my sermon," but instead it is, "Come and see"—if you want to understand what I am saying, then come and see . . . because the words will become flesh.

One of the most influential contemporary incarnations of this pedagogy was born in a Swiss chalet in the 1950s, in the home of Francis and Edith Schaeffer, who opened their hearts to others, first a trickle, then a stream, and then a river of twenty-somethings who made their way to the mountain village of Huemoz, taking part in a holy rhythm of work and study, of meals and more, day by day being drawn into a place of intellectual and moral seriousness where the most important questions of life and love were at the center of the community's very *raison d'être*.

One of those who came was David Laco from Bratislava, Slovakia. A vision for the work of educator already having been awakened in his heart after a first year of teaching, he made his way to the English L'Abri in the countryside of Hampshire, another embodiment of the same vision, a community of seekers whose honest questions wanted honest answers.

A natural learner, now a natural teacher—his gifts for both deeply woven into his very being—David began his schooling at the Narnia School in Bratislava, Slovakia, a school visionary in its hopes, creative in its curriculum. He had begun there as a five-year-old, learning to learn in and through the richly wrought "wardrobes" into the way the world is, and the way the world ought to be. Formed by a moral imagination inspired by Lewis's Narnian universe, the classrooms of the school offered a surprisingly coherent account of what was to be learned, even of why it was to be learned—and simply said, the children learned to learn about things that matter most.

Because Slovakia is Slovakia, and not any other place, notably not England or America, the way that schooling is understood does not fit categories that make sense in schools in other societies. Not a "public" school or a "private" school, the Narnia School has formed its own identity in Bratislava, a parent-envisioned school that draws from the city as a whole—and now the C.S. Lewis Bilingual School has done the same thing, offering a more advanced pedagogy for high school students with a full-bodied curriculum born of wonderfully imagined ways to wonder and work. It calls its pedagogy "invitational," with classrooms that are principally seminars in which students learn alongside others by reflection on a text, engaging in serious conversation about what has been read.

Located in a post-communist wasteland born of a severely impoverished understanding of human flourishing, the schools represent something that is honestly good, bringing renewal to the ruins of what was left when the Soviet Union collapsed. Though

Slovakia as a country is full of remarkable beauty, as is Bratislava with its almost fairy tale-like old city, the community chose a place for their children's learning that needed to be reclaimed, over time becoming a signpost itself. While the stunted Soviet imagination produced ugliness wherever it went, leaving miles and miles of apartment buildings built more for automatons than humans, in stark contrast these two schools have made peace with the proximate—very concretely. Rather than tearing down what is, they have reimagined what could be, bringing into being something beautiful for God and for the world.

While the ethos is profoundly Christian, the student body is philosophically diverse, representing the spectrum of serious opinion about what life and learning mean. A school for everyone, and yet a school with commitments about what is real and true and right, it has nothing dualistic—for example, facts and/or values, objective vs. subjective knowledge—but instead a richer vision of education that sees engagement of mind and heart together as the very center of schooling. Everything about the school is embedded within a worldview that is honestly Christian, but in a way that honors the rabbi of all rabbis, Jesus himself, who believed that knowing means doing. The ideas that make the school a prized center of education throughout Bratislava and Slovakia, winning national awards for its innovation and integrity, are written into its understanding of learning, i.e., a belief in the responsibility of knowledge, and so an invitation to think more deeply and seriously, resisting the temptation to dot every "i" and cross every "t" academically, but instead, "if you have ears, then hear."

One of the first students at both the Narnia School and the C.S. Lewis School, David found that his pilgrimage in and through L'Abri substantively formed his hopes for what kind of teacher he wants to be, for what kind of school he wants to teach in. And now with his wife, Miranda, written into his life and love, they are kindred spirits, working together on this more embodied pedagogy born of long hopes, even generational hopes, of those who imagined the schools into being, yearning for schooling as it is supposed to be, for learning as it can be. Together they understand this as a stewardship of their lives, knowing that they have been given gifts which now they are giving away.

So very creative in every way, with its understanding that a school's curriculum is both inside and outside of the classroom, one important face to these dreams-in-common has been the creation of Baraka, a living/learning community of faculty and students at the high school. Taking as inspiration this rich word for "blessing" with Arabic and Hebrew roots, their vision is that "members of the community through shared life will be a blessing to each other and to the broader environment," to the school, but also the city and the society. Apprenticed as he is in these visions, David has taken these same hopes on to the PhD level, now asking questions of deeper consequence, reading with the best minds about the truest learning, which is always over the shoulder, through the heart, as it must be.

Because educational visions are always formed by epistemological commitments, and our beliefs about learning are shaped by our beliefs about knowing, one of the best images of this truth in the corpus of Lewis's writing comes from the final story of Narnia, *The Last Battle,* where the Pevensie children, minus Susan, enter into mortal conflict over the future of Narnia. After the most terrible treachery, the most vile vanity, with a selfism that knows no end, finally the fight is over. Newly awakened to what is next, the children are certain that they have "arrived," that this must be "it," after the last battle. While they think they have come to the end of a new beginning, in no uncertain terms they are told by Aslan, the Lion above all Lions, "No, this is not it yet . . . further up and further in." Yes, something, but not yet everything—proximate it is.

With the prescience of good parents who were also educational visionaries, these schools were named in honor of Lewis and his richly formed imagination, giving the world stories that beautifully nourish the deepest realities of the universe in language that even the littlest among us can understand—a reality that David entered into as a boy himself. Years later, his own vocation embodies the belief that life, as well as learning, is always and everywhere, *further up and further in.*

Heaven and Earth, and Chocolate Too

Sacraments are windows. Remember to eat this, to drink this, Jesus says, because then you will begin to understand the mystery of the universe, of your place in history, and most crucially, of God himself, incarnate in the life, death, and resurrection of Christ—and in that Eucharistic moment, bread and wine become sacramental, giving us windows into the meaning of heaven and of earth, and most importantly, of the way that they become one.

If we have eyes to see, we are by grace drawn into knowing more deeply the most important things of life.

The best teachers are that for a reason, and when they come to the same conclusion, wise ones listen. That the Russian Orthodox Alexander Schmemann believed in the same universe that Dutch Calvinist Abraham Kuyper did is fascinating: "all of life is sacramental" for the one, and "every square inch of the whole of reality" for the other, both believing in a way of seeing that was comprehensive and coherent. In a different way, in another time and place, yet for this same reason, the French philosopher Simone Weil came to the same conclusion, seeing the truest study as sacramental study. When we see that heaven touches earth within the concreteness of our academic labor—in her evocative image, "learning to pay attention" to what is really there—we then understand the meaning of aesthetics, of biology, of economics, of history, of mathematics, of philosophy, of politics, of psychology, of sociology, and more. A profound insight, its truth runs its way across the curriculum of every school and university, affecting every vocation and occupation across the range of human relationships and responsibilities. The sacramental becomes the thread that weaves its way through the whole of life, our love, our learning, our worship, and our work.

Having grown up within the "sainted" history of the American Southwest, with its long highways connecting the glories of

Colorado and California, its grand valleys alongside their great mountain ranges, I breathed air that was Spanish-influenced—San Luis and San Joaquin, Sangre de Cristo and Sierra Nevada, and much more. Whether one has ears to hear or not, there is a memory of transcendence that lingers across the grandeur of that part of America. Cities like Los Angeles, San Francisco, and Sacramento were the touchpoints of my life—reminding me of "the angels," of St. Francis, and of the "holy sacrament"—orienting me to where I was and to where I might be going, a geography of heart and mind.

But apart from forays across the border, I had never traveled into Mexico, the land that was south of the Southwest, until an invitation came to speak in Mexico City to a gathering of folk from throughout the world whose own lives were embedded in a long love for students, men and women from every continent giving their lives for the next generation. A year earlier I had taught a class in Washington, DC, on vocation, and at the end of four weeks, a man asked if we could talk more, which we did, the next week and the next week, over the next year. The senior advisor to his organization's president, eventually he asked if I would enter more into his world of work, asking me to speak on the question of vocation to his colleagues who were meeting that year in Mexico City.

In the great airport, people upon people bustling about, hurrying this way and that, I looked and looked for a sign with my name—and finally saw it, breathing a sigh of relief! On that ride to the hotel began a conversation I am still having with Victor García de la Torre.

A business student at a university in the city, he and I found that we both had an honest interest in chocolate. For him it was that his grandfather had a ranch that grew cocoa, and for years he had planned to take up his grandfather's legacy; for me it was that I was involved in a project with the Mars Corporation, makers of M&Ms and much more, in which we were trying to rethink the business of business. We talked and talked, through the streets of the city, surprising each other with our kindred spirits, beginning to see that we were asking the same questions and paying attention to the same hopes and dreams. He promised to bring me some of the family's chocolate the next day, and as I put my head on the pillow, I smiled . . . and I drifted off into the night.

When I gave my lectures the next day, I told a bit about Victor and his intriguingly robust vision of vocation, one that began with the challenge of good work for everyone who worked, for those who were employees and for those who employed. Drawing on language of the common good, of the importance of honest pay for honest work, of offering employment to those most unemployable, of a deep sense of stewardship for the trees themselves, he was amazingly articulate about his sense of responsibility for his grandfather's company—and yes, he brought me his chocolate. Even though it was packaged and wrapped, I could smell its richness!

When his studies were done, he wanted to immediately take up the family legacy, continuing production of the cocoa, finding ways to bring it to markets nationally and internationally. But that was hard, harder than he imagined, given all that he did not know about the ins-and-outs of the marketplace. He had read books about business, but he had not yet learned to do business, and Victor decided to enter into the work of management consulting, wanting to apprentice himself to the "best of the best" in Mexico and beyond. His job was to understand what made companies do well, and on the other side, what made companies falter.

Those were important years for Victor, the sifting and sorting of self that takes place in the twenty-something decade, making choices about who we are and why we are, and what we want to do with our lives. Done with school, entering into the new world of work, Victor stumbled into the bright lights that were his to navigate, trying to find the footing for a good life. Making his way through the next years was difficult, with the challenges of work and family illness, and at a certain point he came to the end of all he knew, all that he had trusted. By the happiest of graces, he met Lila, and with love in their hearts they began a life together, moving to Monterrey, and in time welcomed a baby into their hearts and home. As he deepened skills at work, he found himself increasingly thinking through where and how he wanted to work. The management consulting took him here and there, offering more responsibility as he learned to analyze the ways and means of business, all the while feeling the increasing weight of the context for his calling and career, knowing that the choice of a people in a place would be critical for the flourishing of his family.

"I want to spend my life on things that I love." Very simply said, but a challenge for every son of Adam and daughter of Eve. At our best and truest, while we long for everything, we choose for something, knowing that we will have to make peace with the proximate, with something that is honest and true, good and right. There are deep loves that run through Victor's heart: his wife and children, the good work of his life, his grandfather and father in the business of their lives, his commitments to doing business a certain kind of way, his place within the community of Monterrey, his citizenship in Mexico full of hope for a healthier economic and social ecology, and all of this given coherence by his honest faith.

Where this will all go, God alone knows.

But what is true for Victor is that he knows that chocolate matters—because everything matters—that its smell is, in his own words, "like heaven," as if heaven and earth touch in the wonder of chocolate, its taste and texture bringing delight. And like countless pilgrims before him, he sees himself on a journey, one in which he is learning about God, about himself, about being a husband and a father, about the work of work, and about growing ideas, seeds as they begin, but becoming mature trees over time.

It is a good story, one written into the generations of families throughout history—a grandfather's long labor of love taken up by his grandson who feels called to care about cocoa. Bringing the beauty and mystery of chocolate to people who are hungry for something more than mere consumption, he understands that they are hungry for something sacramental, to taste and see what happens when heaven touches earth in and on our very tongues.

The Good Work of an Approximator

Ideas have legs, and more often than not they run into history, in time becoming history.

For those watching the world, the years between the 1950s and the 1980s were ones of terrible tumult in Iran. In this nation long suppressed by the royal regime with the aid of foreign powers, particularly the United States government, the Shah Mohammad Reza Pahlavi was finally overthrown in 1979, a "people's revolution" of sorts, the very secular West surprised by the intensity of religious fervor among the Islamic clergy led by Ayatollah Khomeini. And as with revolutions the world over, in time the oppressed became the oppressors.

A son of Iran, from a family with generations of life in the marketplaces of that predominantly Muslim society, Ehsan Samei came of age during this cultural revolution. Seeing and hearing the unimaginable, he found those years to be ones of disenchantment, knowing that what had long been true for his family and for him could no longer be. His boyhood over, at age 12 he was thrust into questions of allegiance and identity earlier than most, the maturity of manhood forced upon him by the events of his time and place. What then did it mean to be Iranian? What is Islam, after all? What now will I do with my life?

Already a serious student, a lover of both music and science, he spent his adolescent years exploring his great loves, deepening commitments to ideas about the world and how he wanted to live in it. Not seeing a possible future in Iran, Ehsan chose to continue his studies in the United States, going here and there for the next decade, his interests becoming more focused, and early in his career he was invited to join the faculty of the Duke University Medical School as a medical physicist, over time becoming the Distinguished Professor of Radiology, directing its Center for Virtual Imaging Trials.

We met one day in the Research Triangle of North Carolina, the geography where the cities of Chapel Hill, Durham, and

Raleigh touch, on a weekend retreat in which we were seriously pondering the meaning of vocation, and decided to take a walk around a lake, talking about many things—and as sometimes happens, that conversation had consequences. A friendship was born. Having grown up a million miles from each other, we found that we saw the world in similar ways, his questions being mine, and mine his.

A son and a brother, a husband and a father, he is also a physician and a physicist, spending the days of his life at work in the hospital and its laboratories, working to understand medical imaging for the sake of those whose very lives depend on remarkably sophisticated technologies that "see" us in ways that have never been imagined.

But for human beings throughout history, having eyes that see is a challenge. Do we see? And what do we see? With his years of experience, leading his university and now his own professional academy of colleagues across the country, Ehsan acknowledges that at his best he is able to see "approximately," that the imaging available is "approximate," an image of a reality that is beyond the technology's highest capability. As he says, "I can 'see' your knee, but I can never 'see' your knee as it is." Yes, the complexity and wonder of a knee can be seen, but only seen through a glass darkly—or even through the wonders of X-ray, ultrasound, and MRI technologies.

Surprisingly thoughtful about the work of his life, he has given himself to social, cultural, and theological reflection on the world at large, and on his research in particular. With intellectual agility he walks between theories of cosmology and biology, between anthropology and medicine, knowing that his integrity as a scientist and an academician requires an interdisciplinary commitment if it is to be done well—"seeing" being the complex task it is, one that is necessarily physiological but also philosophical, seeing through the eyes of the heart as we must do. Having mentored hundreds of students, future physicians or physicists all, he wants them to understand their work as "approximators" in their theoretical modeling, imaging the knee but unable to capture the function, observing something but not the thing itself, ". . . seeing one dimension exquisitely well, but knowing that we do not see everything." Why? He describes his work this way:

> *The body's and organs' anatomy and function possess many dimensions. In medical imaging, we strive to capture and view those dimensions as best as we can, yet the best is never perfect, and further, as we capture one dimension, we leave many other dimensions unrepresented.*[43]

In the world in which we live and move and have our being, the work of the medical professions *is* because of what *is not*, i.e., as human beings we are frail and finite, and in the end, the Latin words are ours, each one of us: *memento mori,* we too shall someday die. Whether we get our help from a rural medical clinic with earnest but limited resources in Kenya, or we are able to find our way into the Mayo Clinics of the modern world with their world-class insights, at our best we hope.

But *hope* is a hard word in the twenty-first century, more sure than we should be that all things are possible. The right time, the right place, the right person, the right resource . . . and what cannot be done? Acknowledged by his peers as unusually gifted, the recipient of awards the world over for the excellence of his ability, Ehsan has made the word "approximation" the key to understanding him and his work, making peace with its reality as he gives himself away to his patients and colleagues far and near. He knows, and yet he does not know.

If he loved science as a young man, Ehsan also loved music, and he was as serious about the one as he was about the other. Not surprisingly, he was drawn to the intellectually rich compositions of Johann Sebastian Bach, through time aware that the music was embedded within a mind that was genius, sensing "the absolute" that he had lost in the way the Islamic Revolution tore his homeland apart; in contrast, Bach's music

---

[43]Conversation with Ehsan Samei.

was a mysterious echo, an "approximation" of that absolute. As a young flautist, he mastered the master, preparing for a public performance of one of Bach's iconic pieces for the flute. The night before the grand occasion he went through his repertoire one more time, his mentor paying close attention—and all of a sudden he heard, "You cannot play this music, Ehsan!" Shocked, knowing that he knew every note as it had been written, he heard the words, "Yes, you are playing the notes, but I cannot hear the cross of Christ in your playing—and to play Bach one must hear the cross of Christ."

For someone raised as a Muslim in an Islamic society, Ehsan could not understand his teacher's lament. The performance went on as planned, but he was perplexed, knowing that there was more for him to know. Over time, largely through the friendship of folk who incarnated a life born of "the cross of Christ," he came to believe himself, entering into a life of honest faith grounded in mere Christianity. And it was in that context of his membership within a community that had decided that the idea of vocation needed to be explored more fully, if they were to be who and why and what they needed to be in Durham, North Carolina, that we began a conversation that continues on.

Ehsan has had his own pilgrimage: a Persian whose young loves have formed the contours of his life, choosing science as a vocation, but being profoundly affected in his deepest being by Bach's insight into the meaning of music, of what it must be if it is to be beautiful and true, understanding that art and science are inextricably connected—". . . like dimensions of reality, each trying to reflect it as close as it can, never perfect, and each exposing only one facet of that multi-dimensional reality, just like medical imaging . . ."—giving distinctive expression to what one believes to be most real, most true, most right.

There is a simply stated, if very surprising humility in Ehsan's longing to understand the worlds that he loves. But humility too often seems out of place in the academy, though the wisest ones throughout history have understood that it is the first virtue, where a good life and a godly life begin, knowing one's frailty and finitude, eschewing the arrogance that is so easily ours, pushing back against the pride that so often consumes us. His hard-won insight is that at his best he is an "approximator," keenly aware that the technological advances he makes still only enable approximate judgments about the health of patients—knowing something is true because he has seen what can be seen, but knowing even more deeply that he has seen something, and not everything.

More Justice? More Mercy? More Humility?

"I would like to acknowledge that we are gathered on the traditional, ancestral and unceded territory of the Salish, Squamish and Musqueam Nations."

Wherever one is in British Columbia, every public gathering begins with these words—remembering that there were "First Nations" living in the Pacific Northwest before the British began exploring a world that was new to them, expanding their empire onto yet another continent. Sometimes educational, sometimes political, sometimes social, these words surprise only those who are visiting Vancouver and beyond; those who live there know them by heart.

What is this place and who are its people?

Flying into Vancouver, BC, one is immediately aware that this is a geography that was once known and loved by native folk whose aesthetic was neither English nor European. From the airplane doors to the customs area, the walkway goes through forests and wetlands that represent the sea and sky, the forests and rivers of a land on the very edge of North America—so far away from Nova Scotia and New England, from the Carolinas and the Gulf Coast, from the American Midwest and Southwest. Descending by escalator into the airport, visitors are greeted by two red cedar "welcome figures" inspired by Coast Salish traditional images of an eagle and men with salmon artfully becoming motifs which depict the theme of flight, and all of this the world's largest spindle whorl mounted on a cascading waterfall. "Astounding" is a good word, and "very beautiful" too.

Vancouver in the twenty-first century is a city of the world: About half its population are Asian, mostly of Chinese origin, but there are also many of European descent, whose history still dominates, the city still flying the flag of the British Commonwealth. There are growing numbers of Indian peoples and even Latin Americans too; the world at large has moved into the most expensive real estate in North America. With its moderate climate, it is known to the rest of Canada as their "Hawaii," with its stunning natural beauty bringing together both snow-covered mountains and the deep blue ocean, appealing to women and men the world over, each one longing to belong. With all of these peoples and more, even more mysteriously and profoundly it is never not the ancient home of the Salish, the Squamish, and the Musqueam nations—and if that older history was forgotten for too long, it is now remembered whenever and wherever the city meets.

Everyone in British Columbia—the name itself a window into a history that still is—lives by and with the King on its money. Every jug of milk, every liter of gas, every sandal and shirt, every sailboat and set of skis, every car and house, every salary and benefit, is accounted for by the Royal Family of England, and it is a history with blessings and curses.

Especially in the twenty-first century, *colonial* and *colonialism* have become weighted words, carrying meaning that is only more and more so understood by the people of the earth. There are no nations that do not have histories without someone sometime choosing to conquer and overwhelm. There are no innocents here, because it is the story of history, and always a messy story it is, with push and shove, aggression, greed, and power more often than not the deeper motivations that made Alexander be "Great"; that made the Roman Empire spread to every corner of the Mediterranean and beyond; that is the story of Genghis Khan with his far-flung forces making all of Asia his; that made the kingdom of Persia an empire extending throughout what we now know as the Middle East; that gave the power of control to the Oyo Empire in western Africa, subduing peoples wherever they could be found; that inspired Spain to send missionaries, and soldiers too, to Mexico, beginning in Baja California and then into Alta California with its somewhat "sainted" story of expansion; that brought into being an idea of "Britannia," where the sun never set on its global reach. The stories go on and on because history goes on and on. Yes, again, this is history and it is messy.

It was into this story that Monica immigrated to Vancouver, moving with her family from Hong Kong to a city already home to thousands of Chinese. But though it was now home, so far from the familiarities of her birthplace, even as a young girl she felt the burden of being an "outsider" as a non-white person, which is difficult for anyone, but for a little one even harder. Always earnest, always studious, she was every teacher's hope, listening carefully, reading critically. In her adolescent years she began taking seriously the environmental challenges for a globalizing, modernizing political economy, and she volunteered at a salmon hatchery, already wanting to live into the meaning of her studies. And in those same years she began bearing the historical weight that came with understanding the reality of "First Nations" peoples for whom her new home had long been home, knowing that her Asian "difference" from the dominant culture was only exacerbated for the native peoples whose very existence was a difference that unsettled everyone. When she went on to study at the University of British Columbia, these questions became the questions that gave curricular coherence to her undergraduate years, offering the beginnings of a vocation that she has pursued ever since.

Her professors encouraged her to ponder a career in diplomacy, which for her Asian immigrant community would have been quite acceptable. But Monica had a vision for public justice that became the thread connecting her interests, ones that could not be easily answered in her young-adult heart. She went to the nation's capital city of Ottawa, hoping to find a way to bring her academic loves into a kind of work that would make sense of a life, and in those years diplomacy was transformed into public service, giving her room to think about different ways her deepening commitments could find vocational expression.

The ten years beyond adolescence were difficult years in their own right, as she still sorted through her responsibility for what she was beginning to know. "Public service" was not the way into the more lucrative occupation that would be honored by her parents and peers, and she found herself between the proverbial rock and a hard place, having been raised with the responsibility of honoring her family by and with her life, but knowing that the questions that gave life to her heart were more for a healthy civil society than for the corporate towers of Canada.

And Monica decided to pursue graduate study in public policy, still eager to understand the complex relationship of climate and energy policy, with honest concern for the First Nations of Canada, and British Columbia in particular. After time in Germany on a fellowship that allowed her to learn about another nation's public policies, she returned to Vancouver as a negotiations analyst for British Columbia's provincial government in its relationship to its indigenous peoples.

It was in those years that she became my student for a time, entering into a graduate program of study that asked questions about the nature of vocation for the common good. Still "every teacher's hope," with her seriousness about ideas and their meaning for life in the world, she stood out; it was plain that every book we read, every conversation we had, she understood in relationship to the work of her life, which was focused on "the marine space"—fishing and water rights—for the First Nations. Now immersed in intergovernmental relations, she spends the days of her life pursuing more justice to be done, more mercy to be shown, more humility to be embodied, in and through the public square of the coastland life of Burrard Bay and beyond, which is substantially the cultural / economic / political / social world of Vancouver.

More justice? More mercy? More humility? In the now-but-not-yet world which is ours, the world where the creation itself groans for what it longs to be and become, Monica spends the days of her life on a vision for what could be and should be, believing with her whole heart that "reconciliation is both past-looking and forward-looking"—as she puts it—therefore by necessity called to address the complexity of human longing and need, while knowing that she can only do what is hers to do. With a self-awareness that is unusual, she knows that, "My vocation is born of the hope that we can do some things differently . . . we can negotiate differently . . . we can renounce arrogance, choosing humility instead."

And because the labor of her life has public meaning, the virtues of justice, mercy, and humility have structural and systemic implications for the people of her place, with moral meaning for everyone. In the wonderful if wounded world of the Pacific Northwest that is Vancouver, British Columbia, they are habits of heart that run through Monica's very being, yearning for *all* to be made right as she is, but making peace with *some* things being made right—and with that, at least most of the time, she is able to sleep at night, her heart still alive with honest hope for what someday will be.

Proximate Faith, Proximate Hope, Proximate Love

Hints of hope, and love in the ruins—they are words of life, and words of longing.

One of the biographies of Walker Percy is poignantly titled *Pilgrim In the Ruins*,[44] and one summer I spent days pondering the story of his life—from the heir of generations of economic and social privilege in the South to being the son and grandson of men who killed themselves. Leaving his home within the larger Percy family for undergraduate study at the University of North Carolina, he went to Columbia University for medical school. But before he was finally done he contracted tuberculosis, and he was never able to become the physician he planned to be. With terrible deaths and painful disappointments, what he had

[44]Jay Tolson, *Pilgrim in the Ruins: A Life of Walker Percy* (Simon and Schuster, 1992).

imagined would be trustworthy had not been, and over the next twenty years the story goes on, threaded through with anxiety and longing, first trying this and then that, wanting to write but finding no one who wanted to read him . . . seeing himself always as a pilgrim in the ruins of life and the world.

Even with the acclaim and honor that were his as he became "Walker Percy, the profoundly gifted American novelist," he was never free from the sorrows of his early life, never free from the experienced memories that had so shaped his soul. But remarkably, surprisingly, he kept going—perhaps with a proximate faith, a proximate hope, a proximate love—settling into a long life with his wife in Covington, Louisiana, worshipping and working week by week with a holy rhythm that was its own reminder of his vocation as a hint of hope in this frail world, spending himself on behalf of neighbors near and far, entering the needs of those next door even as he wrote with painful honesty about the human condition, knowing that his best work would be his way with words as an essayist and novelist, the literature of his life as "love in the ruins" in a time and a place that was not what it was supposed to be.

And that of course is the story of each one here, pilgrims in the ruins that they are. Different people in different places, but from every corner of the earth men and women who keep on keeping on, longing for what should be, making peace with what can be, each one committed to seeing and hearing and feeling the world like God does, as human beings must, as human beings sometimes do.

6

A LONG-LOVED LOVE

There is a design, an alignment to cry
Of my heart to see,
The beauty of love as it was made to be
—"Sigh No More" / Mumford and Sons[45]

Sometimes there are tender tears.

Several years ago, on a flight across America I watched the film *Coming Home*, born of the genius of Zhang Yimou, the celebrated director whose work over the last generation has changed the character of Chinese cinema. One more time he has told a tale about being human amidst the ruins of the Cultural Revolution, allowing the world windows into what it meant to live in and through those years of heartache and wound.

The story of a family stretched taut across the years of modern China, the film begins as the Cultural Revolution is losing its way, still oppressing and yet gasping. A mother and her daughter have suffered deeply because of the imprisonment of their husband and father, a professor who 20 years earlier was in the wrong place at the wrong time, and like thousands upon thousands was wrongly sent to a labor camp to be "reeducated." When he is finally released, he comes home, eager to see the ones he most loves, only to find that his wife—played by Gong Li, Yimou's favorite actress—cannot remember him.

Something has happened to her memory, traumatized as she is by her years of loneliness, and tragically, she does not

[45]"Sigh No More," title track of the Mumford and Sons album *Sigh No More* (Glassnote Records, 2009).

recognize her husband. Try as he does, with gentleness and persistence over days which become years, her mind cannot be awakened; something has been broken that in this life will not be healed.

What we see through the lens of the heart that is Zhang Yimou is the gift of "a long-loved love," as Madeleine L'Engle has poetically put it. Deeply wrought, this is the love that everyone longs for—we yearn to be known, and still be loved, even and especially in our frailty.

Reflecting on the film, I remembered a visit to China years earlier when I was asked to give a lecture at the Beijing Film Academy, the school where Yimou studied. "Good Stories, Good Societies" I called it, speaking to an auditorium full of students and faculty, with a translator beside me who took my words and made them his. Arguing that there is an integral relationship between "good stories" and "good societies," that we can never be the one without the other, I drew on the American novelist Walker Percy, whose deep wisdom has shaped my life—"Bad books lie—they lie most about the human condition"—and the Czech playwright-become-president Vaclav Havel, whose vision has also formed mine: "The secret of man is the secret of his responsibility." And then I talked about China's best filmmaker, Zhang Yimou, offering several of his best movies as windows into my thesis, doing my best to help them see that bad films always lie—they lie most about the human condition. In contrast, the best films are ones that imaginatively set forth a responsibility born of love as the very heart of our humanity.

There were hundreds of serious, gifted students, and when I finished they asked honest questions wanting honest answers. As one young woman put it, "How can we know the truth of the human condition?" That began most of an hour of questions, each one probing the most important things—and of course, I loved them, longing to spend days with them.

Yes, sometimes there are tender tears. Everyone understands this, because there are moments along the way of life where we weep; we cannot *not*. Pilgrims in the ruins we are, each one of us, going further up and further into the brokenness of life, we more fully face the wounds of the world, and most tenderly of all, our own wounds. Always psychologically complex, sometimes they are born of political misery too, and this only adds layers to the complexity.

Most of us will not have concentration camps to change the course of our lives, though we will know the sorrows of the world in ways that are differently severe. To know the world and still love the world is the most difficult of all vocations—and yet it is what it means to be human, fully and truly human. But to choose that will cost us, which is why, sometimes, there are tender tears.

To Take Delight, To Give Grace

If the film *Coming Home* is its own profoundly experienced story of a long-loved love, stretched to almost unbearable tautness in the psychological and social drama of the story, every one of us knows this too, even without the complexity of contemporary Chinese political conflict—at least if we are paying attention to our lives and the lives of those around us. We long for that too, human beings being human beings as we are, to be honestly known and honestly loved, again and again and again, year after year after year.

Over many years I have been drawn into many weddings. Through my 20s and 30s, even into my 40s, I was asked to be a groomsman; but over the last decades I have been asked to give wedding homilies. As I am not a pastor with clerical responsibilities, I do not "marry" people in that sense; instead I have been asked to reflect on the meaning of marriage, knowing the full-of-hope couple as I do. And so I have—from the Carolinas to California, and places in between.

The following are excerpts from three homilies, completely unique moments worthy of celebration, and yet the same too, as new husbands and wives pledged their troth to each other with the greatest hopes ever imagined, committing to their own long-loved loves.

Family and friends, brothers and sisters . . .

In the history of Colorado this is an important week, a momentous week. In papers all over the country pictures of the Great Sand Dunes accompanied the news that America has a new national park. The San Luis Valley and the state will change, as people come from every corner of the earth to see the wonder of wonders that so surprisingly graces the western slope of the Sangre de Cristos.

The news was specially intriguing to me, as I was born a few miles away from the dunes in a little town called Monte Vista—and a "mountain view" the town does have, 250 miles of glorious peaks. The sights and sounds and smells have shaped me in the deepest ways. Nowhere do I have such a profound sense of belonging as I do in the southwestern corner of this Southwestern state. The air, the sky, the mountains, yes, even the dunes are etched into my memory of the way the world is and ought to be.

But Great Sand Dunes in Colorado? Anyone who has traveled across the front range, wound their way through South Park, passed Buena Vista, and eventually driven down into the far reaches of the San Luis Valley with its famous "gun barrel" of a highway, remembers the strangeness of the sand dunes. What are they doing there? What happened? A 9000-foot valley, 14,000-foot peaks . . . and a deposit of sand so immense, so dramatic, that we must call it GREAT.

It is one thing to see them across the valley, but quite another to encounter them face-to-face, with ears and eyes full of their unmatched grandeur. As beautiful as they are from afar, to step onto the dunes and begin to walk is an altogether different experience. Oh, the first steps are not so hard. But a half mile, a half hour later, the word "great" has become real; it has taken on weight and meaning that is only understood by those who have stepped in and walked up—who have chosen to walk for a while, perhaps even to live for a while, in the Great Sand Dunes themselves.

Marriage is like that too. From a distance the idea seems wonderful, the possibilities grand, but it is only as a man and a woman step into its reality that marriage becomes real, that we begin to understand its weight and meaning.

In the history of Colorado, this day, this hour, also has its own great importance. Dear Kate, dear Joel, God in his glory, the angels in their splendor, the mountains in their majesty, your family and friends in their affection, together we stand as witnesses to the words you will give, one to the other, promising faithful love until death do you part.

You will make promises in these next minutes that will form you: heart, mind, soul, and strength—for the rest of life. By God's grace, generations will be shaped by your commitment. It is not too much to say that the history of the world, now and into eternity, will be different because you have decided to become husband and wife.

But the words you offer must be made flesh. They cannot remain abstract. Rather they must be entered into, lived in and with, to become real. It is only as you step into them that you will know what they mean, that you will understand what they require of you.

Family and friends, brothers and sisters . . .

Two weeks ago my wife Meg and I were in California, the Golden State, the land of my growing-up years. Its weather, its glories of mountains and valleys, desert and sea, its sights and sounds and smells, seem so very right to me. We were visiting my family, especially my parents, whose sixtieth wedding anniversary is in a few weeks. Unbeknownst to Meg, I had arranged for a night away together, just the two of us. We drove over to the central coast, through Paso Robles and the golden hills with their distinctive oaks trees, to Cambria, where I had picked out a room looking over the ocean.

So romantic it was! There were rose petals in the shape of a heart upon our bed as we entered the room. The late afternoon sun shone through the coastal fog. Simply said, it was amazingly beautiful, a view to hold onto for a lifetime.

The next morning we lingered over our breakfast, opening windows and doors onto the Pacific Ocean and its grandeur. As we settled down with our tea and muffins, what should rumble along the lonely road between us and our prized view? A California Conservation Corps truck, with workers determined to spend their morning fixing the path along the cliffs! With lament, I looked out, walked across the road, and asked: "Can't you move?" A shake of the head was my answer, and I sighed. When we got ready to leave later that morning, Meg picked up the notebook for the room, page upon page of memories of past guests for whom the room had been magical. Many had come for anniversaries; we were there to celebrate 29 years of marriage. Musing over our morning, she wrote about both the incredible setting, and the obstructionist truck, observing that it reminded her of our marriage: wonderful, but not perfect.

Wonderful, but not perfect.

Dear Nate and Susan, this day you enter into marriage, becoming husband and wife, pledging before God, and your family and friends that you will forsake all others, and find your deepest human happiness in this multifaceted relationship as friends and lovers, parents and grandparents—in and through it all discovering the meaning of your marriage vows. Over the years it will be full of wonders, yes, wonderful—but it will not be perfect.

Of all that I might choose to say this day, of all that the community of Christ's people which is your community must say to you this day, simply, from the heart, we offer this wisdom: You will need to learn to deal with the reality that your marriage will not be perfect—even as you rejoice in its wonders.

On a day like this, your wedding day, a day so long imagined, so long longed for, where so much planning has made it be "just about perfect," it may be hard to take into your hearts the importance of what I am saying. And that is okay. It is a glorious day, and rightly so. All day long, in every way, for every person—especially for you.

But someday, maybe even tomorrow, the metaphorical California Conservation Corps truck will pull up in front of the perfection, and you will have to decide what you will do then. We all do. It is a conversation in my heart and in my marriage that never stops.

Family and friends, brothers and sisters . . .

Happy families are all alike; every unhappy family is unhappy in its own way.

These famous words begin a famous story; in fact they are the first words of a great story. While I shy away from superlatives, many of those who make judgments about the greatest books believe that the best novel ever written is Anna Karenina *by Leo Tolstoy. Maybe it is.*

What I do know is that the book has long been a gift to young friends on their way to marriage, often to a young woman, sometimes to a young man. Mine is a worn copy, read and read and read again.

Tolstoy's great gift was his moral imagination, seeing and hearing the human condition with remarkable grace, with remarkable truth. With words that are unmatched in all of literature, Anna Karenina *is the tale of two loves, of two marriages, of one that stumbles badly, ending in the most sorrowful of tragedies, and of one a marriage born of glory and wonder—like yours is this day.*

And wonderfully, Tolstoy tells the tale of a wedding, a wedding so beautifully imagined that we all ought to go home tonight and read it aloud. I know of no author who comes as close to seeing the meaning of marriage being born. On one very special day, a much-anticipated day, it is as if heaven comes to earth as the woman comes to the man, the two becoming husband and wife. Most profoundly, over its hundreds of pages it is a story about the reality of life and love, about the truth of the human heart, about who we are and why we are as human beings, about what makes for the feeling of love and what makes for a long-loved love.

These words are worth pondering because they are the genesis of hope for this day. "Happy families are all alike." Of course there are differences, thousands and millions of differences; but good families are good for the very same reasons. Affection and honor, commitment and patience, forgiveness and more forgiveness . . . in uncountably unique ways, these habits of heart make a family a happy family, because they also make a marriage a good marriage.

David and Emily, dear ones that you are to all of us, this is a day of glory upon glory, wonder after wonder . . . families, friends, flowers, hours and days of planning, all with hope for you on this wedding day that is yours—prayed into being by parents and grandparents, by those whose inheritance of faith has preceded you over generations and centuries, praying for you, longing for their love to be made full as you take up their legacy of commitment and trust.

They too, the cloud of witnesses they are, stand here on this day, yearning with hope and smiling with gladness on your desire to love and to be loved, promising your hearts to each other on this beautiful April afternoon.

Given my disposition to say something special and unique at each wedding, I always wonder about the people and the place. Who are they? Where are they being married? What about this moment has weight for the words I will offer? Thinking through how to truly honor the glory of the day, with all of its planning, all of its longing, remembering in a particular way who it is that will stand before me, wanting to say something to them that has not been said before.

But try as I might, my wife, Meg, says that I always say the same thing.

Chagrined at least, and probably somewhat offended, I am sure that I have not. But when I am able to hear, she draws me back into my words, reminding me that, one more time, I offered this wisdom, hard-won as it is: For a marriage to flourish, for a marriage to be honestly happy for both husband and wife, there must be both delight and grace at its heart. *To take delight and to give grace*—day after day after day.

In the homilies above, different as they were, imagined for every couple as once-in-a-lifetime words just for them, eventually I reflected on the proximate character of all of life, and all of love. Having now been married for most of my life, having watched many marriages along the way, it is clear to me that those whose marriages flourish do so because *delight* and *grace* are woven into the tapestry, that they have become—even proximately—integral to the meaning of its meaning. And the marriages that falter? Though a thousand thousand stories could be told, it is the failure to remember delight, the failure to remember grace, that is the cancer that kills what once was. In the wounded world that is, the words need each; they profoundly depend upon each other.

And after all the words of true honor, I have asked, "You have now given the most meaningfully imagined words ever, offering your very souls to each other. If you knew that by God's grace, you will have found proximate happiness together in twenty-five years, would these words still be yours?" I never ever want to say anything that would dampen or discourage, but I want to nourish in them a hope that will not disappoint because it is born of honesty about what is and what is not possible in this now-but-not-yet world. Or to remember again the deeper themes woven through this book: How will you work out with love the meaning of the story of your own marriage within the reality of the story that is more than you, beyond you in every way?

To put a point on it—are these promises of faithful love worthy of an honest happiness, a touchable happiness? Is something that is real and true and right "worth it," even if you do not get everything? Even if the next days and weeks and years are not as "perfect" as the wedding day?

Because, of course, they will not be, because they cannot be.

Longing to Know, Longing to Be Known

"She knew him as he was, and loved him."

There are no more powerful words in literature and life than those seven words of Wendell Berry's. For every human being in whatever century or culture, wherever we are born, wherever we live, we long to know and to be known, to love and to be loved; in fact there are no longings and no loves that are deeper.

Mysteriously born of Father Adam and Mother Eve, naked and not ashamed as they once were, we are like them, for blessing and for curse. We will do the most honorable and most sacrificial in service of that kind of knowledge, yearning to be known and loved at the same time; but we will also do the most dishonorable and selfish, wrecking our hearts and the hearts of everyone we touch, wounding with our wounds with the disordered longings and loves that are ours, imagining that intimacy can be manipulated, insisting that our wants are our needs.

Whether we are married or never married, we are made for community, for a common life. Humanity at its heart is a bi-unity; male and female together are the image of God—"in the image of God he made *them*." To be human is to live into that reality, to live within that reality. In a profound way, we are not fully ourselves apart from each other. We are never autonomous, individuated selves; that is only and ever fiction. As poetic as it may sound, no man or woman is an island. We need each other to be ourselves, and that is as true for humans as humans, as it is for men as men, as it is for women as women.

And when we scratch below the surface of every heart, we all know why Berry's words are so true. From *The Memory of Old Jack*, very literally as the novel is the long, last day of Jack's life, remembering the hours and years that were his—as a boy, as a young man, as an older man, and finally as an old man—that Rose "knew him as he was, and loved him"[46] was as dear a memory for him as any that he had, longing as always to be

[46]Wendell Berry, *The Memory of Old Jack* (Counterpoint, 1999), 100.

known like that by someone somewhere. Orphaned as a child, spurned by his first love, awakened to another, to feel alive again in someone's arms, being seen as himself, the man that he was, gave him a reason for being for as long as it lasted, and longer.

No one of us can be Old Jack, and we should not want to be. A man born of his own unique joys and sorrows, one of the many who are the Port William Membership of Berry's fictional small town of a universe along the Kentucky River, he desired what we all desire, to be known and to be loved. In fact, there was no desire stronger than that—and yes, as must be, it was for blessing and for curse in his life, and Berry does not shy away from that more complex reality.

But it is also true that he is just like us, that we are just like him. We have the same longings, and through the years of life we make choice after choice, in hope, knowing, but more often *not* knowing what our choices will mean—and yet, we still hope, choosing our ways into the future with hope.

This is as true for me as for anyone, my memories being mine, as Jack's were his.

I can remember the slow movement of heart and soul, mind and strength, as I became aware of the girls of my world. Their eyes, their smiles, the way they were and the way they were not, the notes along the way in early adolescence from someone's trusted friend, "So-and-so likes you"—and being both perplexed and puzzled, pondering what the words meant. What was changing within me? Why had I once been a happy little boy who had girls who were friends, now becoming a bigger boy who began to wonder about having a girlfriend?

Those next years were mostly hits and misses, questions with not very good answers. When I was emerging out of boyhood into the next years of my life, discovering the world of worldviews, beginning to think more seriously about everything—yes, about the world, about the ways of the world, about ideas and their consequences, about beliefs and their meaning, about everything I cared about and why I cared—I began to think more seriously about girls.

Who were they? What were they? How could they mean so much to me?

One early commitment I made was to reexamine what I thought about them; before I got to the arts, to politics, to economics, to the meaning of history, I thought that I should rethink girls, given the amount of attention I gave to them in my 19-year-old heart. Having made my way through the previous years with a clear distinction between friends who were girls, and girlfriends, I began to feel in the deepest way that that was not fair and true. That it was not right to say about someone, "Oh, she's just a friend!" dismissing any serious interest in her because she was "only a friend," that friendship was only and ever second-best.

And then I met Meg, who by her very being made my thinking more complicated. What would I do now, knowing what I knew? The wondering was born of true wondering, the convictions were born of true convictions, and yet, and yet they were untried. The words would have to become flesh—but could they, would they, did I really want them to be?

Over the next years I dug more deeply into what I believed about all of life, and about the reasons of my life than I ever had, consciously working to understand the complex dynamic of metanarrative to narrative in my own life. If this was really true of the whole of history, of all of reality, then what did it mean for the way I thought about the girls of my life who were becoming the women of my heart? To put a point on it, what did it mean for Meg?

Even as a very young man I found that people who liked being married were most of all friends; in fact, when all was said and done, it seemed that marriage was a long friendship. A very unique friendship, a friendship formed of the most profound commitments, a friendship with responsibilities that were deeper than any other, a friendship born of a revelation of self that was unlike any other relationship . . . but still a friendship. At that point in my life I could only look into what seemed true; now, after years of marriage, I know more of why friendship is at the heart of being husband and wife. The affection and respect, the love and longing that make for true friendship are the same realities that make for true marriage. If male and female we are, a bi-unity at the very root of our being, then the promises and wonders that make marriage marriage only deepen what is true for the whole of life, in all of the friendships that are the relationships of our lives.

Meg and I knew that we were good friends who were getting married, simply said. Never having been "boyfriend" or "girlfriend," we had honestly tried for friendship, seeing it as what was ours as a man and a woman, not married. Not as "second best," but as what God had called us to as human beings, married or not married, male and female who were together the image of God—and it was only over time that we slowly found our way to the exclusive intimacy of marriage, a kind of knowing and loving that is both unbound and bound, free to be fully "me" and yet only because it comes within the contours of commitment.

Because we all long for relationship, a longing to belong that is as deep and powerful as any desire, friendship is integral to being human—again, married or not married, across the whole of life. On the last day of his life, born of Berry's great insight and tenderness, Old Jack lived through the memories of his years, some that were as happy as a man can be, and others that made him weep. Threaded through every moment was the grace of friendship, a man known and loved by his community, and once very wonderfully, "known as he was."

But what was true for Jack is true for us. As rich as relationships can be, and in one sense must be, in our frailty there is still disappointment, always, falling short of and for each other. The poignancy written into Old Jack's memory is that he knows that his family and friends have mattered to him; his "membership" in their common life has made him who he is and why he is, from the beginning of his life to the end of his life—even as he is painfully aware of the sorrows of his life, necessarily embedded within his community. That cannot not be, for Jack, or for any one of us.

Friendship matters for our flourishing as human beings, and the wise ones of history have almost all weighed in on why this is true—from Epicurus to Emily Dickinson, from Plutarch to Bill Watterson, from Socrates to George Washington, from Euripides to Thomas Aquinas; but here C. S. Lewis has the last word: "Friendship is unnecessary, like philosophy, like art. . . . It has no survival value; rather it is one of those things that give value to survival." Starkly said, and yet in the reality of life, friendship is integral to life, longing to know and be known, longing to love and be loved. Male and female he made them, and in their togetherness they find their humanness. We are never ever islands.

Through the years of his life, from the heartache of childhood to war-torn terror, as Lewis grew up into the one the world now knows, he was a friend, perhaps first and last. Famously, we know some of his friends as "the Inklings," who hiked together, read together, who lived a life together. Longing to know, longing to love, longing to be known, longing to be loved—late in life he found himself surprised by joy through the unexpected friendship of an American woman, and in the next too-few years his love for her became the source of his greatest happiness and his greatest sorrow. He found himself in her, and when she died, he lost what he had found. For its brief, shining moment, was their love real? Was it true? Yes, a thousand times, a real love, a true love, a proximate love, but it was *something* that never became *everything*.

Looking for Love in All the Wrong Places with All the Wrong People

A phone call, a conversation, a hesitation of the heart, and then a man walks into an hour and a half with a woman who in the words of the world was a highly paid prostitute. He is quite earnest if innocent, she is so silky and sophisticated, and we all wonder what this story will be. The achingly honest South African film *Discreet* is an unusual window into the profound truth that we long to belong, and we are able and willing to do just about anything to find our way into the companionship of relationship.

"If it's not too much trouble, I just wondered whether we could talk for a while first."

That was not her expectation, having agreed that her body and time had a price, supposing that he is simply naive, not knowing what he has paid for—and she is very willing to try anything that will move their moment from talk to sex. But he insists that he wants a conversation about things that matter to him. Identity. Love. Sexuality. Truth. Most deeply of all, he wants to know her, and to be known by her, as awkward and strange as that is for the skillful seductress who knows her business very, very well.

For the length of the film, the man and woman engage in the most fascinating repartee, back-and-forth, talking and more talking, her ever-willing for more, sure that in his heart of hearts he wants something that he cannot say; but instead there is a surprising honesty and vulnerability that both slowly offer, finally telling each other their real names. Since the beginning of time names have been central to who we are, to why we are, and to what we do with our lives; trusting the other with "who I am," something beautiful might unfold between them, even without all of the literal and metaphorical weight of "going to bed." He has tears, she has tears, and they do not appear to be anything more or less than real.

The film goes on, but what matters here is to understand that they so deeply long to be loved that they will imagine the most fabricated universe of hopes become words, gasping for the possibility that someone somewhere will honestly care about them. That is why he came, the very conflicted soul that he is, and that is why she does what she does, the very conflicted soul that she is. When the credits roll, it is painfully true for all with eyes to see that there is a grain to the universe, a way to be honestly human, completely and truly human—and when we resist that reality we suffer, stumbling over our loves, disordered as they too often are.

And that is no surprise—remembering Augustine—because it is in the ordering and disordering of our loves that we either flourish, or not, and the best stories we know always tell this tale.

A century ago Sigrid Undset won the Nobel Prize in Literature for the grandeur of her writing about the people and place of medieval Scandinavia. Best known for her work was the novel *Kristin Lavransdatter,* a story about "Kristin," "Lavrans' datter," beginning in her earliest years as a blond-headed little girl, the delight of her father's eyes, following her through to the end of her life; not yet married, married, then a mother, finally a grandmother.

The first in the trilogy is *The Bridal Wreath*, which follows Kristin from childhood into early womanhood, from the one whose very being made her father smile with untold happiness, to the one whose choices made her father groan with heart-wrenching grief. As a girl she was unusually willful, and that disposition deepened over time. When she began to be interested in the boys of her life, every young man's eyes looked on her with longing—and she knew they did. Like fathers immemorial, Lavrans hoped for his daughter's truest happiness, and as she began to grow into a young woman, the fourteenth-century man that he was began choosing a husband for her, an honorable man, a trusted man, a man to whom he could give his daughter with confidence that she would be husbanded as he expected her to be.

And he seemed to have chosen well. The families were friends, the boy and girl having grown up together as friends. Now a young man, Simon was well respected and hard-working, and an honest affection was at the heart of their relationship. But friendship was friendship, and it could not be more, at least within their relational universe. When she falls head over heels for Erlend Nikulausson, the very dashing heir to a large, neighboring estate, everyone but Kristin knows that he is not worthy of her. The first of the trilogy ends with their marriage, the young woman sure that she has sealed her heart with happiness, her parents certain that she has entered into a life without love, at least without the permanence and protection of love born of commitment.

I can still remember reading this first story, intrigued by its premise, but in coming to the end I was not sure if I was willing to continue on. The stories that I love must be grounded within the world that is really there, a moral universe in which meaning and purpose, accountability and responsibility are realities; and when Kristin's disordered love of self had cast a pall over everyone, my heart shivered, knowing that autonomous individualism is a fiction whenever and wherever it is imagined—whether fourteenth-century Norway or twenty-first-century America. And because it is fiction in life, when it is fiction in literature it is bad fiction, and not very interesting. Lies about life, and love, are wearying.

The second story is the long life that becomes Kristin's, married and a mother whom we come to know over the next decades, a tale told with remarkable honesty. *The Mistress of Husaby* is the unfolding of the meaning of her choices through the years, her slowly beginning to live into the wisdom and fears of her parents as she comes to see what they saw, in and through her experience of Erlend's inconstancy and infidelity. As wife and husband, they have a life, and they become parents to many children; and yet they spend their years in the loneliness of their longings. The trilogy comes to a conclusion with *The Cross*, which are the years of the Black Death, devastating in its far-reaching destruction with the deaths of over 50 million people in Europe and more in Asia and northern Africa; and as must be within Kristin's family, the griefs of the wider world become her very own, terribly her very own.

When all is said and done, there is a grace woven into the story of Kristin's life, but it is formed from the grief that has been hers, now seeing more clearly the meaning of her own life, the meaning of her own marriage. Her choices as a young woman have been threaded through with honest joys and honest sorrows—as the best stories always are—and as we read over her shoulder and through her heart we have lived with those same joys and sorrows, sometimes laughing with her laughter, but often mourning with her mourning.

As reluctant as I was initially to keep on with the trilogy, when I finished the last book I was sure that I had just read some of the best books ever written. Beautifully, artfully imagined, with a narrative richness that is rare, and yet page after page rooted in reality, a story so very true about who we are as human beings, full of profoundly complex loves that are so easily disordered, disordering our lives, our great hopes sometimes becoming our great heartaches.

"Trifles make the sum of life"—simple words, and yet they are at the heart of life.

Years ago I spent several days in bed, more sick than I usually am, and through the next long hours I lived within *David Copperfield* by Charles Dickens, coming to know the characters whose story it is, intrigued in every way by the author's unusual gift. David himself, of course, but then Edward Murdstone, Mr. Barkis, James Steerforth, Tommy Traddles, Aunt Betsy Trotwood, Mr. Micawber, Little Emily, Peggotty and his nephew Ham, Uriah Heep, Dora Spenlow, and Agnes Wickfield, dear Agnes she was and must be. As I had canceled a trip because of my illness, the next week I went out, and everywhere I was found David's friends were there too—in shops and stores, sitting in cafes. All day long my life was populated by the people of Dickens's classic tale, ordinary people in ordinary places with ordinary lives. Profoundly, in the most Dickensian way, the story is about the meaning of vocation, the complex and rich idea that that is, about the nature of growing up into the world, the slow unfolding of one's life and loves, of what one cares about and why, of the choices one makes over time, sometimes foolishly and then sometimes more wisely.

David is married twice in the novel, two women and two loves. Dickens describes Dora in almost poetic fancy. So bright, so light, so full of cheer and joy, and early on she wins David's heart, certain that he has found the love of his life. With her tiny, yappy dog who is almost not a dog, David and Dora settle into their honeymoon days full of youthful happiness. But with the saddest sorrow those days are short-lived, Dora's exuberance stronger than her stamina, and too soon she becomes ill, too soon she dies.

While Dora is cared for in her last hours by a nurse in the upstairs bedroom, David is downstairs looking into the fireplace, his soul sighing, feeling the weight of his young love very painfully, knowing that it will not last much longer. And as he ponders all of this, the days of great joy and the days of great sadness, he concludes that "Trifles make the sum of life."

So struck by those words, so true they seemed to the life I knew, I began to think about them, and to talk about them. A year later my wife, Meg, gave me a sampler for my birthday with those words stitched and stretched across the frame, and now for most of our life together they have graced our dining room, a reminder to everyone who comes to our table of an enduring reality of life under the sun: It is the little things that matter most. Across the whole of life, from the most personal to the most public, it is the little things, the trifles, that in the end define one's life. Not our grand ideas or great words, but the ways that we live together morning by morning, evening by evening, day after day, year after year.

But as we sigh with David over Dora's death, we slowly by slowly begin to hope for him that he will finally see dear Agnes for the woman she has always been, the kind and patient, thoughtful and wise friend that he knows her to be, that everyone knows her to be. Finally, making his way through his mourning as a good husband must, he remembers to remember Agnes, whose steady affections for all who are in need he begins to see in a new light; and the woman that he knows becomes the woman he loves, and that love brings forth a marriage, a long friendship of affection and respect growing into a deeper kind of affection and respect, one that makes sense of vows to love to love, until death do us part.

While Dickens never wants sadness for David, or for Dora, it is true that those of us reading his wonderful book can see what David does not see; and what we see is what Dickens sees too. With David's understandable immaturity as a very young man, his eagerness to love overcomes his own better self, the deeper, truer self that he becomes with the sorrow of years. When he groans, we groan.

But the truest truths are perennial, and what was London in the nineteenth century could be St. Petersburg too, as much Boston as it is Mexico City. Longing to love, longing to be loved, we are frail people who too often stumble over our hearts, wanting everything, too often losing what might be for what we want to be. While it may seem possible to fall in love and then get married—which was David's great hope—in reality we get married, and then learn what love requires, which is always and everywhere an honest satisfaction with something that is beautiful and true, even if it is not everything.

I smiled.

"But you need to look at the recipe!" Not so long ago I was in the kitchen of someone I love dearly, intending to make a simple breakfast of pancakes for her family. I had found the flour, the eggs, the oil, the milk, and the bowl—what more did I need? A recipe, she was sure.

But having made pancakes for almost eons, I knew. More of this, some of this, a little bit of that, and mix it up, seeing, feeling the consistency of the batter as it came into being, knowing just what it needed to be. Not very complicated—and yet to someone else it was. I suppose recipes are like that. To make most anything that is both something we want to eat and is good to eat, we need to know what ingredients are called for in order for it to become what it could be, perhaps even what it should be.

When I found the book *Recipes for a Perfect Marriage* in a used-book shop on Capitol Hill in Washington, DC, I was simply browsing, seeing what I might see, but the title intrigued me, and I brought it home, hoping that "the perfect" in the title had nothing to do with the story—and it did not.

In this surprisingly imagined novel by Morag Prunty, her story is at one and same time two stories: of a thirty-something woman in New York City who has labored long and hard for the coveted position of food editor for a national magazine, and also of her grandmother with whom she spent the summers of her growing-up years in the small Irish village from which her mother had come. A gifted writer, from the first page on the author weaves a tale of two women that is sometimes playful, but more often than not is an aching account of the loves and longings that make marriage a marriage.

Recipes and the food they make is the substance of the story, quite literally, with each chapter beginning with a family recipe, passed on from the Irish grandmother to her granddaughter, whose vocation has been formed through the hours and years she has spent watching with anticipation and pleasure her grandmother at work in the kitchen. She learned to love good food as she learned to love her grandmother, whose gifts are always in the background of her writing about making food for the wide world.

But there is metaphorical meaning too, the recipe for soda bread being easier than the recipe for "a perfect marriage." Amidst the glories of her life in New York City, going here and going there, stepping into important meetings for this and for that, spending her evenings at parties celebrating life upon life, the young woman wants to be married, yearning for a man who will be to her the way her grandfather was to her grandmother. A perfect husband, a perfect wife, a perfect marriage.

And she finally finds a man, an Irishman of all things, from a large Long Island family who live far away from the excitements of her busy life in the city, where the hours of her days are full of busy people whose lives are full of busy work just like hers. He is a basically good man, born of folk who have always loved him; but his world is not her world, and from the beginning of their marriage she wrestles with discontent, certain that he will never measure up to the excellence of her grandfather, whom she watched for all her growing up years be the best husband a wife could ever want.

When her grandparents die, as the lone grandchild she inherits the responsibility for their earthly possessions, and to her surprise she finds a box full of journals and letters from her grandmother. From that point on the story becomes more complex, chapter by chapter offering windows into these women's lives, already separated by generations, now the gulf of death between them—and we read along with the granddaughter the story of years and years and years of unhappiness, wounds that never healed marking the years of their marriage.

The more she reads, the more she understands that the grandparents she adored, and whom she *knew* that she *knew*, had a long and yet terribly difficult marriage. As a little girl, as a young woman, she had loved an image of what she wanted to be, not the reality of what was. How could two people who were different, who disagreed deeply, who disappointed and hurt each other, still care for each other, choosing for love again and again?

"When you are young, feelings are your truth; love is how you feel. The years have taught me that love is not an emotion that you feel about someone, but what you do for them, how you grow with them." And as must be, the granddaughter begins to see that her grandmother was like her, a woman very much like her, once a young wife with her young hopes strained over the years, forming a heart that was invisible through the summers of their labors of love together in the Irish kitchen.

Recipes for a perfect marriage? It could not be because there never are perfect marriages. What we find instead is a novel about the meaning of marriage, glorious ruins that we are, so full of hope and yet so full of hurt. How can we hold them together in one bed? How can a home be made from such complexity? With surprising candor, with unusual tenderness, this is a story that reminds all of us that something honest and true is worthy of being called a *marriage*, even if the marriage is never everything that the pretense of perfection promises—and if we have eyes that see, that is a gift.

"I am coming to see that it is not so much a question of finding the right place, the right time, the ideal marriage. Neither life nor happiness hinges upon such things. It is wholly within. It is response to what is given. It is choice."

Those are the words of Anne Delaney, whose story is the novel *Strangers and Sojourners,* one more book by the Canadian Michael O'Brien, whom I have been reading for years during Lent, wanting him to probe my heart, to ask questions that are hard for me to answer. The setting is British Columbia during the middle years of the twentieth century, and it is told from the perspective of an Englishwoman who emigrated to Canada following her experience of World War I, eventually finding her way to a crossroads in the middle of great forests and mountains hours north of Vancouver, where she becomes the teacher in a one-room school house.

Over the next hundreds of pages we see the world as she does, from her early days knowing and being known in the little forestry/mining village of Swiftcreek, on through her years of marriage to an Irish immigrant who himself wanted a new life in a new place, their love making a family with characteristic hopes and heartbreaks, the truest suffering born of the truest love—

and of work and more work, everyone pushed to the nth degree by the circumstances of their lives. With his unusual insight, O'Brien explores the deepest places in his characters, but then of course our deepest places too, if we have ears to hear.

The idea of responsibility, thinking through one more time our *ability to respond,* has become a central question in my life. We make choices, and that we do matters immensely; the possibility of vocation is the very reason that it is a reality. The Latin *vox* and *vocare* are words that communicate "communication," that someone has said something, and that we can hear; "vocal" is from that same root. At the very heart of our humanity is our responsibility; we are made able to respond to the world around us, able to respond to the pushes and shoves of life, and profoundly, even if very mysteriously, able to respond to God, who is there and who is not silent.

The best stories are always this story, which is why Percy insists that bad books lie about the human condition; grievously, they do not tell the truth about who we are and why we are. The karmas of the East and the West miss this tragically, and the novels from these traditions reflect that great loss, in their different ways insisting that everyone and everything is already decided, that choice is a fiction, that we are "beyond freedom and dignity," in the language of Western materialism, while everything that seems to matter most in Eastern pantheism is illusion, even and especially our human agency, that we can and do make honest choices that have consequence in history. In the strangest ways, Hinduism and evolutionary materialism kiss each other at this very point.

But our humanness cries out for something more. In our very bones, we know better, which is why we are drawn to stories that are born of a responsibility rooted in love. For Anne, the girl who slowly, slowly becomes a woman in O'Brien's novel, it takes years of life for her to begin to see the truth about herself and her world: "Neither life nor happiness hinges upon such things." For her, for us, the twenty-something years are ones often full of the highest hopes, looking into what might be in every area of life—

meaningful relationships, meaningful marriages, meaningful work, meaningful citizenship. And yet we fall short, because perfection is a fantasy in the reality of this now-but-not-yet world. But can we make peace with something, with something honest and true, wonderful and good—even if it is not perfect? A weighty question, and a weighty answer.

How do we respond to what is given? Will we love? How will we respond to the hurts and wounds that come with intimacy? Will we learn to love to love?

The painful pilgrimage that is Anne Delaney's is the long story of *Strangers and Sojourners*, generation after generation ordering and disordering their loves, sometimes getting something right, sometimes getting it all very wrong; her life is much like ours, her loves much like ours. With long grace she bears the weight of her loves, true as they are, born of her own body as a wife, as a mother and a grandmother must, the story being the story of these relationships, each one its own ache in her heart. And therefore we listen carefully to the hard-won wisdom that becomes hers, offering to us the reality of her life and ours.

"It is a choice." Always it is a choice—to love, to respond, to choose responsibility born of love.

A Long-Loved Love

So deep our longings are to love and to be loved, and yet every one of us feels the hurt when what we most want is not found. At the very heart of who we are are our hearts, as from our hearts everything else comes. We see from our hearts. We hear from our hearts. We feel from our hearts.

And when our hearts are hurt, we hurt.

That is true in the best of relationships, the longest of loves—which is why I began each of the wedding homilies with words about the weight of love, even of very earnest and honest love. Climbing into great sand dunes as a metaphor for marriage . . . acknowledging that even our highest hopes bring about wonderful but not perfect relationships . . . seeing ourselves as the finite and frail people we are, stumbling our way into the stories of happy marriages and families. These experiences are not unusual; rather they are the realities of Everyman and Everywoman. In fact, for everyone I know well enough to know, this is true to the way it is.

Looking back on the pilgrimage of our love, so thoughtful as we wanted to be about the integral relationship of friendship to marriage, longing for the gift of our friendship to thread its way into the meaning of our marriage, we yearned for the stars, for a kind of extraordinary excellence between us that would not disappoint, that would not wound—and that lasted a few days into our honeymoon. "You think that?" and "You think that?" Neither of us could believe the other could possibly see the most important things about God and the world so differently!

And yet we did, again and again and again.

Now being married for most of life, we know the greatest happinesses and the greatest heartaches, their realities running through our years together—wonders upon wonders, and wounds after wounds. Both are true, both are woven into the tapestry of our love. In fact, clay-footed as we are, there have been hours and days when we have been without words to and for each other, so hurt that we can only be silent, alienated from each other into feeling lost to God and to each other. Will we talk again? Can we talk again?

Now knowing ourselves better than we once did, eventually we come back to the poetic vision of Madeleine L'Engle, to her seven poems "to a long-loved love." Those words, so honest, so tender, so true to who we are, true to who we want to be, we have allowed to be our words, knowing that we are unable to say what must be said, what needs to be said.

In the story told with tears in *Two-Part Invention*, born of her forty years of marriage, a long love brought to a tragic end by the cancer of her husband, L'Engle artfully reflects on the profound richness of married love, even as she opens her heart for all of us to see its griefs and sorrows. Knowing that she knows, entering into the graces of the words of her heart, has been a balm for our hearts.

Because you are not what I would have you be
I blind myself to who in truth you are.
Seeking mirage where desert blooms, I mar
Your you . . .[47]

There is more of course, beautifully more, profoundly and poetically more, seven poems to and for "a long-loved love," an image that has now become central to everything I believe about what marriage can be and should be.

But if these heartfelt words come from her poetic imagination, she has written more autobiographically about the story of her marriage in *Two-Part Invention,* from the days of "Aah" so full of hope at the beginning of their love, to the years of hard work that marriage is, "a two-part invention" requiring the best we are, the best we have, if we are to enter into the "long-loved love" of a good marriage, a happy marriage.

Two artists they were, embedded in the professional worlds of New York City, Hugh an actor, Madeleine a writer. So eager to know the goodness of commitment and intimacy, the confidence of promises made to be kept . . . and over years and years they loved their way into that hope, their callings taking them into different places with different people, coming home night after night, year after year, with longing for each other, knowing each other, and yet and yet . . . feeling the weight of their knowledge, aware that they were "strangers" too, as Adam knew Eve, yearning for a love that "struggles to break through the hidden lovely truth of me, of you."

To read over their shoulders and through their hearts is a wonderful gift, but one that comes with our own tears as we listen to their love, slowly coming to a heart-wrenching end with the year-long battle against cancer, a heartache that makes everyone groan as they groaned. With surprising brilliance and candor, L'Engle tells this tale in "two parts," one the forty years of their life together, the other the last year of their life together,

---

[47] Madeleine L'Engle, *The Weather of the Heart* (Harold Shaw Books, 1981), 16.

twining their long love together with the final year of their love, giving us a window into both, the forest and the trees of a long-loved love.

We have often given both books to those with young love before them, hoping that the surprising honesty will be a good gift for years to come as they began to climb their way into the meaning of their own marriages, as they begin to experience the reality that wonderful marriages are possible even if perfect marriages are not, and as they see themselves in the best stories we know, feeling the weight of their longings to know and to love, to be known and to be loved.

What Do You Love?

Good books are honest about who we are because they are true to what it means to be human—and they are often eloquent as well, sometimes even beautiful. They are the gift of twining ideas and words together that draw us into our deeper selves, not asking us to flinch, not requiring us to blink; rather they insist that the eyes of our hearts be open to what is and what is not.

But living with truth like that is hard, for a thousand reasons. So very broken the world is, so very broken we are; there is tension for all of us, as there was for L'Engle, loving her long love even as she knew she was saying goodbye to him—and the longer we read the more certain we are that their tears have become our tears. In their own different ways, the poetry and the autobiography offer a window into the reality of narrative and metanarrative, unusual as it might seem, and yet very ordinary as it is. When they are taken together, we see into the moments of a life made sense of in light of the whole of a life, one year of marriage within the story of forty years of marriage. In one poem we ponder with her the challenge of knowing and not knowing this person who shares our pillows and our beds, as she draws on the oldest story she knows, and this becomes the ground from which she could make sense of the story of her own very modern marriage. And somehow all of this is mysteriously bound together in one life and one love.

Love is such a many-splendored word, a word full of imagined and unimagined expectations. We ask it to be and do a thousand things, wanting it to mean so much to us, to mean so much for us.

The great teacher Augustine of Hippo understood this 1500 years ago, and once again we remember his soul-searching question, "What do you love?" asked amidst the ruins, the very literal ruining of Rome. Seeing that what mattered most to us is centered on what we love, and then the way that we order what we love—the whole of life brought into being and carried along by what we love—of all the questions that could be asked, he saw it as the defining question, its meaning coursing through the centuries, a lens for the wise who long to live well in times and places far from the Mediterranean world from which the question comes. But why does this matter here, among words about friendship and marriage, about relationships and sexuality, about the nature of long-loved loves?

Unless we get this right, even proximately right, we will not get anything else right. In the pilgrimage of my own heart, I knew that if God could not be trusted with the girls of my life, how could I trust him with the arts, the economics, the politics of the world? If it were going to be a worldview, it had to be a way to see the world, every square inch of it. If I could not make more sense of what I thought most about as a young man, then how would I ever make sense of what would become mine as an older man—a public world, a wider world with relationships and far-reaching responsibilities that required the eyes of my heart to know and love in ways that I never imagined, and some days never wanted?

These are the stories we know because they are the stories of our world, being told time and again—because this is the life we know, being lived again and again. What are Shakespeare's stories if not plays about human beings who are, more often than not, born of disordered loves? Because we are perennial people, we all miss—ambition and vanity, a lust for love and prosperity, jealousies of all kinds—and then miss again, pretending that someone or something has meaning that cannot be, in the world that is really there. Think of *Quest for the Holy Grail*, one of the first novels ever written, a story of loves found and lost, of true courage and terrible cowardice, an ancient tale told to us in and through the Knights of the Round Table, their lives singularly theirs, and yet, lives we know so well. And what about 500 years later with *Romeo and Juliet*, *The Merchant of Venice*, *Much Ado About Nothing*, *Macbeth*, and on and on. Every one a love story, of loves ordered and disordered; sometimes we laugh and sometimes we cry, comedies and tragedies that they are. What are Jane Austen's novels if not the same stories, "love stories" each one? A different time and place than Galahad and Guinevere, a different time and place than Shakespeare imagined, but the same reality of ordered and disordered loves makes the stories ones we read again and again. *Pride and Prejudice* and *Sense and Sensibility* are nothing if not two more in a long line of stories of love hoped for, sometimes found and sometimes not, as true in medieval Europe as in contemporary China, as true for King Arthur and the queen who has forgotten her promises, as for a professor and husband whose wife has forgotten that she is married.

In the reality of life in everyone's world, we have no other stories to tell, because these are the stories of life in the world—which is why we keep reading them, year after year, generation after generation. We see ourselves in them, knowing more keenly than we ever want, the proximate character of our deepest hopes, of our truest longings. At our best we find honest love, sometimes a beautiful love that is a true love, but never ever do we find a perfect love.

7

WOUNDS AND SCARS

Ring the bells that still can ring
Forget your perfect offering
There is a crack, a crack in everything
That's how the light gets in[48]

—Leonard Cohen

Bicycling barefoot along the California coast has been one of the great gifts of my life.

Spending most of my growing up years in the Golden State, I loved the days and months without shoes, imagining that that was the best of the best—and over time I began biking on the beach, the seascape as far as my eyes could see, feeling the ocean wind in my face and the sun everywhere I looked. Almost glory.

But as strange as it may sound, it is rare for me to go for long on those beachside paths without thinking about wounds and scars, because for me biking means remembering a terrible night.

A long time ago when I was a college student, one evening I was on my way to study with friends, biking of course. It was dark, and I was new in the neighborhood. Years later I am still not sure what happened, but I had an accident. What I do remember is being on the ground, unable to get up, finally hopping to a street light, and seeing that my left foot was bleeding badly.

Eventually I made it to my friends' apartment, and as undergraduate men are prone to do, they laughed at the blood, taking me to their bathtub where we tried to wash my foot off—

---

[48]Leonard Cohen, "Anthem," *The Future*, 1992.

but it kept bleeding, for a long time. Slowly, we decided that I should go to the emergency room. For the first time since birth, I was in a hospital needing someone to pay attention to me, and after a restless night was told that I was going to have surgery. I do not remember being told for what; perhaps they did not know the answer. At the end of that day I woke up through the fog of anesthesia with a leg-long cast molded in an awkward angle so that I could not move anything for the next three months; my severed Achilles tendon needed time to heal. On that innocent night, I had ripped it apart, and it was a mess.

A semester later I had to learn to walk all over again, and it took me another four months to walk unselfconsciously, without thinking through the movement of my foot, ankle, and leg. Most of life later, I can walk, swim, and bike, but not much more. The wound has healed, but the scars remain; faint now, no longer the raw stitchwork they once were, but my foot is still numb—and whenever it is touched by me or someone else, I remember that awful night so many years ago.

As wounding as that injury was, as scarring as it was, the older that I am, the more people that I meet, the more places I go, the more of life I see and hear, the more complex the wounds and scars become, for all of us. A broken world it is. Our bodies get hurt, but so much more does too. In Dylan's plaintive poetry, *everything is broken,* and we feel the weight of those words in our own bones. We bear physical pains, but we also bear psychological pains, ones that tear away at our very souls.

While our own sorrows often seem more than we are able to bear, when we pay attention to our neighbors and friends, looking down our streets into the cities of our lives, listening as we must to stories of human beings all around us, we are drawn in—for love's sake—to the wounds and scars of others. And then if we open the eyes of our hearts to the wider world of nations and peoples, we begin to see that some of the saddest of sad stories are from systemic wrongs that overwhelm hope with a heartache that is more political and economic, social and historical, and more often than not, with no resolution in sight.

Even the creation groans.

None of us get off. Everyone is broken by and with the world. Every friend I had in those college days has suffered in ways that were unimaginable in our more innocent years, some in fact very grievously. There are no exceptions. And given the life that I have with the work that I do, every room I walk into, wherever I go, I assume that everyone in the room bears a pain—some a lingering hurt, some a deep disappointment, while others have known cataclysmic grief that changed everything. No one I know well enough has lived long without wounds and scars, on some level in some way. We are wounded people in a wounded world.

And yes, given the way that I am, I thought of all this and more, bicycling barefoot along the California coast.

But . . . it matters to acknowledge that *I was biking* along the beach, and that is not nothing. On that long-ago night when I ripped my Achilles tendon apart, making a bloody mess, I did not bleed to death on the dark street, nor did I live my life crippled as I would have a hundred years earlier. Instead, a wound and a scar, with a numbness that will last as long as I live, and yet there has been healing, enough so that I can do many things, even if not everything. With the terrible trauma of the accident, and the long recovery, I learned to walk again, a proximate healing.

A Sacred Speech

Wounds and scars are everywhere, if we have eyes that see.

Wars and even rumors of wars bring terrors, wreaking havoc whenever and wherever they come. In my own city, in my own neighborhood, there are lingering memories of a civil war that ripped apart a nation not yet a century old. Though every history is more than complex, a twining together of peoples and places that are more than we know, drawing on the strands of human life that are economic and political and social, as well as ecclesial and theological, the American story is one born of its own unique hope and heartache—and the human calculus from that reality is history, the history we know and the history we only imagine.

When Asiatic peoples slowly made their way across Arctic ice floes, following the winds in their long walk into North America, they had no idea what they would find. And hundreds and thousands of years later, most of that story is beyond us; we do not know, other than that their histories were ones of glory and ruin too, human beings as they were. Over time that migration made its way through the Americas, the long land it is from what we now know as the tip of Alaska to the tip of Argentina, with different tribes and tongues making homes here and there, East to West, North to South—and every story of every people was one of glory and ruin. When centuries later Europeans found their way across the Atlantic, "discovering" a new world, landing on the shores of an unknown land, it was already home to native peoples, and history being history, there was and is never "a land without a people for a people without a land," not then, not now.

And because history is messy—always a story of glory and ruin, missional callings mired with military ambitions, political reach with economic growth—when the first settlers came to the Eastern seaboard of North America, the expectation of financial reward was written into the equation. Ships were commissioned for that purpose, and whatever was required to meet that end would be done. The First Nations' peoples would be removed, and to plant the fields and harvest the crops other nations would be enslaved to work the long days so that cotton and tobacco could be sent back to Europe. Given that most who first came to the "new world" were adventurous, willing to make new lives in new places, those first years and generations were marked by remarkable entrepreneurial imagination, with an economic and political creativity that the world had not known; and yet there were tears too, a weeping over what once was, a weeping for what still might be. That is the history of these United States.

History being messy again, eventually America went to war with itself, the question of slavery being at its heart. If the forced trafficking of human beings from Africa to the Americas was a poison pill the United States swallowed in its earliest days, generations later a horribly, terribly bloody civil war was its result, the North and the South at war.

Abraham Lincoln came to Washington, DC, as that conflict bubbled into being, scalding the young nation with battles and battlefields and leaving over 600,000 citizens dead. His years as president were necessarily ones of unimaginable weight, watching a great wound fester, knowing that his people were willing to fight to the death over what "America" was meant to be. In his Second Inaugural Address in 1865, he finished with this charge, looking out from the Capitol as far as his eyes could see, speaking to everyone with ears to hear.

> *With malice toward none, with charity for all, with firmness in the right as God gives us to see the right, let us strive on to finish the work we are in to bind up the nation's wounds, to care for him who shall have borne the battle and for his widow and his orphan—to do all which may achieve and cherish a just and lasting peace among ourselves and with all nations.*[49]

In my years in the city of Washington, I have visited the Lincoln Memorial time and again, sometimes by myself, often with a visitor from out of town, insisting that they come and see the greatest of our memorials. And so we walk across the Capitol Mall at night, seeing the stately monument lit before us, walking up its grand staircase to read Lincoln's words that are inscribed in the stone walls: "to bind up the nation's wounds."

They are worth remembering, for the generations. In his address to the American people at the beginning of his second term, in 700 words he drew on a remarkable moral imagination, as mature in theological insight as with political judgment. With an eloquence without peer he spoke into his place in time, word by word, sentence by sentence, setting forth his understanding about what America was, and what America must be.

---

[49]The Inaugural Address of Abraham Lincoln, delivered at the National Capitol, March 4, 1865.

One of those who listened to Lincoln's powerful speech that day was Frederick Douglas, the most passionate voice for the enslaved African-Americans of the mid-nineteenth century, a man whose words rang out across America and the world. When Lincoln saw Douglass in the crowd of supporters who gathered at the reception in the East Room of the White House, he said, "There is no man in the country whose opinion I value more than yours." And Douglass replied, "That was a sacred effort." And it was; sometime later he reflected, "I have always been a man; but that day I felt like a man."

Terribly, tragically, one month later Lincoln was killed for the courage of his convictions, his speech ennobling many and enraging others, an assassination that still scars us as a people.

In the ironies of providence, the war had come to its own sorry end six days before Lincoln was murdered. The official war was over, but the reality of the civil war still worked its way in and through America. While we were done with the war, the war was not done with us, and a century later the same issues brought forth the civil rights conflicts of the 1960s, cities burning with rage over the unresolved "civil war" of the 1860s. Now generations later, into a new century, we still stumble badly over the systemic wrong that we seem unable to leave behind.

Wounds leave scars.

Wounds Hidden, and Not

Not so long ago I hosted an evening on Capitol Hill in an historic nineteenth-century home. We called it a Vocare Evening, "a conversation with consequences," in which educators from throughout the Washington, DC, area came together for dinner to talk about the work of their lives.

We drew on a monograph by Wendell Berry, *The Hidden Wound*, a very personal reflection on his family's complicity in the slave trade, his great- and great-great-grandfathers' tobacco farms in Kentucky made possible on the backs of men, women, and children who had no choice other than to awaken one more day into one more year under the literal and proverbial whip of his forebears—the "two hundred and fifty years of unrequited toil" as Lincoln described it in his address. He argues that the "wound" is a complex one. Yes, there is a wound that still wounds for those who were enslaved, a wound that must be remembered; but he then presses the thesis that "the hidden wound" is one that has wounded those who enslaved other human beings.

> *If the white man has inflicted the wound of racism upon black men, the cost has been that he would receive the mirror image of that wound into himself. As the master, or as a member of the dominant race, he has felt little compulsion to acknowledge or speak of it; the more painful it has grown the more deeply he has hidden it within himself. But the wound is there, and is a profound disorder, as great a damage in his mind as it is in his society.*[50]

That is a difficult argument to hear. But with characteristic wisdom, Berry understands that history and heartache must be told together, remembering that everyone is wounded, both those who bear the burden and those who burden, both who feel the whip and those who whip.

That night we talked about its meaning for the vocation of teacher in the city of Washington, with its incredibly multicultural demographic—the nations of the earth coming by the hundreds and thousands to the capital city of the world—and perhaps most poignantly with historic white and black populations equal in size throughout the city. Public schools, private schools, elementary schools, high schools, teachers and principals, years of experience in every different kind of school, together around the table, each one asked to think aloud about Berry's insight in light of their own institution and experience, and about what they had learned about teaching in the face of "the hidden wound."

[50]Wendell Berry, *The Hidden Wound: Patriotism and the History of Prejudice* (Counterpoint, 1970).

The conversation we had that night could be had all over America, in small towns and big cities, north and south, east and west—because the wound still wounds, sometimes and in some places leaving deep scars.

Birmingham, Alabama, is a city that embodies this tragedy, by its name a memorial for the greatest losses and the deepest longings in American history. One hundred years after the terrible civil war that tore apart America, the streets of Birmingham still felt the lash that Lincoln spoke about, with long-established laws that were meant to grieve and hurt, systematically repressing the formerly enslaved peoples who had been brought from Africa to America. If there are names that still bring tears, Bull Connor is one, perhaps preeminent among too many, the ironically misnamed "Commissioner of Public Safety" for the city during the decades of the civil rights movement before and after the 1960s. Known for turning on fire hoses against his own citizens, for turning dogs loose among his own citizens—Negroes as they were called, "Blacks" as they became, African-Americans as they are—his bullying ways made Birmingham a flash point for the ongoing horror of racism in the United States.

Enough so that Martin Luther King Jr was jailed under Connor's watch, writing his famous "Letter from Birmingham Jail" behind bars, imprisoned because of a peaceful protest on the city's streets. Profoundly eloquent, a letter born of the yearning of generations before him, King's words were primarily for the leaders of the "white" church, calling on them to pay attention to what was going on in America, in the South in particular, and in Birmingham specifically. Not unlike Lincoln's inaugural address, there is historical and political gravitas in his letter, his long wrestling with theological conviction woven together with social commitment. Reading him years later one can only respond with awe at King's remarkable insight into the complexity of the human heart embedded in the complexity of history, with rare grace calling for more honesty about the state of race relations in Alabama and beyond.

One morning several years ago I was asked to speak in Birmingham at a citywide breakfast on what the recovery of a vision of vocation could mean for the renewal of the city, and I chose to quote from King's letter. Even remembering that day, I sigh, sometimes feeling very deeply the burden of ideas, knowing that they can be both blessing and curse, yearning that my words would become flesh for those people in that place, somehow a gift to the city. Speaking at the 16th Street Baptist Church in downtown Birmingham, known throughout the world for the horrific bombing one Sunday morning in 1963, the malicious murder of four little girls who were walking down the stairs from their Sunday school class to the sanctuary for worship, I was deeply sobered. To walk into the building now, generations later, one feels the weight of history, its iconic and tragic identity echoing through time—and we cannot not tremble.

At the heart of King's letter was the longing that the white church leaders would have ears to hear, that the long suffering of formerly enslaved people would be seen and heard for the moral morass that it always was, for what it always would be apart from a sense of responsibility for what is and for what should be, awakened by strange grace. In the most simple terms, for Blacks to be seen as neighbors to be loved, that love had history and economics and education and politics written into its meaning. Yes, that the good words of faith had to be made flesh in time and place, in cities like Birmingham throughout the South.

That year the film *Birth of a Nation* came out, artfully if painfully insisting that America listen to a different story. After all the glories of antebellum culture are remembered, with its New World refinements in architecture and ethos, the truer story is that from beginning to end it was an economy built on the backs of slaves. The film is a hard story of a horrific time in our history, with violence begetting violence, always an eye for an eye and a tooth for a tooth, with grief and blood screaming across the screen, insisting that we remember to remember the on-the-ground reality of slavery.

I wanted those there, the good folk of Birmingham that they were, gathered to hope and pray for their city, to know that we were going to have an honest conversation about what had been—so I lingered over the film as we talked together.

But then I told of my own coming-of-age years, of stepping away from what was expected of me, of my wrestling with questions about what I believed about the world, and about my place in it—and in that time of self-interrogation I met John Perkins.

A son of the South himself, born into a sharecropping family in Mississippi, John was thrust into the crucible of our long civil war over the meaning of "America." Could it be, would it ever be a home for the once-enslaved peoples from Africa? Or would they always be second-class citizens, less than human in every way that mattered most to being human? After his older brother was brutally murdered by a policeman in his hometown, John left the South and moved to Los Angeles—a story of amazing grace, as the best stories are—where he found reasons for his own being, ones that brought him back to Mississippi for the rest of his life. From the hardscrabble experience of his family—being raised by grandparents because his parents were no more, through his own refiner's fire—came a deep well from which he began to speak about being the son of slaves, the grandson of too many slaves, over time writing good book after good book, each born of his unusual wisdom and passion about the world that not only can be, but should be.[51] And I was drawn in, as his vision was for the whole of life, every square inch of life. Nothing ivory-tower, as that could never be John, but rather for a hope reaching into everything that makes life life.

All of this and more found its way into my address that morning, where then I quoted from King's letter, which concludes with these words:

---

[51]Beginning with *Let Justice Roll Down* in 1976, John Perkins has now authored twenty books.

> *If I have said anything in this letter that is an understatement of the truth and is indicative of an unreasonable impatience, I beg you to forgive me. If I have said anything in this letter that is an overstatement of the truth and is indicative of my having a patience that makes me patient with anything less than brotherhood, I beg God to forgive me.*[52]

And because this was Birmingham, I finished by offering a native son, Walker Percy, the physician who became a novelist, unusually gifted at diagnosing the soul of our society in his stories about these United States, whose image of "hints of hope" has rooted itself deep within me. Being where I was that morning, with the weight of history in the air we breathed, I tried to speak between two worlds, the life and times of the citizens of Birmingham through the last generations and centuries, and those who had come that morning wanting to think aloud and together about the flourishing of their city, in particular about what the recovery of the idea of vocation could mean for the renewal of their city.

Could we become "hints of hope"? That was the reason for being behind the breakfast, imagined into reality by a group of remarkable people who call themselves *In Spero,* who with deep longing for the renewal of their city believe in "restoration, reconciliation, and redemption, because beauty is what will transform the world." Nothing cheap could be said about them, gathered as they were from across Birmingham that morning, representing a spectrum from the city—racially, economically, professionally. There was too much on the line, too much history bearing down upon us, too much that still needs to be done. And every idea would be terribly complex, with difficulty that would be discovered as the ideas began to have legs, with social implications, economic implications, political implications, ecclesial implications, cultural implications. In the

---

[52] Martin Luther King Jr, *Letter from Birmingham Jail* (Harper Collins, 1984).

most profound way, all of these arenas of human life are mixed up in ordinary human experience, defining and refining each other, shaping and reshaping each other. Our lives, our ordinary lives lived out in ordinary places, are right in the middle of this, longing as we are for the world to be different, for our cities to be different, even and if that means proximately so.

But could we step in? Would it be possible to reimagine a people and a place that believe in visions of vocation that would leaven the life of Birmingham, taking its past seriously while taking its future seriously too? If we could pray towards that, if we could work towards that, something might change, and the words "intractable, impossible" would no longer be ours, because we would have chosen something honest and true, something more just and more merciful. Yes, we would have chosen to be hints of hope.

The Vocation of a Wounded Healer

"And when I saw him, he smiled."

If the wounds of the world are often institutional and structural, social and systemic, they are also always profoundly personal. They have names of human beings, young and old, male and female, each one a story of sadness, a story with longing, hoping that what is will no longer be. And while the aches and heartaches are global and universal, stretching across the cosmos, at some point they must be named for them to mean what they must mean. For example, most people in most places struggle to find compassionate, competent medical care, simply said—and sometimes in some places, by surprising grace, we see the vocation of healing incarnate, where the truest needs are met with the truest care.

Todd Wahrenberger has lived his life into that calling, making choice after choice for the sake of his neighbor, especially those who cry out in their many-faceted pains, physical and psychological, social and historical. The chief resident in his medical school program, the world was open to him: he could do this, and he could go there, practicing medicine anywhere, but what would he do? Already of unusual intellectual grace, the eyes of his heart aware of pain and hope, he spent the summers of his medical school training with physicians who had chosen to practice their healing arts among the underserved of the city of Pittsburgh, Pennsylvania. And because all of us learn the most important things, the habits of heart that become *us* over time, "over the shoulder, through the heart," Todd's apprenticeship in learning formed his soul, teaching him to see and to hear, to know and to love, right in the middle of his deepening understanding of medicine, shaping skills with a surprising seamlessness.

When he finished his years of study, he opened a clinic on the city's Northside—under the shadows of the city's iconic baseball and football stadiums—across the river from the gleaming downtown in a neighborhood of complex and unusual need, its houses and streets full of people who did not have access to the kind of medical care people must have if they are to be well. Over the years he came to love his patients, asking questions that went deeper than the ones doctors usually ask, ones that probed heart and mind, soul and strength, for the sake of healing for the human being as a whole being—which sometimes meant he would pray with those who came, knowing that at his best he was an instrument of grace.

And then came a day when the Sisters of Mercy called, wondering about his interest in a new work that they wanted to build on the other side of the city's rivers, the Southside, underneath the trolleys that move people up and down the hills looking over the Golden Triangle of downtown Pittsburgh. This would not be the same work, but it would draw Todd's deeper vocation into another occupation, that of leading a new clinic devoted to those who lived on the streets of the city, especially those who suffered from mental health problems. It was not an easy decision; he and I talked for hours in that season of serious discernment as he eventually joined in on this new hope to take care of those whom almost no one even knew existed.

Street people, but schizophrenic street people. On some days we might see someone like that, though mostly we do not for all kinds of complex reasons, some having to do with who we are, some with who they are. But in fact, for Todd and his clinic to do its work, week after week they go out into the city, finding folk under the bridges of a city that has more bridges than any other city in America, first simply listening to those they meet, giving the gift of true attention, wanting these unseen human beings to know that they too matter—made in the image of God as they are—and then asking the questions that can be asked, trying to understand what can be understood.

And because this has been his life for most of his life, he is no longer surprised by who he meets and what he finds. There are few surprises, and yet every person is new, again. In a severe-weather shelter one night, bringing his heart and his skills wherever his work takes him, Todd began treating a thirty-something man whose face was worn with life at its bleakest. When Todd began to ask the questions he asks, the man told his name, which awakened in Todd memories of a young child whom he had cared for whose mother had taken him to the Northside clinic years earlier—and here he was again, still full of need, still full of hope. These stories go on and on because these are the stories of Todd's life every day, every night, the life that he keeps choosing again and again, in this place with its people.

But "choosing" is a weighted word, because our choices are complex. Why do we choose what we choose? Why do we see what we see? And how do we learn to "see"? Yes, this is a question about Todd, but it is a question for all of us. Apprenticeship in learning is the deepest pedagogy, the truest pedagogy. Words have to become flesh for us to understand them, because the Incarnation is not only the heart of Christian theology, it is a genius pedagogy. Nothing we learn that matters much do we learn any other way. At the first moment when Jesus could have offered something else—a book, a lecture, a seminar—he simply said, "Come and see. . . . If you want to understand what I am saying, then you need to come and see, to see the way that what I am saying is embodied in my life."

While the history of professional and vocational learning is largely this, from cobblers to plumbers, from lawyers to pastors, the world of medicine has held onto this reality as closely as any other. No one even imagines studying hard, passing the exams, then immediately entering into the work of healing; instead, written into the meaning of medicine is that it is learned in apprenticeship, *over the shoulder, through the heart.* From the most general skills to the most specialized practices, the younger learner must learn alongside the older teacher. We call this "residency," a choice to learn from someone whose insights are more deeply formed through years of practice; always a conscious choice, and always a required choice for those for whom health care is the vocation of their lives. Not only did Todd choose time and again to learn medicine with those who focused on the underserved, a decision that is a crucial window into the character of his calling, but also in his work he has entered into a longer apprenticeship, one that spans the centuries, echoing its way across time and place.

But again, why do we see as we see? Why do we choose what we choose?

The answer is complex, because *we* are. Always eager for more, characteristically willing to ask harder questions, Todd has been willing to linger with harder answers, a habit of heart that is as deep within him as any. It is not difficult to trace the vision and skills that carry him into his days to good stories of good people who have in their own unique ways been healing incarnate, from his medical residency, on and into an embodied tradition that has been passed down generation by generation through the Sisters of Mercy, of one healer teaching another healer, from Dublin to the far reaches of the earth, even to the streets of Pittsburgh.

In the early nineteenth century Catherine McCauley was born into a family that as a family did not last long. Her parents both died when she was a girl, and with her siblings she became part of other families. As she came into adulthood, Catherine was "adopted" by a generous and visionary family who offered her a home for the next twenty years. The husband was a Protestant and the wife a Quaker; their house became her house, their hopes her hopes, their kindness her kindness, their openheartedness her openheartedness, and through the years her Catholic convictions gave increasing coherence to her life, answering the deepest hopes of her heart. When these good people died, to Catherine's surprise she was bequeathed their whole estate.

Feeling the importance of continuity with those who had loved her with such remarkable hospitality, Catherine chose to use her new wealth for those in her city—those whose hopes and hurts most did not even know. The family home became a home for others, and the money that was now hers became the source of her ability to walk the streets of Dublin, seeking out those with needs, making sure that the city's forgotten knew that someone had not forgotten.

In the next years she became Sister Catherine, and over time her vision of health and hospitality became the Sisters of Mercy, a community of women moved by the same heart for those without any hope of help. In the late 1800s the Sisters of Mercy came to Pittsburgh, bringing their work of healing to the newly industrializing city, its steel mills offering employment to thousands of immigrants from Europe—the Irish first, then the Italians, and then to wider Europe, to any and all who would come. With social commitments to wellbeing and welfare being almost nil at the time, health care was largely income-based: Those who had, had, and those who did not, did not—with those just off the boat the least able to find medical help for themselves and their families.

And not so long after the sisters came with healing in their hearts, Mercy Hospital was birthed, institutionalizing Catherine McCauley's own vocational pilgrimage into a calling for a new people in a new place, to see and hear the needs of the city of Pittsburgh. The work that was begun continued on into the grand but always hard-edged story of Pittsburgh as the industrial capital of America in the twentieth century, known throughout the world as Steel City—at least into its recent decades, when the city stopped making steel. Remembering Wendell Berry's thesis about our life together in the marketplace, the "lesser economy" ground to a halt in the face of the "greater economy" of reality. What seemed plausible and possible to the steelmakers was never seen that way by the steel barons; and the reverse was true too, painfully so. Their mutually abetted, go-for-the-jugular business practices could not be sustained in the world that is really there.

And when Pittsburgh lost its steel, the city's downtown changed. No longer was the U.S. Steel building the iconic master of metropolitan architecture, high in the sky announcing its economic dominance to any who needed to know. Instead, that same building was renamed by the new magnate as UPMC: the University of Pittsburgh Medical Center. If Carnegie had found a way to overwhelm the city and its steel a hundred years earlier, UPMC followed the same story, taking over hospital after hospital, each distinct and different health system "forced" to become one system by the *realeconomik* of the twenty-first-century marketplace—and eventually Mercy Hospital was lost too, unable to continue to offer its unique care to the city because the financial costs were too great.

But this large loss for Pittsburgh became a financial windfall for the Sisters of Mercy, who by habit of heart chose to step into the needs of the city, again. If they had come to the Steel City as it was in the late nineteenth century, one hundred years later they responded to it as it now is. If caring for a steel economy-based population had been their calling, as the twentieth became the twenty-first century those in greatest need were those left behind in the new high-tech and high-touch economy—and for too many life on the streets became a way of life.

It was into this new moment in the history of Pittsburgh that Todd was called into a practice among the most needy of the city. Anglican he is, and therefore born of the liturgical promise-in-prayer to "love and serve You with gladness and singleness of heart." Those who know Todd describe him as someone marked by a surprising joy and characteristic eagerness that is uncanny even as he works very hard, every day hard in a new way, as the complex weight of his work is often overwhelming.

Of course there is the again-this-day work of listening and responding, of knowing and caring, but there is also the everyday labor of love that is more administrative, the unending paperwork, the fundraising for hopes and dreams, all written into the work that it is to make health for all more what actually is than what might be. And what carries him every day into the Southside neighborhood is a deepening responsibility born of love, and from that most local of all medical care into concerns for the health-in-common for Pittsburgh as Pittsburgh. As his insight into the public health of the city has deepened, he has been drawn into the most serious national conversations about what health means for Americans and America.

Hear the question again: Why and how do we begin to see what we see? Especially why and how does someone called to care as a medical professional move beyond "professionalism" into a deeper calling, that of a healer giving himself to human beings, complex and wounded as we are—especially as the more we know about ourselves and the world the more we understand the reality of frailty—our own, painfully, and the world's, painfully.

Substantively, that is born from those whom we choose as our teachers, and that is as true for Todd as for anyone. We learn what matters most in that way, always. But everyone and everything is complex—and because most of life is autobiographical, for blessing and for curse, there is more to Todd's story than one might imagine, not altogether surprising as it is. Like most Pittsburghers, he is a son of the city, from generations who have lived on its hills and beside its rivers before he ever came to be. That history is his, his blood bleeding "the 'burgh" from his first days. But his own family was, in a weighty word, dysfunctional, terribly so, a wounding place for a boy to be born, for a young man to learn to be a man. Alcoholism and abuse were the raging waters in which he swam, and while horribly hard on everyone, it bore down on Todd, who longed for more, for something more whole, even for something more holy.

By good grace he found his way into the lives of good people in good places, drawn in by an undergraduate experience that engaged him in heart and mind, teaching him to know what a pre-med student must know; and also teaching him to see the whole of his life and the whole of life through the lens of meaningful faith, born of a belief in the God of heaven and earth who loved the most wounded among us, even and especially so scarred as we sometimes are. This story is never not Todd's story, its great hurts his hurts, its great hope his hope. He sees what he sees and hears what he hears because of who he is, which is a story of remarkable sorrow and remarkable joy, together. For all those reasons and more, he has been my physician, the one I have chosen to care for my health, trusting him with my life, with all that I have been, with all that I am and with all that I will be.

One day along the way of many days, an older man came up to him in a tent community under one of Pittsburgh's bridges. He was obviously sick, his needs crying out for care, and Todd saw that he had been terribly wounded, with blood on his beard and a broken jaw. Because medical care for those who need it most has been his life for most of the years of his life, Todd knew who the man was, having treated him for decades. Asking the questions that are his, he found that the man had been pushed and shoved miserably, and finally assaulted with a hatchet, leaving him terribly hurt.

Todd took him in, finding the care he needed within the Mercy Clinic's system, a "medical respite center" that is an enhanced homeless shelter for the injured and vulnerable, a place to be cared for by people who care. Months later, his wounds no longer grievous and him more healthy in every way, he told those in charge that he wanted to see Dr. Wahrenberger again.

"And when I saw him, he smiled." The simplest of words, perhaps, but they capture the heart of Todd's life and work. His long years of offering healing to the neediest of the city have earned him the most humbly given honor—*a true smile*—coming from the most heartfelt gratitude. In Pittsburgh the unimagined and unknown of the city are those who live under its bridges, and by great grace they know that someone cares for them, that someone will come, that someone will touch their hurt, that someone will move heaven and earth to bring healing for their pain. All might not be made well, but the best care possible is given, in hope. A proximate healing, yes, and that is a gift.

We never do more than that, our lives and labors stretched between what is needed and what is possible; we are, after all, wounded people in a wounded world, each one of us called to be "wounded healers" in and through the vocations that are ours.[53] But as rich an image as that is, it is sobering too, requiring us to rethink who we are, why we are, and what we do with our lives; yes, requiring us to reimagine the very nature of vocation. At its heart it is born in the meaning of the Incarnation, which is the centerpiece of Christian theology—the vocation of Christ was and is that of a wounded healer. Those who follow him into the world are called into that same vocation, in imitation of Christ, who as the Word become flesh came into history to take our bent hearts and our broken bodies into himself, making us holy and whole. But the portal into this promise is through the sorrow and tragedy of Golgotha, our healing made possible because of the cross of Christ, the death of death. As the wise Puritan teacher John Owen wrote for the generations, it was "the death of death in the death of Christ." Poetically put, profoundly true, in the wounding of the world Christ was wounded—the promise from Genesis 3 on—offering healing to the world through his wounds. These are deep waters, but they are the ones in which

[53] The image of "wounded healer" comes from both J. B. Phillips, a translator of the New Testament in the mid-twentieth century, and more recently from Henri Nouwen, the professorial pastor to people the world over.

we are called to swim, being the very contours of reality for us, defining the character of vocation for us.

In thousands upon thousands of different ways, this is as true for all of us as it is true of Todd Wahrenberger. Bearing his own wounds, binding up the scars of the city that he has long loved, he makes this his vocation—one more day, one more year, taking the pain of Pittsburgh into himself, its most complex and perplexing troubles becoming his own reason for being, the *raison d'être* that has taken him into the streets of the city, day and night, for the years of his life.

The Art of Precious Scars

There are moments along the way of every life when we meet someone who is a deeply kindred spirit. What they see, we see. What they hear, we hear. What they feel, we feel.

Years ago I was asked to speak to a group of artists in New York City on the vocation of the arts, on the responsibility of artists in and for the cities of the world. Already a friend, Makoto Fujimura invited me to spend an afternoon with him in his gallery, where his paintings for the Four Gospels at the 400th anniversary of the King James Bible were on display. Gladly I joined him, and for most of an afternoon we slowly made our way through the gallery, him explaining to me the work of his heart. We lingered here and there, me asking questions, him telling me all that I hoped to know about this one, and then that one—until we finally stopped before a large canvas which he had titled "Kairos Christos—The Tears of Christ."

I looked at his work, taking it in in every way that I could, and then looked at him, and he began to draw me deeper into his own way of making sense of making sense. Born of his reading of John 11, it is the story of the death of Lazarus, and Makoto wanted to capture what for him had become the very center of his commitments about everything that mattered most to him. I kept listening very carefully, because I had never ever heard someone see the story as I did. For him, and for me, the story of the weeping of God before the tomb of Lazarus had become the crux of faith, of his faith and my faith, both of us concluding that if this chapter were not in the Bible, neither of us could imagine wanting to be a Christian. In the most profound sense, in the most deeply rooted way, this was the line in the sand for both of us. Either the God of heaven and earth wept over death, over its destruction of what was meant to be, over its distortion of what should be; or we would choose for the nihilism of "nothing matters that much," because nothing could.

That starkly beautiful painting of "The Tears of Christ" became the frontispiece of the Four Gospels, now known all over the world for its artful grandeur, drawn into the liturgies of congregations everywhere because of its painterly insight into the meaning of Matthew, Mark, Luke, and John. No longer surprised, I can only smile when I see the very large book held up for all to see and hear the Gospel read again and again and again, week after week after week, knowing what I know of the heart and mind of the one whose beliefs and gifts brought it into being.

But the frontispiece? Simply because everything else that matters, matters because of the tears of Christ.

Seeing the horror and sorrow of death, God said, "No!"—and wept. As the text reads, he wept not only because of his compassion for Mary and Martha, feeling their feelings so deeply within himself, but also because he was angry at the abortion of his good hope for human beings in his world. The world that he intended to be was no longer the world that was. People died; even his own friend Lazarus died. That God cared as he did, crying as he did with tears of sadness and rage, meant everything to Makoto and to me.

In and through those years he and I kept talking, even sometimes working together on common hopes. Though we are different, though we are differently placed, I have come to trust his vision, knowing that what he sees and hears and feels will draw me in—even as his work and mine are not the same at all.

But in listening to him reflect on his work, I'm keenly aware there is always tension, for in a bent world, a broken world, there must be. Is it possible to hold together wonder and wound? Can we see and hear the terror of life in the world and at the same time give ourselves to the truest beauty that can be imagined? Human beings as human beings feel this—and artists do too, with their characteristic "feel" for what is to be felt, when we learn to pay attention.

Makoto brought into being a book of great beauty, yes, but even as he wrote the introduction for the Four Gospels he reflected on being in New York City on September 11, 2001, living with his family in Tribeca, blocks from the horror of that day. After walking amidst the ruins, not knowing all that had happened, needing to know whether his family was safe, overwhelmed by the grief of the city, he created artistic windows born of the Gospels and their forceful articulation of the crux of history in the life, death, and resurrection of Christ—with the first page being his painting "The Tears of Christ." To say it as simply as can be, if God did not weep over the brokenness of history, knowing the weight of every heart, then why and how can anyone believe that God is God? And have any honest interest in a word from God?

That instinct about who God is, and who and why we are, is also seen in the oeuvre of his art, the range and scope of all of his work—always graceful, always intriguing. And it is seen in Fujimura's deepening interest in the ancient Japanese art of "kintsugi." Described as "the art of precious scars," it is as poignant a portrayal of hope as we know, artfully embracing the relationship of wounds to scars in the very craft itself. With his unusually eloquent wisdom, he explains,

> *Kintsugi, the ancient Japanese art form of repairing broken tea ware by reassembling ceramic pieces, creates anew the valuable pottery, which now becomes more beautiful and more valuable than the previous, the original, unbroken vessel. . . . Kintsugi does not just "fix" or repair a broken vessel; rather the technique makes the broken pottery even more beautiful than the original, as the Kintsugi master will*

> *make the broken work and create a restored piece that makes the broken parts even more visually sophisticated. No two works, done with such mastery, will look the same or break in the same way. . . . The Christian gospel, or the Good News, begins with the awareness of our brokenness. . . . Christ came not to "fix" us, not just to restore, but to make us a new creation. . . . The biblical vision of the new world accompanies the reminders of the wounds of Christ. The resurrected Christ still bears the wounds of the resurrection.*[54]

Beauty out of brokenness. Never not broken, and yet and yet, surprisingly beautiful too.

A very visible wound, but a choice to make something new from the scars themselves. They are because they must be, but they will become something new too, an honest healing of what was, now made into what could be, of what might be.

If Fujimura has chosen to make this art his own art for a thousand good reasons, he stands in a line of the best artists we know, the filmmakers, novelists, poets, singers, and songwriters—and yes, the painters, each one gifted to see and hear the world in and through the vocational vision written into the nature of his or her own work. Story after story, our best storytellers see the same world: Shakespeare is known for his comedies and his tragedies; taken together, they are the stories of who we are. Bach, with his grand musical compositions marked by incredible complexity and wonder, insists that we offer "faint hallelujahs" in response. Hugo, with his profound understanding of who we are as human beings at our worst and at our best, the most glorious and the most ruinous, crafted novels that are as good and grand as stories can be. Van Gogh's brush strokes created the landscapes of life that remember the most ordinary human beings with the most ordinary loves, in

[54]Makoto Fujimura, *Art and Faith: A Theology of Making* (Yale University Press, 2020), 44-45.

and through every day deeply wrestling with his own longings. Dostoevsky is honored for his heart-aching exploration of the self-deception that runs through the human heart, even as he knew that truth sets us free, finally free. Sayers offered her gift of seeing into our darkness through her murder mysteries, while at the same time threading her tales with honest hope. Berry and Percy draw upon their unusual ability to hold together the greatest happiness with the greatest grief, set within the contours and culture of the American South. U2 gifts us their unique vision of music that raises the roofs of the world, even as it searches our souls, never not asking "How long, O Lord?" with heartaching perplexity, inviting everyone in attendance to become a member of a global concert, singing the songs of Zion all over the face of the earth. We do not have important art that is less than that.

In his *Silence and Beauty* it is clear that Fujimura has spent years of his life pondering the artistic vision of the novelist Shusako Endō, specially so his very difficult book *Silence*, the painful account of seventeenth-century Jesuit missionaries to Japan, asking the hardest of all questions that human beings ask and answer.

The contemporary composer Arvo Pärt presses into the same dilemma in his profoundly imagined music, a vocation that is captured in the study *Arvo Pärt: Out of Silence*, an analysis of the integral relationship of his beliefs about God and the universe, and his art, so allusive, so beautiful, so rich, each composition one more effort to musically remember that the deepest, truest source of his work is in his cruciform faith, a way of seeing all of reality in and through the death and resurrection of Christ.

To affirm that God is there is its own line-in-the-sand commitment about reality; to then argue that God is not silent presses even more deeply into our most deeply held beliefs about what is, and what is not. But these are the great questions of the human heart, asked and asked again in every time and place. While it is one thing to acknowledge the existence of God and the plausibility of transcendence, it is even more to argue that he has spoken with meaning about the meaning of life in the world. These are our questions, always, the great conundrums of every man and every woman.

Endō understood this, raising the stakes with his novel about human vocation in the world, about one's sense of calling to care about the world for Christ's sake—and then he was plagued by the possibility that God has not spoken after all, that there is in fact no calling because there is no caller. Pärt wrestles with this too, working his way out of the despair of a silent God and a silent universe into a holy and proper confidence that there is beautiful music to be made, that there are songs that take us to the deepest places of our hearts, notes woven together that remind us that there is not only a God, but that that God has spoken, his songs playing through our experience as ordinary people in ordinary places into the universe and beyond.

And Fujimura sees this too, believing as Endō believed, believing as Pärt believes, taking the questions of life as seriously as they can be and must be, with remarkable ability giving the gift of beauty—in the very face of anguish and grief and pain and silence—his paintings and writings wonderfully reflecting the truest truths of life in and through the work of art itself.

If we have eyes to see, we will.

The Gift of the Proximate

Always and everywhere, the proximate is a prism into the painful reality of wounds and scars. From the historical, political, economic, and social in the generational heartache of racism, the task of binding up a nation's wounds becomes one of a very long labor of love . . . from the cultural and national indifference brought into being by the assumption that *realpolitik* requires prosperity for my people against prosperity for your people, of wealth for me and mine over a true commonwealth . . . from the surprising transformation of wounds that have become a vocation for the sake of a city, for its forgotten citizens, whose scars are taken in for love's sake . . . to the sense of calling to take up the mysterious place where beauty and brokenness are twined together in the work of art, with images of a cosmic tension that is at one and the same time full of the greatest heartache and the greatest hope, with tears remembering to remember that the grief of God is the crux of what honestly is and of what honestly might be—and yes, from beginning to end the grace of walking into the years of life with a wounded tendon that was literally ripped apart, so bloodied and broken that its hurt could not and would not be fully healed in this life.

Apart from the gift of the proximate, we have no way of keeping our hearts alive, either as persons or as polities, either as human beings who long for healing or as cities and societies who stumble and stumble again over systemic wrongs that generations cannot unravel. To find a way forward requires that we see ourselves and the world truthfully, being honest about what is, at the same time hoping for the day when all will be real and true and right; it is an expectation of the future which actually shapes the way we live into the wounds that otherwise only damage and debilitate—making us feel stuck in moments that we can never get out of because we cannot make sense of the senselessness of the sorrow, the ache of the tension we live with being so great that we cannot see a way forward.

For Everyman and Everywoman, for every one of us, we live stretched taut by that tension, needing to make peace with the proximate, with the hope of something that is honest, knowing in our bones that everything that needs to be made whole is not yet ours in this world of the now but the not yet.

8

SOMETHING MORE

It's like in the great stories, Mr. Frodo. The ones that really mattered. ***Full of darkness and danger they were. And sometimes you didn't want to know the end. Because how could the end be happy? How could the world go back to the way it was when so much bad had happened? But in the end, it's only a passing thing, this shadow. Even darkness must pass. A new day will come. And when the sun shines it will shine out the clearer. Those were the stories that stayed with you. That meant something, even if you were too small to understand why. But I think, Mr. Frodo, I do understand. I know now. Folk in those stories had lots of chances of turning back, only they didn't. They kept going, because they were holding on to something. That there is some good in this world, and it's worth fighting for.***[55]

—J. R. R. Tolkien, *The Lord of the Rings*

Before the brightness of the morning sun began to overwhelm the city, I biked miles for an apprenticeship in learning and life, listening for hours, and then my longing to understand was met by the master's patient attention, him taking me seriously, him taking my questions seriously.

In my dropped-out years, leaving the world of higher education for a time, entering into the adventures of "extra-academic education"—living and learning in places far and wide—one summer I found my way to the Valley of the Sun, the city of Phoenix, Arizona, where with my bike and my backpack I entered into the tutelage of a philosopher, Surrendra Gangadean. Remarkably articulate, always profound, a careful and critical thinker about all things, he opened himself to my questions, day after long, hot day.

---

[55]Tolkien, *The Lord of the Rings*, "The Two Towers," "The Stairs of Cirith Ungol," 711–12.

Of all that has come and gone since that summer, I remember that we talked most days about the questions "What is real? What is true? What is right?"—each a lens into the meaning of meaning, of metaphysics, epistemology, and ethics. By then I was persuaded that they were more than abstractions, beyond the pale of honest interest of honest people; but instead, they were crucial for the forming of a good life and a good society, whether a person or a polity imagined them to be, or understood their meaning as meaningful. Through those days of summer we talked through the world with a searching honesty, him the professor, me the student with questions that had taken me from the confines of the classroom to the push and shove of learning from life.

I wanted to know, simply said.

To know what was real, what was true, what was right—and we wrestled our way through the questions and their answers, for as long as we had energy. But as we pressed into these perplexities, with persistent insistence he probed me to think even more deeply, with his quiet earnestness insisting that "expectation affects program." This was confusing at first, but the longer I listened, the more we talked about the philosophers and philosophies of the world, their diverse ways of making sense of making sense—from the pantheisms of the East to the materialisms of the West to the theisms of the world—and I began to understand.

What we believe to be true about the future has meaning for the way we live in the present. And that cannot not be. As true for Hindus (the family of faith into which Surrendra was born) as for Buddhists, as true for Marxists as for evolutionary materialists, as true for Jews and Muslims as for Christians, *expectation affects program,* our beliefs about the eschaton, about the future of history, about the future of life in the world—whatever it may be, whatever form it might have—form and shape the way we live in and through the moments of our lives, "affecting" our convictions about what is real, what is true, what is right.

Once upon a time Calvin and Hobbes offered all of us windows into the world, and surprisingly—given the popularity of the cartoon—into the meaning of life. One day the Boy and his Tiger are walking through the woods, and Calvin says, "'Live for the moment' is MY motto," followed by, "You never know how long you've got! You could step into the road tomorrow and—wham—you get hit by a cement truck! Then you'd be sorry you put off your pleasures! That's why I say, 'Live for the moment.' What's YOUR motto?" With characteristic nonchalance, Hobbes says, "Look down the road," and walks on—and if we have ears to hear, we smile.

Where are we going? What is ahead? *Eschaton* becomes a very important word, whether we are pantheists, materialists, theists, or even little boys with their tigers. If everyday life is only and ever illusion—as pantheism argues—then the here and now does not have moral meaning, because the future has no hope, "illusion" that it is. If life is only and ever about the nothingness of a meaningless existence—as materialism insists, remembering our reflections on Coupland and Nietzsche—then why would anything other than "eat, drink, and be merry, for tomorrow we die . . ." make any sense of what does not make sense? If life in the present moment has meaning because it is framed by a metanarrative that begins and ends with the coherence and congruence of heaven and earth, a sacramental cosmos, then that has consequence for the moment-by-moment experience of ordinary people in ordinary places.

Because it is true that our longings and loves are determinative, making us "us," they are the threads that become the fabric of the future, whatever we understand the future to be.

Pilgrims We Are

Growing up in California as I did, the name John Muir seemed to be everywhere: schools in his honor, forests in his honor, even an organization, the Sierra Club, in his honor. And while I spent many days as a boy hiking in the Sierra Nevadas, my father taking me into the wonders of the majestic mountains, as I grew older my understanding of Muir evolved, asking questions as I was about the meaning of my life, and of life itself. From what I read it seemed that he was probably a transcendentalist, sympathetic to Thoreau's vision of the unity of all that is, an American version of pantheism. Yes, he loved Yosemite, but this was California, and his organization was the Sierra Club! He must have worshiped the mountains he loved—why else would he have loved them as he did? There never seemed anything of transcendence twined with truth that I heard about him or his work.

Surprised I was then, years later, to see a fascinating photo of him as an older man, clear eyes, white beard, a walking stick, with these words.

> *I don't like either the word [hike] or the thing. People ought to saunter in the mountains—not 'hike!' Do you know the origin of that word saunter? It's a beautiful word. Away back in the middle ages people used to go on pilgrimages to the Holy Land, and when people in the villages through which they passed asked where they were going they would reply, 'A la sainte terre', 'To the Holy Land.' And so they became known as sainte-terre-ers or saunterers. Now these mountains are our Holy Land, and we ought to saunter through them reverently, not 'hike' through them.*[56]

If this were isolated, words standing alone among the many words of his life, we could dismiss them as poetic and metaphorical. But instead it seems that for Muir there was

---

[56] John Muir as recounted by Albert W. Palmer in *The Mountain Trail and Its Message* (The Pilgrim Press, 1911). As Muir said of himself about the history of the word "saunter," "I am a naturalist, not an etymologist," acknowledging the debate about the word's origin. "Saint" and "land" are clear; what their relationship was to each other in medieval Europe as the word came into being is less clear. The dictionaries are not definitive, though in searching the oldest English dictionaries, one can make a case for Muir's reading.

something profoundly sacramental about the way he saw the world, a surprising seamlessness in what he understood about what and why he loved the Sierras as he did. Where would this have come from?

And so I read more, learning that by the time he was an 11-year-old boy in Scotland, already a lover of the adventures that the outdoor world offered, he had memorized most of the Old Testament and all of the New Testament, which in itself is astounding. His family immigrated to the United States at the end of his childhood, settling in Wisconsin. There, he lived and worked into his 20s, then started his study at the University of Wisconsin just as the American Civil War was beginning. The cultural clash of the war seemed a long ways from him as a son of Scotland, and only knowing the woods of Wisconsin, after two years of study he dropped out, moving to northern Michigan, with its proximity to Canada. When the war was over, he began a journey across America, deep into the South, ending in Florida. Finally, he found his way to California, first in its vast San Joaquin Valley, and then up into its grand mountains, the Sierra Nevadas, which he loved with an unusual love.

Over time he became America's best-known naturalist, in and through his years inviting the nation to love what he loved, his notes on his sauntering life becoming books which we are still reading. Listening to Muir in the twenty-first century is much like reading Wendell Berry, who speaks so tenderly, so profoundly, of the wonders of the world, of his farm along the Kentucky River with its meadows and trees, full of adoration for what has been created by a Creator—and in fascinating fact, there is a remarkable resonance between the two, a century and a continent separating them. Different people, different places, but their common commitments shape their affections, the loves that form their lives. To see, to hear, to smell . . . the complex beauty of life in the natural world, a wonderful world, a world worth caring for and about.

Whatever happened in Muir's long life, wherever he went in the many miles he walked, he was shaped by Scripture, the ground of his very being biblical, his way of seeing and hearing the world rooted in the revelation of God in and through his word and world. That seems clear. And while the twenty-first century sees him as one of America's great explorers, he saw himself as a man sauntering through the mountains and meadows of the Sierras, his understanding of the character of the cosmos and the meaning of history shaping what he saw wherever his feet took him, wherever the eyes of his heart lingered, a pilgrim on holy ground he was and always would be.

Wherever we are on the face of the earth, whatever we believe about the meaning of our lives and the meaning of life, we are pilgrims, like Muir—and not surprisingly, our best stories are always stories of journeys, from here to there, and sometimes back again. Most of us will not know the countryside of Scotland, the woods of Wisconsin, or the Yosemite Valley as Muir did, but we live our lives born of our own loves, the longings of our lives leading us through the years of our lives.

And this truth is an ancient truth, eschatological expectation affecting the ways we live as they always do, the question lingering around and over everyone's heart: "Do you have eyes that see?" To see what is really there? To see its meaning? To see what it is, and is not? To see that the deepest truth is that heaven is touching earth, that we are entering onto holy ground?

What is the Exodus, if not a story of a people on pilgrimage? Through their centuries leaving a home in the Fertile Crescent, coming to a land with promise, going to another land for survival, and then 400 years later beginning a long journey home to what they believed was their "promised land." What is the Odyssey, if not the story of an adventure into unknown lands with unknown peoples, all the while the narrator giving the reader historical context so that Odysseus's journey home will make some sense, and it still does, thousands of years later seen as one of the most important coming-of-age books ever written?

The rabbi of the rabbis, Jesus of Nazareth, chose stories about journeys as a way into his teaching; even his best-known parable begins with, "A man was going down from Jerusalem to Jericho . . .," surprising the expert of the law by his refusal to engage in the intellectual back-and-forth of the academy, simply saying, "I will tell you a story." And another of his most-pondered parables is also a story of a journey, of a son who "goes off to a far land . . ." and finally comes home into the waiting heart of his father. These windows into the life of faith are so perennially rich that we tell them, tell them, and tell them again.

Long before Monty Python or Indiana Jones ever imagined their adventure, most of a millennium ago an unknown writer brought into being one of the most important stories the world has ever heard, a story we call *The Quest of the Holy Grail.* Described as "a guide to Christian discipleship" in its most authoritative editions, it draws the reader into the court of King Arthur, with his queen Guinevere and her ladies, and of course the Knights of the Round Table, led by the valiant Lancelot. Commissioned by the king to find the Holy Grail, the knights set off, a pilgrimage for each one and therefore a time for soul-searching it becomes, with questions that probe the deepest places in the human heart, the "holy grail" becoming a path to holiness, a path for a holy humanness.

The centuries come and go, and the stories of pilgrimage continue. One which the world has long celebrated is simply titled *The Pilgrim's Progress,* with its telling of the tale of Christian, who begins his journey full of hopes and questions, then spends his days entering into places we know all too well—from the Slough of Despond . . . to Vanity Fair . . . to Doubting Castle . . . to the River of Death . . . to the Celestial City. So widely read they have been, John Bunyan's images run through our popular consciousness, because the story runs through our hearts, e.g., in Nathaniel Hawthorne's *Celestial Railroad,* William Thackeray's *Vanity Fair*, Tom Wolfe's *Bonfire of the Vanities,* each reflecting on the meaning of Bunyan's images for the reality of life in the world. And more recently, we have read *O Pioneers*, *Ulysses*, *Grapes of Wrath*, *A Handful of Dust*, *On the Road*, *Invisible Man*, *Lonesome Dove*—story after story of journey upon journey.

The stories of our lives are always stories of journeys, of a beginning and then an end—an end that we hope for, and at other times an end that we resist. But whether we are Hebrew patriarchs or Greek heroes, whether we are knights pursuing holy grails, whether our paths take us through sloughs and fairs and castles, wherever the pathways go far and wide, in and through every story that is a good story we are pilgrims, *sainte-terre-ers* each one, the steps we take always in light of the places we are going, expectation affecting program as it does, and must.

A Telos In Our Hearts

Human beings as human beings are made with a *telos* in our hearts; even Hobbes knows that, stating for the generations that he is looking "down the road." We do, because wherever we are in history, whatever time and place are ours, we cannot forever still the sense that there is something more to life than what we see and hear—awakening day by day wondering what is next, wondering if there is something "next" which more often than not is a good enough reason to get up and go off into the world again another day.

Truth be told, whether most casually or very seriously, written into our humanness are dreams of what could be, of what might be, even of what should be. Yes, there is something about being human that makes us think about tomorrow, hoping that it is better than today . . . often stumbling over ourselves as we do, ordering and disordering our longings, full of desire as we are for something that we can hardly even talk about, sure and yet not sure of what we are looking for.

For as long as we have put our dreaming and wondering into print, human beings have given their best selves to imagining cities and societies where everything was finally right, where everything was as it ought to be—and because at our truest we understand that the individual and the community must be remembered together, the determination to think through the critical relationship of *me* to *we* was written into these works. Found at the heart of Aristotle's work, they were Plato's questions too, because these are the questions of human beings in every time and every place. The good, the good life, the good society—that was virtue at its highest, that was happiness at its fullest.

In historic Chinese culture, there is no one honored as Confucius still is, his philosophical vision still forming and informing the peoples of Southeast Asia. With its commitment to "tiananmen," a window into cosmic harmony where heaven and earth meet in time and place, it teaches a way not only for individuals to flourish, but for societies to flourish too. The historic Tiananmen Square in Beijing, long known as "the Gate of Heavenly Peace," is meant to be a public place which remembers that there are "mandates from heaven" which have consequence for people on earth. The truest truths being true everywhere for everyone, the heart of the Confucian ethic is, "Do not do unto others what you would not want others to do unto you." An ethic for one life, yes, but necessarily a social ethic too, one with meaning for persons as well as polities—and its hope? A harmony between heaven and earth. Human beings cannot imagine any other world, longing for all to be well, all to be as it ought to be, all to be as we want it to be.

This is true too in the Hebrew and Christian tradition, which has long set forth a time and a place where "lions will someday lie down with lambs," where justice and mercy kiss, where our loves and longings will be ordered in ways in which we are most virtuous and most happy because we are living lives coherent with the cosmos, where the hope of holiness is profoundly woven together with the hope of humanness.

If the gifted cultural critic Christopher Lasch captures this in his book *The True and Only Heaven: Progress and Its Critics*[57]—seeing into the Enlightenment promise of more and more and more—and calling its bluff, then the remarkably able and wise political theologian Oliver O'Donovan sets forth his reading of

[57] Christopher Lasch, *The True and Only Heaven: Progress and Its Critics* (W.W. Norton & Company, 1991).

human history in *The Desire of the Nations: Rediscovering the Roots of Political Theology*.[58] Taken together, these volumes offer contours for understanding what it is in us that longs for a story that makes sense of the stories of our lives, not only personally but publicly.

Both books are described by serious readers as "magisterial," because they are that. Drawing on the most important sources, philosophically and theologically, culturally and sociologically, in their different ways they argue with unusual insight that we long for something more than what we know. While Lasch is searchingly critical of the Enlightenment's secularized eschatology of "progress," he also understands that we long for the good, for good lives, for good societies. What are the conditions that are required of us to get there? On the other hand, O'Donovan is as serious about serious things as anyone anywhere, a scholar's scholar who takes up the meaning of our public life within an intellectual discourse that courses through the centuries, thinking theologically about our deepest desires for the way the world could be, profoundly rooted in his beliefs about the way the world someday will be.

Too honest to be "idealists," both men wrestle with the world that is in its finitude and frailty, and yet identify a deeper hope for a future born of what ought to be in our homes, our neighborhoods, our cities, our nations. Wary of misplaced hopes, of misdirected longings, they stubbornly insist on a future hope born of eschatological expectations that are more profoundly formed. Lasch is sympathetic to transcendence and truth, but not altogether sure what that would mean in terms of particularized religious beliefs; O'Donovan is committed to the vision of the new heaven and a new earth that is the climax of history within the biblical reading of reality, the story from creation to consummation. To read them together is to engage in a richer conversation about the way that expectation affects program, about the ways our very humanness cries out for

[58]Oliver O'Donovan, *The Desire of the Nations: Rediscovering the Roots of Political Theology* (Cambridge University Press, 1999).

something more than "eat, drink, be merry, for tomorrow we die." We want our lives to be about something that matters; we long for our lives to be written into the tapestry of history, into the meaning of a meaningful universe.

One more time it is the interconnectedness of metanarrative to narrative that is integral to what it means to be human. All over the face of the earth we experience the fullness of that tension between the way we make sense of everything and the way we make sense of our own lives—and some answers are better than others. Remember the contrasting murders in the stories of *Cold Mountain* and *Calvary*? One absolutely meaningless, the other just as terrible, but somehow sacramental too—and for human beings who want to see the whole of life as lived before and with God, the idea of the "sacramental" allows us to see, even mysteriously, more of the ways that heaven and earth touch in this very now-but-now-yet world in and through the vocations of our lives.

And human beings long for this—as true for the most ordinary people in the most ordinary places as it sometimes is for the kings of the earth too, human beings that they are. Almost a thousand years ago the King Louis who became Saint Louis lived with these same questions, torn by his royal responsibilities on the one hand, and on the other by his sense of responsibility to God to be a just and merciful ruler of the French people.

Wherever they are to be found in the history of nations, kings and queens stumble over the meaning of power, their "divine right" to rule over the people perplexing at best, and a reign of unholy terror at worst. True of Egyptian pharaohs as for Aztec kings, of Chinese emperors as for African chiefs, on into the most modern and secular leaders of the modern world who make themselves "gods" in the most bullying and manipulative, dictatorial and tyrannical ways, there is a necessarily messy relationship of "heaven and earth" in the dynasties of history. Who is speaking? And on what authority?

For all of these reasons and more King Louis became known during his reign as "the penitential monarch," willing to live a surprisingly simple life born of true repentance, while at the same time being the ruler over what was then the most powerful nation on earth, France ruling the late-medieval world of the eleventh to the fourteenth centuries. How is it possible to be both at the same time? Can we understand the idea of vocation as deep enough to give coherence to all that I am? to all that I am responsible for? As messy as one's moment might be, as complex as one's responsibility is?

Louis's life was lived in the cathedrals and palaces of Paris, even as he also lived his days among the Cistercians, a renewal movement in the Church of the twelfth and thirteenth centuries, men and women committed to the new wineskins of deepened faith, hope, and love. *How can I hold together my sense that life at its truest is about something more, while at the same time honor my duties as heir to the throne, the political steward of vast power and wealth?*

Called a just man, a man of honor, he made proximate progress for a more honest public square, insisting that royal officers render justice without distinction of persons, that they refuse all gifts for themselves or their families, that they not levy any fine without judgment, therefore establishing the presumption of innocence in the courts. More could be said about this Louis who was a good man, though never a perfect man, always the king as he was, always the penitent that he was.

Many in the modern world would wonder at choices he made in the pilgrimage of his faith, for example, spending a literal king's fortune acquiring "the crown of thorns" as the description of the day described them, and then his determination that they required more glory than the Cathedral of Notre Dame provided. Staying within the royal neighborhood of Île de la Cité at the heart of Paris, he made the decision to commission Sainte-Chapelle as the place to honor the prized reliquary, the crown of thorns.

A surprising and perplexing choice, and yet most of a millennium later, is there a more beautiful place on earth?

The "holy chapel" took seven years to build, and while 900 years later we do not know the builder, he was someone whose great gifts imagined into being a building whose stones and ceilings frame windows that are glory upon glory, from beginning to end telling the story of God through the story of Scripture—in a word, the metanarrative of biblical revelation, what the theologians call the history of redemption.

Whatever conversations there were between architect and king, what came into being was a holy place for a holy story. Window after window offers one more moment in redemptive history, from the Old Testament on into the New Testament, a wonderfully artful pedagogy that draws one into the Story of All Stories. And while it is also true that the windows tell something about French kings, a remembering here and a remembering there, those smaller stories are written into the larger Story, each narrative written into the metanarrative.

We do not know what King Louis wanted, nor do we know if Sainte Chapelle satisfied his desires. What we do know is that his palace was next door to the building site, and that he was a monarch who was also a penitent, a ruler of a nation who also longed to be a holy man, seeing his work as a responsibility from God for the sake of his people, his own vocation written into the mission of God for and on the Earth. To see something of that through the glass darkly of a human heart requires beliefs about God and the world that are grounded in something more than the hubris and vanity that seem part and parcel of political power always and everywhere.

Story-formed we are, all of us, for blessings and for curse. For every peasant, every pauper, every architect, every artisan, every cleric, every king, being human means that we see and hear the world through the lenses of our hearts, narratively born, metanarratively formed. Our deepest longings for the "true and only heaven" of the universe, the greatest desire of every person and polis, thread their way through who we are, why we are, and therefore the way we live our lives. In some way, on some level, the medieval monarch King Louis knew that, by fiat bringing into being a sacramental wonder, Sainte-Chapelle architecturally embodying this reality for history, its very existence a signpost for the ages that there is a Story that makes sense of every story, and that the heart of every story is that heaven will someday come to earth.

On Earth As It Is in Heaven

The journey to Nagaland is long and winding, high in the mountains between the worlds of India and China, but for those who live there, it is the true center of the universe.

As far from Mumbai and New Delhi as it is from Beijing and Shanghai, this mountainous region borders Bangladesh, Bhutan, and Burma (now Myanmar), its two-lane roads finally making their way into the homeland of the Naga people. A complex story born of its many tribes and many tongues, so far from anywhere than most have ever imagined, a geography that is uniquely beautiful in the world; and yet its history is tragically familiar: the push and shove of wars from outside and inside through its centuries. The first records of a people in this place go back thousands of years; its strategic location on the way between great empires has made it perennially contested ground.

Every nation that is has known this story: ambition and greed, the overreach that insists on me over we, on mine over ours, the longing for dignity and identity overwhelmed by hubris—in Africa and Europe, in the Middle East, in North and South America, and in Asia, the vast ground that runs from Mongolia in the north to India in the South. In the mid-twentieth century, with horribly myopic political irony, its neighbor to the south betrayed the Naga people's emerging social identity by forcing it to become part of larger India, blind to its own newly found freedom from British rule. During the conflict over this in the 1950s India sent 500,000 troops to quash the Naga hopes for self-determination, and 75 years later Nagaland is an Indian state. Generations later, its poetry and stories are filled with the memories of this terrible terror; it has not been forgotten because it cannot be forgotten.

But it is also true that the Naga people have experienced the fullness of their future as a distinct and unique place on the face of the earth, their history with India notwithstanding. More than a million citizens call it home, their hopes having become incarnate in particular places with particular people like the Dzuthotso Tunyi family, who for centuries have called these fertile mountains "ours." Generation after generation they have brought their sons and daughters into being with the same sense—*we belong to the land and the land belongs to us*—and because we love this land we will care for this land, cultivating the soil, planting seeds and seedlings, in hope.

Farmers as their forebears were before them, the Tunyi family stewards the hillsides of their home village, which is an hour-and-a-half from the capital city of Kohima. With Nagaland's moderate climate they grow flowers and fruits throughout the year, their affection for what is theirs passed on again and again, learned across time from a grandfather to a father to a son, the good work of farming always seen together with the hard work of farming rooted in hard days and sometimes terrifying unknowns, their long love a vocation to cultivate the world that is theirs.

Where does this sense of responsibility born of love come from?

Like the best words always are, "cultivate" is a word from somewhere, its textured companions being "cult" and "culture," grounded in an etymological and philosophical richness that matters, if we are to understand what "cultivate" is about. Whether in the Fertile Crescent of Mesopotamia, the rocky hillsides of Ireland, the lush lands of Central America, the steep mountainsides of Switzerland, the green vastness of sub-Saharan Africa, the miles and more miles of America's Midwest, the carefully tended valleys of Indonesia, or the terraces of Nagaland, to cultivate is to care for, to develop, to plow and plant, to water and weed, and finally to harvest. And as that is true in the most agricultural ways, it is true more metaphorically too, with its own rich meaning, *viz.*, to plant a vision, and over time to grow it into being. In its several ways, this is a universal longing of the heart.

But however we use the word, to cultivate is always a word set within the words *cult* and *culture*. Do we worship the earth as *divine* or do we use the earth as *ours*? Those are very different words and worldviews. Or instead do we love the earth, caring for it because "the earth is the Lord's and everything in it"? The way we understand "the work" of our lives grows out of what we believe about the meaning of our lives, our "cultic" commitments about everything that is—in heaven, on earth, and under the earth. Not surprisingly, the word "cultivate" is about the way we answer the questions "What is real? What is true? What is right?" They are the deepest questions, and our lives are answers, whatever we believe about the questions and their answers.

As agricultural and attentive to what is most local as the Tunyi family has been and is, they are also surprisingly engaged with the wider world, intellectually and socially, academically and professionally, and yes, theologically, a reality threaded through human existence, acknowledged or not. In fact, it would be hard to distinguish one from the other: their sense of political participation in the hope and history of Nagaland, and their unusually rich philosophical commitments about the nature of a good life and a good society embodied as it is in their village and for their land.

And while there is clearly a deeper familial vocation to seek the flourishing of Nagaland principally by caring for the land that is theirs—growing persimmons, bougainvilleas, taxus baccata, cherry, hollocks, sunflowers, marigolds, and zinnias, and keeping bees too, for the local as well as the national markets—not surprisingly, among the six siblings they are different people with different gifts and different occupations. One daughter works for the Naga government and another in healthcare, one son is in business, another son is a physician, another son a political scientist, still another son a theologian (that son became my student, sent by his family to study the meaning of vocation, and who introduced me to his family) but together, having learned to see and hear the world over the shoulders and through the hearts of their father and mother, they have a common calling to cultivate the land that is theirs, and the culture that is theirs.

Again, where does this sense of responsibility born of love, come from? What is the hope at the heart of the Tunyi family life?

Generations ago the Tunyi family left behind the animism of their ancestors and were drawn by grace to belief in the God of heaven and earth, the maker of everyone and everything. Transcendent and yet immanent, infinite and yet personal; neither the divine spirit of animism nor the god of everything everywhere of pantheism, but the One whose very being, in the words of the Book of Common Prayer, is always to have mercy, the hope at the heart of every heart. This is the God who loves the world and who invites the world to love him. This is the God of heaven who loves the earth.

That possibility was life-altering, transforming the Tunyis' understanding of what it meant to be human in the world. Of love and life, of marriage and family, of work and worship, of politics and history, and of the land, the land they have loved for a long time—no longer praying to the land, to the divine spirit present in the land, but now praying for the land, for this God of grace and mercy to bring into being a coherence between heaven and earth, for what is in heaven to be on earth, a prayer for a sacramental cosmos, a world in which everything has sacramental meaning, holy ground as it was, as it is, as it will be.

Sunrise and sunset, the growing seasons of the year, the seed and the soil, the rain and the sun, the harvest too, and most of all, human beings, made in the very image of this God of mercy who cares about his world, who by the greatest grace became incarnate in this world because he loved this world—their view of life, and of the whole of life, was transformed as they became followers of Jesus the Christ. Christian by confession and creed, they became committed to working out its meaning in and through their lives, their reason for being becoming the telos of their days, giving meaning to why they worship and work, day after day, season after season.

With the family's commitment to good work, to good education, to good healthcare, to good politics—always expressed in the most local ways, always with an eye to the world beyond—there is a humility about what ought to be and yet is, even as they give themselves to what could be and someday will be, expectation affecting program one more time in one more place.

Several years ago a group of kindred spirits, Nagas each one, banded together in the name of "A City On a Hill"—remembering the image of John Winthrop and the Massachusetts Bay Colony in 1680—planning for conversations of consequence across society, longing for their life together to be a signpost of something more honest, more just, more true. With seminars on leadership, the gospel and social justice, forgiveness and politics, economic opportunities, demographic imbalance, challenges for the next generation, vocation as mission and calling and more, they gathered to think through the questions of their time in history. *We know where we have come from, we know what is before us now, and we know we must come together in this moment if we are going to see our country become more of what it needs to be.*

No arrogance about all that should be, or about all that they planned to do, but rather something true about what might be; yes, something more proximate, the expectation of what could be for the nation of Nagaland that would shape the ordinary lives of ordinary Nagas, both personally and publicly. We do not do better than that because we live in no other world than that, whenever we are and wherever we are.

The Tunyi family was there, of course, taking their part in the day and beyond, committed to being Naga, committed to what it will mean for Nagaland, their loves shaping their lives. Winthrop would have been surprised, seeing his hope still rippling through history, the longing of his heart for what might be, having found its way into the lives of a people in a place far away from anyone or anywhere he had ever known. History at its best is that history.

The Journey's End

There is a sainted story written into the American Southwest, far away in every way from California and the Sierra Nevadas . . . from Paris and France, and the king who became a saint . . . from the highlands of Asia and the Naga people whose people long for a future that is an honest window into heaven on earth. But because it is history, a true history, it is messy, history always being messy, as California was and is, like Louis and his city and nation a thousand years ago, like the Naga people and their place—like every other moment in time, stories of both glory and ruin, the thread of something more holy threading its way through every people in every place.

This story is one that we know, and do not know, most of it passing by generations ago. In the eighteenth century one group made its way from what was New Spain (now Mexico) into what we know as New Mexico, and then Colorado, following rivers and mountains northward, seeing what had never been seen by Europeans. They called the river the Rio Grande, and the mountains the Sangre de Cristos and the San Juans, remembering something of the ecclesial and missional genesis of their quest to "name" the new world—tragically, for the most part having no eyes to see that others were already there, with histories and hopes to which the Spanish were largely indifferent, pushing and shoving their way into the dominance which they assumed was theirs by divine right. Yes, history is messy.

And two hundred years later, I was born into this world, in the beautifully named town of Monte Vista set in the middle of this sainted story, the San Luis Valley of Colorado, with the Sangre de Cristos and the San Juan Mountains rising up from the valley floor, their majestic contours giving definition to this place and its people. I have no deeper sense of home than here.

As a boy I spent summers with my grandparents, who then had a ranch west of this valley, 160 miles across the San Juans, between Durango and Cortez, where the mountains meet the mesas of the Great Southwest. Those are days woven into my sense of being, and I can still remember sights and smells that are so "me" that in some deep sense I am still that little boy . . . carried by the breezes across my face as I took into my heart the aspens quaking in the wind.

My grandparents were gifts to me, opening their hearts to my desires, allowing me to have adventures that most of my peers could never have imagined. A life with cows and calves, and the bulls that must be . . . with frogs too and their surprisingly tasty legs . . . watching with patient delight the rodeos that I brought into being . . . allowing me to meet the grown-ups of their lives, their friends becoming my friends . . . teaching me to pray about things that mattered now in light of things that were still to come . . . and more and more. Because my grandfather bought cattle, he also sold cattle, and one week he drove to Denver for that purpose. Without a doubt, if I had a hero in those years, it was him, and the longer he was gone from the ranch, the more I missed him. Having been told by my grandmother that he was coming home "today," I waited and waited and waited, for as long as a little boy could possibly wait.

And then I walked down the hill, leaving the house and barn and corrals, across the cattle guard, and began my way into town on the dirt road that I knew would take me there eventually, sure that my grandfather was on his way home. How could he not be *almost* there?

I walked, and walked, the little steps of a five-year-old making their way, at every bend looking to see if I could see him . . . loving him as I did, longing for him as I was. One mile, then two, then three, and finally four, and there he was, his red cattle truck coming up the hill! The years have come and gone since then, but I can still remember the glad welcome he gave me. He was "home" and I was "home" with him; his response was decidedly different from that of my dear grandmother, who had no idea where I had gone, and who made sure that I knew that my yearning for him did not relieve me of her worrying about me!

Yes, the little boy that I once was, whose longing I still remember, so aware I was of wanting and wanting my grandfather again. . . . And now most of my life later I have lived into my longings in ways that I could never have imagined in those days and years. Marrying a woman that I met in the mountains of Colorado, a father I have now been, a grandfather I now am. Life is like that, and boys and men are like that, as is every girl who becomes a woman. We are like that, human beings that we are. To know us is to know our longings, and even the littlest ones among us have them. As we grow, they do too; they are distinct within us, unique to us as they are.

In the last century, two of the best storytellers to ever live gave themselves to stories about journeys and the longings from which they came, their books becoming surprisingly important for readers young and old all over the world. C. S. Lewis opened up the wardrobes of his own rich imagination with his *Chronicles of Narnia*, the seven stories about times and places where it was possible to be "always winter but never Christmas," while J. R. R. Tolkien began with *The Hobbit,* followed years later by *The Lord of the Rings,* from the very first words a journey "there and back again" into a universe of dwarfs and dragons, magic rings and more. For most of life Lewis and Tolkien were the best of friends, Oxbridge dons by day, by night writing about adventures into worlds that were both beyond ones that we know, while at the same time worlds we know as well as we know ourselves. With affection and respect, they even read their manuscripts aloud to each other, sometimes hearing a great "yes!" and sometimes a deeply felt "no!" as they responded to each other's literary worlds, iron sharpening iron around the table of their pub. And when they were done with the conversation for one more week, they took up the tasks that were theirs, off into the world of their work embedded in the deeper vocations that were theirs, called into journeys of mind and heart that became great gifts to history.

Journeys are like that for everyone everywhere; they are life, and they tell the story of life.

While my growing up in America's Southwest is a million miles from Lewis's along the Irish Sea, we are both sons of Adam, our desires so deep within us that we cannot be known apart from them. For a boy who became his own man, the longings of his life shaped the years of his life. While his writings are voluminous, his insights and interests ranging across the world—from the most playfully profound children's stories ever, to the remarkably articulate account of his faith in his BBC radio broadcasts and autobiography, to a prized contribution in the Oxford History of English Literature Series, to the remarkably perceptive retelling of a Greek tale, to his Space Trilogy exploring the deepest questions of human life under the sun, and much more—in his writing Lewis persistently pursued the question at the heart of every heart, the question of longing, understanding, as the wisest ones always have, that it is in our longings that we are most completely known. What do we want? What words do we give to the yearnings that are so deep that we can hardly speak of them?

Those with only a superficial understanding of Lewis imagine a life that was not his—this achievement and then that honor, success upon more success, fame after great fame. But any more honest reading reveals a deeper truth: He was an ordinary man living an ordinary life, one marked by the truest joys and the truest sorrows, bearing both in his own bones. Grieved beyond words by the devastating death of his mother, as a boy sent off from his home in Northern Ireland to a Dickensian boarding school in England, wounded so badly in World War I that he was hospitalized for months, and all that within the first 20 years of his life, experiences that awakened in him desires for something more than he had known, a time and a place in which he could find the happiness that he believed in, but one that seemed beyond what was believable.

He called it joy, a longing for joy.

And in his autobiography he remembered that it was joy that he pursued in and through everything that he did through the first decades of his life, eventually being profoundly—in the most soulful way—"surprised by joy," finally and fully finding the long longing of his heart in the realization that the God of heaven and earth could be known and loved, and that he could be known and loved by this same God.

But that joy was hard-won, requiring a "pilgrim's regress" for Lewis; his story formed an analysis of life against the grain of the universe, and of what it means for both selves and societies. He wanted more than that, and yet he could not identify what it was, or where it came from. At important points along the way Lewis began drawing on the German word *sehnsucht*,[59] knowing that it captured something that was at the very heart of his heart in a way that was not found in the English language. Almost impossible to put into words, it is "the inconsolable longing in the human heart for we know not what. . . ." An idea made word that is so very human, so very knowing of what it is to be human.

Lewis had known losses that would not be healed in this life. His mother had died, and for him that meant his childhood happiness was forever lost—and given the reality that most of life is pretty autobiographical, he never got very far from that wound, so very tender as it would always be for him. When he wrote about another boy's fears in *The Magician's Nephew*, we hear the story as one written by someone with an unusual sensitivity to what it feels like to be afraid of one's mother dying, and even more about what a young boy would do to keep his mother alive. In a word, he would do *anything*, because the

---

[59]C. S. Lewis, *The Weight of Glory* (Macmillan, 1949), 12.

longing was so deep. Nothing else mattered more than that his mother lived.

In the final story of the Chronicles of Narnia, *The Last Battle,* the children of the great adventure come to the end of history, the final conflict of heaven on earth, and are surprised by what they find, knowing and not knowing what it is they now see and hear. Hoping, and hoping even more, they wonder if they have come to the place of their deepest desires. Is where they are in fact all that they have longed for? Aslan, the one who has led them through their long journey from its beginning to its end, says to them, "Further up and further in," telling them that there is still more, that in coming through the stable door, the quest has come to an end . . . and yet, and yet, there is more, a mysterious wonder it will be, forever and forever, recognizably Narnia but a renewed Narnia, Narnia as it was always meant to be.

If Lewis understood life, and his life, as born of the longings of our hearts—even when we cannot give words to them—his colleague and friend J. R. R. Tolkien wrote his stories about the same world. They were kindred spirits, deeply, even though they were different people with different gifts with different histories. But the eyes of their hearts saw the meaning of stories in remarkably similar ways, each with a literary and moral intelligence that carried him through the years of life, their imaginations bringing into being worlds that are both beyond us, and so familiar to us. We read them because we trust them. Fantasy but not fantastic, the stories of Narnia and of Middle-earth call us into a sense of self in the world that is true to what it means to be human, true to who we are and to who we want to be. We know the hearts and minds of each character—Peter and Eustace, Frodo and Sam—because that is how we feel too, and we see and hear what they feel. Their fears are our fears, their hopes are our hopes, and yes, their longings are our longings.

While Tolkien is best known for his stories of hobbits—perhaps the greatest literature the world has known—we know him more fully when we read his letters, the correspondence of his life over his years of life. There are windows into family, especially with his son Christopher, that give us crucial insight into the character and wisdom of Tolkien family life, and there are pages and pages of letters to friends, including Lewis, as there are important letters to his publisher and to his public. Much was written about much that mattered most to him.

Surprisingly—and yet not—Tolkien was taken by the meaning for life in this world by what he believed about life in the world to come, his beliefs about the eschaton threaded through his correspondence. In one letter he wrote, "But certainly there was an Eden on this very unhappy earth. We long for it, and we are constantly glimpsing it; our whole nature at its best and least corrupted, its gentlest and most humane, is still soaked with the sense of 'exile.'" Those words are worthy of being read again.

How do we hold together in our frail hearts commitments about the meaning of a Great Story, with the story of our own little lives? Of metanarrative with narrative? So aware of the wounds that have wounded the world, of the wounds that we ourselves bear, we have "glimpses" of Eden, "soaked with 'exile' as we are." The tenderness of Tolkien is uncanny, writing that questions of cosmic importance can only be known when we are at our "gentlest and most humane." And therefore "glimpsing" is a good word, a profound word, a word that is not far from *proximate*. We see in part, and yet we see.

That reality is woven through Tolkien's work. From Bilbo's first steps away from the Shire, all the way to Frodo's departure for the Western Lands, we come to know and love these hobbits, their "humanness" assuring us that the longings we have, while unique to us, are not new longings. For a thousand good reasons, I have lived my life as a hobbit, seeing in these little folk enough of myself to feel at home—I know them, and in a strange way, they know me. For years the contours of their lives have drawn me in. Long friendships. Love for a good cup of tea. Gardening. And adventure too.

When I first read these stories, *The Hobbit*, then *The Lord of the Rings*, I was enamored, deeply affected by who they were, why they were, and therefore what they did with their lives. I did not need to be them, but I chose to learn from them. While the meaning of hope and hubris, and the sifting and sorting of loves are the great threads that are woven through the tapestry of Tolkien's tale, it is Rivendell, the last homely place—where the best meals are eaten, where the most artful songs are sung, where the crucial conversations are had—that gives coherence to the story.

I have taken this world into the sources of my own self—and wanting to know more of the origins of Middle-earth, I have spent days in the Lauterbrunnen near the city of Interlaaken in a beautiful-beyond-beauty Swiss valley, eight miles long and a half mile wide, with 72 waterfalls roaring down its sheer sides from the Alpine peaks above. No one who knows his writing is surprised that Tolkien placed Rivendell in the Lauterbrunnen, his literary imagination inspired by its grandeur. As I walked and biked, I thought about its meaning every day, for Tolkien and his hobbits, and for me. With its geographic and imaginative prominence, the place everyone longs for and never wants to leave, Rivendell is not the end of the story of the *Lord of the Rings,* the *telos* of their travel; rather it is meant to be a grace, a signpost perhaps, of something more, of something still to come.

One has to follow the hobbits through their pilgrimage to understand that Rivendell is a foretaste. Deep happiness and profound rest, yes, the nourishing of heart and mind, soul, and strength, yes, and yet it is not everything. All things are not well in Middle-earth, a reality which makes the story a story, and so Rivendell is given as a gift to keep the hobbits' hearts alive as they keep at the task that is theirs—from the seeming innocence of their calling as the story begins, through to the climax of the great conflict on Mount Doom, all the way back to the Shire, each one longing for the day when all sad things will finally become untrue.[60]

[60] Tolkien's own image of the eschaton, the end of history.

In walking up and down the path from the valley floor to where we have stayed, literally the last homely place in the Lauterbrunnen—a house with ancient timbers, a rushing river, green meadows, and majestic mountains—from morning to night I thought about the meaning of Rivendell, so full of wonder, a place of remarkable joy, and yet at its best, a signpost along the way.

Very beautiful. Very good. Very right. But not everything . . . yes, proximate.

Because it must be. "Bad books lie. They lie most of all about the human condition."[61] True across the whole of literature, the reality that good books tell the truth about the human condition is why Tolkien is read, and read, and read again. Most readers have no idea of the deeper cosmology behind his work, the metaphysical commitments about God and the world that form his vision, but they are drawn in by the sense of honest humanity, of reading about life in a world that they know as well as they know their own.

Wrestling as his characters must, from the earliest decisions about taking up the quest of the Ring, on through their long travail towards Mount Doom with untold adventure and drama at every point along the way, Tolkien chose to create a word to make sense of history, especially hobbits in the midst of Middle-earth's history, their days marked by such deep hope, such great longing, such terrible heartache, such grievous tragedy. And so he imagined into being a word for all of this and more, *eucatastrophe*.[62]

---

[61]Percy, *Signposts in a Strange Land*.

[62]The idea for the word comes in the course of Tolkien's own very ordinary life. In a weekly letter to his son Christopher, he wrote about bicycling with his daughter to church, about his response to a "holy beggar" at its doorstep, about caring for his trees at summer's end, about his conversation with C. S. Lewis and Charles Williams, "a feast of reason and a flow of soul," and his wrestling with the writing of *Lord of the Rings*, struggling to find a word to say what was needed—and finding his way to *eucatastrophe*. "I was there led to the view that [eucatastrophe] produces [joy at the turn of a Happy Ending] because it is a sudden glimpse of Truth, your whole nature chained in material cause and effect, the chain of death, feels a sudden relief as if a major limb out of joint had suddenly snapped back. (. . .) the Resurrection was the greatest 'eucatastrophe' possible in the greatest Fairy Story – and produces that essential emotion: Christian joy which produces tears because it is qualitatively so like sorrow, because it comes from those places where

Coming forth from his own beliefs about the meaning of life in the world, of where we have come from and of where we are going, the word draws on "eu," and "catastrophe," becoming a word that has not been, but is desperately needed if we are to understand the lives that are ours in the world that is ours. What is it? A eucatastrophe is a surprising, even shocking, change in expectations, altering what seems an impossibly dangerous and dire future into one of with a victory born of grace.

No one I know well enough to know lives for long without feeling the consequences of a fallen world, its anguish, its disappointments, its frustrations, its griefs, its miseries, its sorrows, its wrongs. And while sometimes that is more acid rain, slowly by slowly coming down upon us, sometimes it is a terrible shock, a cataclysm that comes completely unexpected. And as that is true for every human, it was true for every hobbit.

Tolkien's tales are not a tragedy, but there is tragedy—and yet as terrible as that always is, it is not the end of the story. As Bilbo, Frodo, and more must find ways to keep on keeping on in the face of terrors known and unknown, they hold on to their hearts, pressing into the calling on their lives through their losses to the final chapter, which was never easy, as the wounds were deeply wounding. Because good stories tell the truth about life, these stories of quest, "there and back again," are embedded within a Grand Story, the metanarrative of Middle-earth, even as they are the stories of hairy-footed hobbits, of elves and wizards, and kings-in-waiting, each one a narrative of someone whose own story is made sense of in light of the Story, as the best stories, the truest stories always are . . . pilgrims that they were, a pilgrimage of the proximate that it was.

And Someday All Sad Things Will Become Untrue

Expectation affects program? From beginning to end, yes, a reality for everyone everywhere.

Joy and Sorrow are at one, reconciled, as selfishness and altruism are lost in Love." Humphrey Carpenter, ed. *The Letters of J.R.R. Tolkien* (Boston: Houghton Mifflin, 2014), 100.

From the unexpected wisdom of John Muir about the sacramental character of the journeys of our lives, from King Louis of France who became St. Louis to the world, who imagined into being an architectural wonder that captures for the ages the hope that someday heaven and earth will touch, to the familial longing of the Tunyis of Nagaland for good lives and a good society, and yes, to remembering the good gifts of my grandparents who taught me to pray and live in light of what someday will be, finally on to the good lives and good work of Lewis and Tolkien, whose own lives brought forth a literature which will echo on into the future because it is so profoundly true about the present—all these and more are ways of understanding the reality that what we believe about what is still to come affects how we live in and through the ordinary days of our lives.

At the end, a final story, the story that is the heart of every True Myth—as Lewis and Tolkien understood stories—the stories that my father the plant pathologist, and that Jozef Luptak the cellist and his community of kindred spirits in Slovakia have chosen to live within, as have each one whose life I have drawn into this book with windows into the whole world, East and West, North and South.

Woven through these pages is the belief that in the Hebrew and Christian way of seeing the world there is an account of history and the human heart that resonates with reality, making sense of making sense in ways that we long for, that our truest humanness yearns after. The metanarrative of the biblical story from creation to consummation is grounded in the most important questions that human beings ask and answer in whatever time and place. Where have we come from? What is wrong with the world? Can it ever change? What will the future be? Wherever we are, whatever we believe, these are the questions of being human.

They are necessarily the questions which are embedded within, and made incarnate in the biblical story, the metanarrative from creation to consummation, in book after book, from Genesis to Revelation, inviting us into a way of seeing and hearing all of life and reality, coming to a proper confidence about what is, and what is not real and true and right.

The Gospel of Luke begins with these words:

> *Inasmuch as many have undertaken to compile a narrative of the things that have been accomplished among us, just as those who from the beginning were eyewitnesses and ministers of the word have delivered them to us, it seemed good to me also, having followed all things closely for some time past, to write an orderly account for you, most excellent Theophilus, that you may have certainty concerning the things you have been taught.*[63]

And from the first chapter on we are drawn into the story of Jesus the Christ—from his mother Mary's great song of surprise, to his boyhood conversation with the teachers of the Jewish tradition in Jerusalem, through the record of generations before him that span the centuries of history, on to the years of living among the people of first-century Palestine, seeing their lives, hearing their stories, teaching them to know and love the world as God his Father does, and finally to his own death and then resurrection.

Towards the end of Luke's narrative, we are given an account of a walk to Emmaus, a village about ten miles from Jerusalem. Two of his disciples are overwhelmed with sadness; all that they had hoped had not happened, everything that they had imagined could no longer be. What now?

By great grace, Jesus joins them, asking what they are talking about. Not recognizing him, they are surprised: "Are you the only one visiting Jerusalem who does not know the things that have happened there in these days?"

The disciples then recount all that they had hoped, and all that had happened to crush their hopes. Perhaps with the holiest

---

[63]Luke 1:1–4, taken from The ESV® Bible (The Holy Bible, English Standard Version®), © 2001 by Crossway, a publishing ministry of Good News Publishers.

of smiles, and yet with divine seriousness, Jesus begins to tell them the Story of Stories, explaining that the suffering of the Messiah was promised—the Eucatastrophe that it was—a great wounding in the very heart of history, and yet not the final end of history, that there was still more to come, more to understand about the metanarrative and what it meant for them, for the lives that were theirs, narratives each one.

They want to hear more, and so they invite Jesus for supper, and in the breaking of bread they finally see him for who he is: "Were not our hearts burning within us while he talked with us on the road and opened the Scriptures to us?" Seeing through a glass very darkly, they did not understand what to make of the heartache, what to do with the tragedy, senseless that it was, a "catastrophe" that it was.

There is nothing cheap here. There was great grief, horrible punishment, a heart-rending death, and yet, it was not the end. Not until the eyes of their hearts were opened so that they could see what they had not seen, hearing the Rabbi of all Rabbis tell them the Story of all Stories, the history of redemption "beginning with Moses and all the Prophets," were they able to make peace with what had happened. Knowing but not knowing what it meant, trusting that the Teacher knew what they did not, they came to an honest belief in the truth of what they had heard, enough so that their "hearts burned" with the realization of its reality.

But to know this story was to become implicated in this story, the weight of its love carrying those who followed Jesus most closely entering themselves into his suffering, his vocation becoming their vocation. A political outcast, "the troubler of Israel" he was called; choosing to follow him meant joining him in life and in death, in his great joys and in his great sorrows, his true happiness and his true heartache, which they did by the scores, the hundreds, and the thousands—knowing that here-and-now was not then-and-there, that there was a sure hope that someday, someday, *all sad things will become untrue.*

For them as for us, we live stretched taut between what we believe about the world and how we live in the world, between what we believe about the meaning of history and the meaning of our lives—yes, between the metanarrative that makes sense of everything and the narrative that makes sense of a life—having to make peace with the proximate all day long, all our lives long.

For some good. For some justice. For some happiness. For some mercy. For some beauty. Real and true and right, each one, and yet never everything.

A Final Word

Common Grace, Common Good, Common Ground

For most of 30 years I've been meeting with two friends every Wednesday morning for a cup of something. Very ordinary people we are, we meet in very ordinary places to talk about the vocations of our lives—and then go off into our work another day, taking up the callings and careers that make us "us."

Over the years our occupations have changed, no longer here or there doing this or that, but our visions of vocation have only deepened, still asking the same questions, still wrestling with the world, the flesh, and the devil for answers that make sense of making sense of what we do and why we do it in the evermore globalizing, pluralizing, and secularizing world.

Place matters, more than we know, the contours of our commitments defined by the rootedness of our lives. That we live in the world of Washington, DC, means that there is something political and public about the vocations that bring us together, binding our hearts and minds through the years. Having chosen to live by the creed of the Clapham community of 225 years ago in England—to choose a neighbor before you choose a house—we work hard at the complex challenges of this city, a city known the world over for its glories and shames, a city which draws people from every corner of the country and the earth who want to put their shoulders to history, longing to change the way the world turns out, for blessing and for curse.

Destructive partisanship, naked ambition, short-sighted political fictions—all this and more make this place unique in the world, neither Sacramento nor Shafter, neither Denver nor Monte Vista, neither Harrisburg nor Beaver Falls, neither Topeka nor Lawrence, and not Bratislava or Nairobi or Singapore or Belfast or Jerusalem or Sydney or Beijing or Mexico City either. Where we live and move and have being sets the tables of our lives and labors, and yes, our longings.

Week after week, year by year we think aloud and together about the questions that are ours, none of which have cheap answers. Because the truest truths of the universe cut deeper than the partisan divide, our deepest loyalties are to something more than partisan wins and losses.

Todd Deatherage, for example, after years on Capitol Hill and the State Department, gives his life away to the Telos Group, whose mission is to nourish understanding of what seem the most intractable issues of the day, the deep-seated, long-suffering problems that run through the Israeli and Palestinian conflict, most recently the horrific and tragic scorching of the land we call Gaza, displacing millions of people from their place; the tragic divide that makes Ireland into two peoples and two places, the bitterness still bubbling below the surface, with boundaries drawn and undrawn, keeping traditions and tribes on one side or the other; and the cultural consequences of the poison pill that America swallowed generations ago, in the slavery of Africans that came into terrible being in our Civil War a century-and-a-half ago, a war that we are still fighting, that still plagues our national well-being. Blessed are the peacemakers? Not in this world, very often at all. And tragically, almost no one in the church or the world is willing to ask the hard questions which are at the heart of his life, preferring more partisan loyalties instead.

And Mark Rodgers is integral to our life together, a neighbor who has been a friend for most of life. Always the political visionary, after years of leadership on Capitol Hill he formed the Clapham Group and the Wedgwood Circle as ways to bring into being literal and metaphorical "tables" for folk who almost never talk with each other. Both for-profits and nonprofits, institutional hopes of both left and right give definition to Clapham; social and cultural visionaries most committed to a common good ask him to curate their conversations, knowing that they simply do not know what is required for an honest dialogue with "the other," those whose political loyalties keep them in different places with different people. Alongside is Wedgwood, which has as its reason for being a renewal of the arts and entertainment in America for the sake of the world, since its beginning believing that the culture is upstream from politics—so that the stories and storytellers of our time matter deeply for the sake of our life together in America and throughout the world. Singers and songwriters, painters and painting, novelists and novels, films and filmmakers, playwrights and plays, and more upon more, each one vision-shaping and reality-defining windows into what it means to be human and into what human flourishing is and must be.

And me? Always the professor at the table, a cup of tea in my hands, thinking with my friends who are my neighbors about the on-the-ground meaning of vocation for our common good, and yes, working away at the questions that are mine about the intersection of faith to vocation to culture. I came to the city to teach politics, and discovered that the questions of the polis were more mine, longing to know more and more about our life together, about the conditions that make for the flourishing of cities and societies.

We are clay-footed people, each of us, seeing something of what is real and true and right, never seeing everything; at our best, we see through a glass darkly, in hope. And not surprisingly, though our deepest commitments are held in common, we do not always agree about the particulars of which ideas must have legs for us to get where we need to go. Twined together, we are different and distinct, sometimes fraying at the edges—but trying again next Wednesday, praying for wisdom for the next week.

But our longings bring us together, hoping for more common grace, for more common good, for more common ground, knowing in our bones that our nation's wellbeing is absolutely dependent upon on it, because cities and societies will not flourish without these commitments coursing their way through our life together, making peace with the proximate in our families, in our work, in our city, in our world.

And all this over a simple cup of something, sipping our way into what we believe about what matters, and therefore what we are willing to do with the days of our lives.

Lord, have mercy, please, we pray.

FOR FURTHER READING

Hannah Arendt, *Eichmann in Jerusalem: A Report on the Banality of Evil*

Augustine of Hippo, *City of God, Confessions,* and *Enchiridion*

Wendell Berry, *A Hidden Wound, Home Economics*, and *The Memory of Old Jack*

Douglas Coupland, *Life After God*

Charles Dickens, *David Copperfield*

Jean Bethke Elshtain, *Augustine and the Limits of Politics*

Viktor Frankl, *Man's Search for Meaning*

Makoto Fujimura, *Art and Faith: A Theology of Making*

Martin Luther King Jr, *"Letter from Birmingham Jail"*

Milan Kundera, *The Unbearable Lightness of Being*

Christoper Lasch, *The True and Only Heaven*

Madeleine L'Engle, *Two-Part Invention: The Story of a Marriage, The Weather of the Heart*

Alasdair MacIntyre, *After Virtue: A Study in Moral Theory*

David Naugle, *Worldview: The History of a Concept*

Lesslie Newbigin, *The Gospel in a Pluralist Society* and *Proper Confidence*

Reinhold Niebuhr, *Moral Man and Immoral Society*

Michael O'Brien, *Strangers and Sojourners*

Oliver O'Donovan, *The Desire of the Nations: Rediscovering the Roots of Political Theology.*

Walker Percy, *Signposts in a Strange Land*

Morag Prunty, *Recipes for a Perfect Marriage*

Sigrid Undset, *Kristin Lavransdatter*

ACKNOWLEDGMENTS

Why do I see and hear the way that I do?

In *The Magician's Nephew*, the story of the beginning of the Narnian universe, C. S. Lewis observes, "For what you see and hear depends a good deal on where you are standing; it also depends on what sort of person you are." There is mystery here, as we know and yet do not know why we believe this, and not that, why this matters to us, and that does not. The deeper reality is that our beliefs about life and the world are twined together with the way we live in the world, because our convictions about what is real and true and right are inextricably connected with our character, the way that we *characteristically* make sense of making sense morning after morning, year upon year, which is of course most profoundly born of the longings of our hearts.

As must be, these pages are born of deeply formed commitments and loves, shaping what I see and why I see what I see. And while my library is full of prized books and more books, works whose words run through all that I think and say and do, eventually words must become flesh for us to believe them. We must see if the ideas have legs—what they mean for honest life in the world, for ordinary people in ordinary places, for men and women with lives marked by the relationships and responsibilities that make us human.

When I began to ponder the proximate, knowing that a book would take years of my life to bring into being, I looked to a group of friends whose lives I trusted, whom I knew shared deeply in the labors of love that have been mine. Todd and Judi Deatherage, Brad and Ginger Gibson, Jay and Eleni Jakub, Jesse and Lara Krohmer, Gavin and Emily Long, John and Ashely Marsh, Russ and Ruth Pulliam, Mark and Leanne Rodgers, Shauna and Phil Schneider, Gary and Cathy York—and in and through everything, my long companion of hopes and dreams, David Kiersznowski.

There are more, of course, the friends whose friendship gives meaning to my life. Andi Ashworth and Charlie Peacock, Jay Barber, Brent Beshore, B.J. and Ray Blunt, Mike Bontrager, Byron and Beth Borger, Beau Boulter, Scott Buckout, Bryce Butler, Randy Caldejon, Georgia, Camp Bell, Uli Chi, Kris Carter, Milan and Bozena Cicel, Susan and Nathan Den Herder, Nathan Dickerson, Carl Edwards, Al Erisman, Bob Flayhart, Brad and Sue Frey, Mako and Haejin Fujimura, Bill Fullilove, Rich Gathro, Brian Gray, Don and Mary Guthrie, David Hanke, Kate and Joel Harris, Jerry Herbert, Cristián Guadalupe Mejía Hernández, Hans and April Hess, Kwang Kim, Bonnie Liefer, Jozef and Katarina Luptak, Sandra McCracken, Brian Mackay, Claudius and Deirdre Modesti, Tod Moquist, Steve Moore, Jim Mullins, Tom and Liz Nelson, Philip Ng, Sam Owen, Bill Palmer, John and Sandie Penrose, Dean and Lyle Peterson, Clydette Powell, Bill Reimer, Mark Roberts, Lisa Pratt Slayton, Fred Smith, Sven Soderlund, Paul Stevens, Pak Wah-Lai, Eliud Wabukala, Todd and Charity Wahrenberger, Chad Watson, Rick Wellock, Mike Woodruff, John and Susan Yates, and Nancy Ziegler.

And heartfelt thanks to the trustees of the M.J. Murdock Charitable Trust, whose stewardship of hope and longing for the communities of the Pacific Northwest is a common grace for the common good; their institutional reason for being included for me a season as visiting scholar, and that gave me time to work on this book. In addition, there are other communities whose visions are mine too, in their unique ways sustaining my own deepest loves as they embody commitments to what should be done on the face of the earth: the Economics of Mutuality Alliance, the Institute for Marketplace Transformation, and the Washington Institute for Faith, Vocation and Culture. Because I have chosen to live my life among communities of lived commitments—in love and learning, in work and worship—these people, like me, have to make peace with the proximate, with something that is beautiful and true, good and right, knowing that all that matters most will not be found in this wounded world that is ours, and yet they persist, in hope.

Because books are necessarily the work of a cast of thousands, of good people coming together with a vision for bringing books into being that should see the light of day, I am keenly aware that there are gifted people who have labored along with me, from beginning to end. So to Jeff Crosby, whose hopes have sustained me for many years, and to Elisa Fryling Stanford, Lillian Miao, Robert Edmonson, and Lexa Hale, I am very grateful.

Finally, to my children and grandchildren, whose very being gives me reasons to wake into the morning, knowing that you are like me, and yet different, longing for what should be, sighing over what is, yearning for what someday will be: May this long labor of love be an honest grace to you, each one of you. And yes, at the end, as at the beginning, deepest thanks to my wife, Meg, who in heart and mind is woven into the fabric of my life, whose editorial insights I trust—and as you are, they are a gift.

About the Author

Steven Garber has been a teacher of many people in many places, including his work as Senior Fellow for Vocation and the Common Good for the M.J. Murdock Charitable Trust, and the Economics of Mutuality Alliance. The founding principal of the Washington Institute for Faith, Vocation and Culture, for several years he was the Professor of Marketplace Theology at Regent College, and he continues on as Senior Fellow for the Institute for Marketplace Transformation in Vancouver, BC. The author of several books, including *Visions of Vocation: Common Grace for the Common Good* and *The Seamless Life: A Tapestry of Love and Learning, Worship and Work*, with his wife, Meg, he has had a long life among family, friends, and flowers in Virginia.

ABOUT PARACLETE PRESS

Paraclete Press is the publishing arm of the Cape Cod Benedictine community, the Community of Jesus. Presenting a full expression of Christian belief and practice, we reflect the ecumenical charism of the Community and its dedication to sacred music, the fine arts, and the written word.